PRESENTATIONAL
SPEAKING
Theory & Practice

Third Edition

Melanie Morgan, Ph.D.

 **Custom Publishing**

Boston   Burr Ridge, IL Dubuque, IA Madison, WI New York San Francisco St. Louis
Bangkok Bogotá Caracas Lisbon London Madrid
Mexico City Milan New Delhi Seoul Singapore Sydney Taipei Toronto

PRESENTATIONAL SPEAKING
Theory & Practice

McGraw-Hill's Custom Publishing consists of products that are produced from camera-ready copy. Peer review, class testing, and accuracy are primarily the responsibility of the author(s).

1 2 3 4 5 6 7 8 9 0   QPD QPD   0 9 8 7 6 5

ISBN 0-07-353604-0

Editor: Tamara Immell
Production Editor: Carrie Braun
Cover Photo: © Corbis
Cover Design: Fairfax Hutter
Interior Design: Karen Fleckenstein, Fleck's Communications, Inc., Peosta, IA
Printer/Binder: Quebecor World

Contents

Introduction to Presentational Speaking

Chapter Objectives

After reading this chapter, you should be able to:

- Explain the differences between public speaking and presentational speaking.

- Explain the elements of effective presentations.

- Understand the different types of plagiarism.

A Northeastern University freshman sat in his uncle's office and wrote the code for a piece of software that caused a great deal of controversy. This simple piece of software changed the music industry forever, and the life of its creator. Shawn Fanning, who had been a quiet and reserved young man, was suddenly thrust into a sea of public discourse, forced to defend his creation, Napster, against huge corporate giants. Napster was a simple piece of software that allowed computer users to share MP3 music files over their computers.

Shawn was suddenly thrown into a media frenzy. He was expected to participate in interviews, make public presentations, and testify in hearings. This average American teenager was suddenly asked to be the "voice of a generation."

While this story may sound extreme, we have no way of knowing what life may hand us or when our circumstances will suddenly become newsworthy. In a blink of an eye, we can go from complete anonymity to sudden fame. There are many examples of these situations in the current news. Take for example John Walsh, host of *America's Most Wanted*. He never expected to be the spokesperson for victims of crime. However, the kidnapping and murder of his young son, Adam, thrust him into this position. Similarly, the nine coal miners in West Virginia who were trapped for days in a mine shaft never imagined on that summer day in 2002 they would suddenly become heroes who were being pursued by the media for interviews and speaking engagements.

All of these examples may still seem a bit removed from some of your experiences, but you never know when life will require you to stand up and engage in public discourse. Your impetus may not be as overwhelming as some of the examples, but your situation may be just as compelling for you. Imagine that you have just bought a new house, only to learn that a nearby processing plant is planning on increasing its toxic output. This would be a situation that would require you to step up and debate the issues in a public forum. You, along with other homeowners, would likely participate in city council meetings hoping to persuade local officials to ban the increase in production.

Still, many of you will not even face this kind of situation. More likely, you will be asked to be the voice of your department within your organization. Perhaps you will be asked to represent your organization in a sales presentation with a potential client. All of these situations seem far less grand than some of the other examples we have discussed, but they still have very important implications for you, your career, or the success of your organization.

This book is designed to help you prepare for common speaking situations that most of us face on a fairly regular basis. Having the ability to express one's thoughts is important to success in any career.

Although your first job may seem a long way away at this point, you cannot underestimate the importance of strong presentational skills to your success in the workplace. This course will provide you with the basics that you will need to succeed in presentational speaking. Not only will you learn theories and skills that are vital in the workplace, but those skills will also serve you well in other courses you take while in college. Many of the courses you take at the university level will require some type of presentation. Use these presentations as practice for the presentations you will make later in your career. All of the strategies and skills you learn in this course will be valuable and applicable to the speaking you will be required to do while in college, whether that speaking occurs in the classroom or as part of a membership you have in some organization. Perhaps you will become president of your sorority or fraternity and will be required to deliver presentations to raise money, increase membership, or even remain in good standing with the university. The skills you learn in this course will help you achieve those goals.

> ## Making effective presentations is vital to career success.

This course and text are designed to present communication theories and research to help you learn the fundamentals of presentational speaking. As part of this process, various guidelines will be presented on how to prepare presentations. Some of these guidelines are very specific. Elements of the presentations will be required to contain particular features. Sometimes, students report that these requirements seem constraining. However, research has shown that these guidelines work in almost all speaking contexts. You cannot go wrong if you use the fundamental guidelines this book and course advocate. Once you become an accomplished speaker, you learn which of the guidelines can be broken or adapted to specific speaking situations. Until then, these guidelines will serve you well and help ensure that your presentations are successful.

Presentational Speaking and Career Success

Making effective presentations is vital to career success. In fact, organizational recruiters report that the fear of public speaking is one of the most common career-stoppers in America.[1] Alan Geenwald, a partner at T. Bresner & Associates, a company that helps executives with presentation skills, says, "Being a poor speaker is the principle reason people don't make it into the executive ranks."[2] A recent article in *The Wall Street Journal* reported that 90% of organizational recruiters surveyed said that good communication skills were essential to obtaining employment and succeeding in the work force. So as you can see, the ability to express oneself well is important for your success. The bottom line is this: You have to be able to express your ideas effectively. It is imperative in the world we live in, whether we are talking about your career or your everyday life. This book will help you take theories of effective communication and apply them to the presentational speaking context.

What Is Presentational Speaking?

By now you have determined that presentational speaking is something that is unavoidable and is essential to success. No matter how much you dread it, it is an inevitable part of academic and professional life. This book has been referring to presentational speaking, not public speaking. So what are the differences? Let's examine some of those differences now.

Presentational Speaking Is More Inclusive

Public speaking can be thought of as a grand presentation. By public we usually mean it is a presentation that affects the community at large. The audience will include a "public audience." Staff meetings don't fall under this category. However, if you have ever attended a staff meeting, you know that the ability to present one's ideas in an organized and effective fashion is important. Presentational speaking includes more typical types of situations that people commonly find themselves facing. Therefore, the term presentational includes both the public type of presentations we often see politicians making, and those smaller types of presentations that occur within organizations.

Presentational Speaking Is Less Formal

Public speaking usually occurs in a formal setting. Speakers are behind podiums and microphones. They are usually dressed in formal attire. Speakers deliver their presentations from a prepared manuscript and the presentation is rather scripted—meaning that there is little room for spontaneity.

Presentational speaking can occur around a table while everyone is seated. The speaker doesn't necessarily have to stand up to address the audience. Most likely, the presentation will be delivered from an outline rather than a manuscript; therefore, the situation is much more relaxed and allows for informality.

Presentational Speaking Is More Interactive

The reliance on manuscript delivery usually means that public speeches rarely adapt to the needs of the audience. Usually, the audience has little chance for interaction with the speaker. Audience members can usually stop the speaker during a presentation and ask questions if they feel they need to. The extemporaneous delivery style of presentational speaking also allows the speaker the spontaneity to talk to the audience and adapt the presentation to the needs of a particular audience.

Presentational Speaking Reaches a Smaller Number of Individuals

Presentations are often made to smaller audiences than public speeches. Public presentations usually reach multiple audiences through a variety of mediums. They are usually videotaped for replay, and the actual words delivered in the presentations are transcribed so that they can be reprinted in the newspaper. So, while you may not be able to see the president deliver his State of the Union Address, you may be able to see it replayed on television, or read the transcript in the newspaper. This extra distribution has the ability to reach a very wide audience.

Characteristics of Effective Presentational Speaking

Now that you know how important presentational speaking is and how it differs from public speaking, let's examine the factors that will make your presentations effective. These three factors are the essential elements in making a good presentation. We will refer back to these elements throughout the entire book. They will help guide you in making many of the decisions that you need to make when preparing for a presentation.

Good Presentational Speaking Is Goal-Directed

Good speaking is goal-directed. Each time you address an audience you should be extremely clear on what the purpose of your presentation is. What exactly are you trying to convey? What are you hoping to achieve? Are you trying to explain a procedure to a group of colleagues, or are you trying to update your staff on new developments in your product line, or persuade a client to change operating systems? Whatever the purpose, the content of your presentation should be driven by your goal. Every decision you make about what to address or what to include in the presentation should be made in regard to the over-arching goal of your presentation. If the material you are considering using doesn't support your goal, don't use it.

Presentations that aren't goal-directed seem muddled and often ramble. The message is unclear, and audiences often leave wondering what they should take away from the presentation.

Before beginning the preparation process, have a firm idea of what you want to achieve in the presentation. After ensuring that the goal is appropriate for the audience and the situation, use it as your guide. Every decision you make during the preparation process should be driven by your goal or purpose. If you follow this guideline, you will

be on the road to delivering a presentation with a clear message that your audience can follow.

Good Presentational Speaking Is Audience-Centered

Good presenters are always aware of their audience. One of the differences between strong speakers and average speakers is the ability to relate and adapt to their audience. You have to know your audience in order to reach them. If you are delivering a sales presentation to a potential client hoping to sell them a new computer operating system and you know little about the types of features that will be most useful to them, you will probably lose the sale.

In order to be successful as a speaker, you must know the attitudes an audience holds about your message and be able to strategically plan for possible differences between your position and that of the audience.

Being audience-centered not only means that you should think of your audience during the planning phase of the presentation, but you should also respond to the audience during the presentation. It is important that you watch for audience feedback and adapt your message as their needs change. For example, if you notice that your audience seems confused by some statistical data you just presented, stop the presentation and explain it in a different way.

The bottom line is this: Good presentations are those that relate to your audience. It is important to make sure that, as a speaker, you are connecting with your audience. If you fail to achieve this connection, it is unlikely that you will achieve the goal or purpose of your presentation. Therefore, keep your audience in mind at every step of the presentation.

Good Presentational Speaking Is Ethical

While the goal of your presentation may have great significance to you personally, you have a responsibility to your audience to pursue that goal in an ethical manner. As the expert on a given topic, you have great power over your audience. They are trusting you to provide them with good solid evidence and sound reasoning. Providing them with anything less is unethical. If you are asking your audience to change the way they eat, then it is important that you present all of the evidence so that the audience can make an informed decision about a change in their diet. This means using supporting evidence that is timely and from respected sources, and refraining from fallacious reasoning (see Chapter 10).

Additionally, make sure the goals of your speech are ethical. You don't want to ask anything of your audience that could potentially cause them harm. This becomes particularly important for classroom presentations. It is unethical to advocate any behavior that may cause potential harm to your audience. While a presentation on how to make a fake I.D. may appeal to an audience of traditional-age college students, making fake I.D.'s is

illegal. If an audience member actually engaged in this behavior, they could be arrested and face serious legal ramifications. Therefore, stop and ask yourself what you are advocating. If it could potentially cause harm to your audience, pursue another topic.

Ethical speakers are always prepared. As we discuss later in the book, it is a waste of time for you and the audience both to arrive at a speaking engagement unprepared. If an audience doesn't get what they are expecting from your presentation, they will be disappointed. More importantly, it is essential that you have prepared thoroughly and are competent to speak about the topic you are addressing. If you are not fully informed about your topic, your presentation could be misleading to members of your audience and cause them potential harm.

Ethical speakers are also honest. Be truthful in what you say. This means reporting statistics in a straightforward manner that your audience can understand, quoting experts accurately, citing sources correctly, using examples that are typical rather than unusual, and using sound reasoning.

Don't make promises your presentation can't deliver. Don't tell your audience that you hold the key to all of their dating happiness if you don't. Be realistic in what your presentation can accomplish.

Plagiarism

As an ethical speaker, it is important for you to know exactly what plagiarism is so that you can avoid it. Plagiarism is taking someone else's words or ideas and claiming them as your own. Plagiarism is a rising problem on college campuses (September 9, 2003—*New York Times*). But plagiarism isn't only an issue on college campuses. Several important leaders in business, industry and education have been caught plagiarizing. Plagiarism is a serious offense and carries stiff penalties. For example, the top editor of *USA Today* was forced to retire under allegations of plagiarism. The editor, Karen Jurgensen, did not even commit plagiarism herself. It was one of her star reporters, Jack Kelley, who was actually accused of the offense, but as the editor she was held responsible. (April 21, 2004—AP)

Types of Plagiarism

Misrepresentation

Misrepresentation occurs when you take something someone else has written and claim it as your own. Buying a speech or paper on an internet site, taking an assignment from a file, or having someone ghost write your assignment for you are all examples of misrepresentation.

This is a serious offense within the academic community and the larger community as a whole. Some students who engage in misrepresentation do so because they are dishonest. Other students get themselves stuck in a situation where they have waited too late to complete their assignment. At the last minute they realize they have not allowed themselves enough time and they rush to a test file and grab an old outline from a former student and put their name on it, and turn it in.

Make sure you don't get yourself into a similar situation. You would be better off turning in the assignment late than suffering the consequences of academic dishonesty.

Cut and Paste Plagiarism

Unlike misrepresentation which pirates from one source, cut and paste plagiarism takes information from several sources and patches it together in one document. Cut and paste plagiarism is more common today for two reasons: first, word processors make it easy to cut and paste things into our documents and second, the internet provides access to a wealth of information on any topic. Instead of taking the ideas of other individuals and putting them into our own words and providing proper citations or putting the information in quotations marks and providing proper citations, the text is pasted verbatim into the new document and no credit is given to the original author.

Just like your assignments in other classes, your presentations must be combined with research and your own ideas. You should conduct sufficient research and be involved enough with your topic so that you can write a presentation that not only conveys information from experts, but provides your own perspective on the topic.

Incremental Plagiarism

Sometimes plagiarism occurs because we just fail to give proper credit for small parts of the presentation. This is usually a result of misusing quotations or paraphrasing incorrectly.

Assume that you plan to give a speech on the consumer advocate, Ralph Nader. You find the following quote from David Bollier's book, *Citizen Action and Other Big Ideas: A History of Ralph Nader and the Modern Consumer Movement:*

> While Nader did not invent the idea of consumer advocacy, he and his associates did radically transform its meaning. Before Nader's appearance, "consumerism" was often a trivialized concept that dealt with shopping for the best bargains and redeeming supermarket cents-off coupons; it did not put forth an analysis of corporate or governmental power. Nor did it constitute an independent "countervailing force" to the enormous power wielded by business in the marketplace and government policymaking.
> From CITIZEN ACTION AND OTHER BIG IDEAS, A History of Ralph Nader and the Modern Consumer Movement, by David Bollier

You like the quote because it captures the importance of Nader's presence in the consumer movement. If you wanted to use the quote as it is, you would need to document it with quotations in your outline and introduce it in your speech in the following way:

> According to David Bollier in his book, *Citizen Action and Other Big Ideas: A History of Ralph Nader and the Modern Consumer Movement,* . . .

You have made it clear that these ideas belonged to someone else and have given credit to the original author.

If you had decided to paraphrase the passage instead, you would simply restate or summarize the ideas in your own words. But, you must remember that these ideas were not your own. Even though you have restated Bollier's ideas, they are not original and you must still give credit to the author. Here is an example of how that passage may be paraphrased.

Nader may not have invented consumer advocacy, but together with his colleagues, he transformed the nature of the movement from one of trivialized pursuits to an independent force with the ability to counteract the power wielded by corporations and government.

While Bollier's ideas are now presented in your own words, it would still be plagiarism if you failed to cite him for the ideas represented in the statement.

Although you would not use quotation marks in the outline, you would still cite the source. In the presentation you might present the quote in the following manner:

> Davie Bollier argued in his book, CITIZEN ACTION AND OTHER BIG IDEAS, A History of Ralph Nader and the Modern Consumer Movement, that, Nader may not have invented consumer advocacy, but together with his colleagues, he transformed . . .

Excessive Collaboration

Sometimes we ask our friends or family to read something we have written for class and make suggestions for improvement. Sometimes, however, we sit down and write the assignment with our friend or family member. While the first example is acceptable, the second is considered excessive collaboration and the work can no longer be claimed as solely your own.

Last semester, two students from this course were discussing their first presentation assignment. They decided they were both interested in the topic of baseball for the first individual informative assignment. They narrowed the topic to new innovations in baseball and went to the library to conduct research. They collected their research together and went back to their dorm and wrote the outline for their speech, together. They constructed a solid outline and turned it in to their instructors. The instructors, who were office mates, discussed the upcoming topics for their student presentations, and discovered that they had received the same outline from these two students. The students were called into a conference, where they admitted to writing the outline together. However, the assignment was not a group assignment and the students were found guilty of academic dishonesty and punished accordingly.

This example is extreme. The two students obviously co-wrote the presentation in question. Be careful that when you ask for feedback or advice from friends that the work remains your own.

Conclusion

Presentational speaking is vital to your organizational success. Remember, the guidelines outlined in this book are appropriate for both public speaking and presentational speaking situations. Regardless of your speaking situation, a presentation that is goal-directed, audience-centered, and ethical has a good chance of being successful. By understanding what counts as plagiarism, you have a much better chance of avoiding this kind of ethical dilemma.

Key Terms

Plagiarism
Presentational Speaking
Characteristics of Effective
    Speaking

Misrepresentation
Cut & Paste Plagiarism
Incremental Plagiarism
Excessive Collaboration

Notes

1. Ligos, M. (2001, June 20). Getting over the fear-of-speaking hump. *The New York Times*, p. G1.
2. Managers speak up for oratory. (2001, May 28). *The Independent*, p. B14.

CHAPTER 2

Audience Analysis

Chapter Objectives

After reading this chapter, you should be able to:

- ◼ Explain why audience analysis is important.

- ◼ Explain and apply demographic audience analysis.

- ◼ Explain and apply psychological audience analysis.

- ◼ Use direct and indirect methods to gather information on your audience.

- ◼ Explain how a speaker can adapt to the audience while preparing a presentation.

- ◼ Explain how a speaker can adapt to the audience during the presentation.

Effective presentations are always audience-centered.

Sarah, a finance major, decided she wanted to deliver a presentation on retirement planning. She delivered an incredible presentation to her COM 114 speaking class. She provided strategies and tips that traditional college-age students could use today to get them on the road to financial security later in life. Her presentation was so outstanding that her instructor asked her to deliver a retirement planning presentation to a civic group in the community made up of business professionals. Sarah gave the same presentation she had delivered in the classroom. Unfortunately, the audience did not respond as positively. Sarah was very disappointed.

What Sarah failed to realize is that good presentations are always audience focused. She was addressing a different audience and her presentation should have reflected that difference. The demographics of her audience, primarily the age of her audience, had changed significantly from that of her class at the university. The civic group was not interested in retirement planning that was forty years away. The audience Sarah addressed was made up of individuals primarily in their mid to late fifties. They needed strategies to meet their retirement needs that were less than ten years off.

Sarah violated one of the golden rules of good speaking: "Effective presentations are always audience-centered." Your presentation will always change based on the unique characteristics of your audience. By adapting to the unique attributes of your audience, you have a better chance of connecting with them as individuals. This is extremely important as an effective speaker. As a competent speaker, you must consider the demographic and psychological characteristics of your audience.

The Importance of Audience Analysis

Audience analysis is one of the most important aspects of any presentation. As mentioned in Chapter 1, it is essential to a successful presentation. We live in a diverse world. The audiences you will come in contact with will be diverse as well. Individuals will be from different parts of the world, will have a variety of different experiences, and will have a wide range of attitudes, beliefs, and behaviors. Part of being an ethical speaker is to understand and appreciate these differences. By anticipating what these differences might be, you can plan a presentation that respects these differences and builds your ethos, or credibility, as a speaker. There are many aspects to audience analysis. This chapter is designed to introduce you to three different types of analyses, along with issues to consider when employing these tools.

Demographic Audience Analysis

One method of analyzing an audience is to examine the demographics that characterize a particular audience and then adapting the presentation to the characteristics associated with those demographics. Demographics may include: age, gender, religion, geographical location, group membership, sexual orientation, ethnicity, occupation, and many others. At one time, demographic audience analysis was extremely popular. However, we now know that we cannot make accurate assumptions about individuals just because they belong to a particular group. Just because I am female doesn't mean that I enjoy decorating or shopping. You simply cannot make those types of assumptions. Placing too much emphasis on demographic audience analysis can lead you to stereotype your audience. If an audience feels stereotyped, they will likely react negatively to your presentation. However, if used with caution, demographic audience analysis can inform certain aspects of your presentation. Let's examine a few of these categories in order to understand how they may inform the way you prepare your presentation. While there are many other categories that this chapter does not address, the analyses of other demographics will be similar to the examples discussed below.

Age

Age is one of the most helpful of all of the demographic categories. When you prepare your presentation, it is important for you to ask yourself: "What are the ages of the individuals that will make up my audience?" We can predict with certainty what events a particular cohort has experienced. For example, we know that young people growing up in the late 1920's and early 1930's were greatly affected by the Great Depression. Therefore, any presentation concerning finances would have to take that event and the effects on that generation into account.

Experiences such as the Great Depression or 9-11 have a deep effect on a generation of individuals. Events such as these shape the way they view life. By thinking about particular events an audience has experienced, you can better predict how they may react to certain policies and ideologies.

By knowing the age of your audience members, you can predict basic concerns they may have as well. For example, college students planning vacations in March or April have an interest in spring break vacations. They are interested in "hot spots" and economical destinations. An audience of professionals planning vacations in March or April is not interested in this type of vacation planning. In fact, this age group would probably want to avoid a "hot" spring break destination. Therefore any presentation made by a travel agent would have to take these differences into account.

Age is such an important variable in adapting to audiences that Beloit College publishes a "Mindset List" for each entering freshman class. This list is compiled to help professors relate to their students. It explains how they may view the world differently from individuals born in different age cohorts because of changes in the world. You can visit this list at http://www.beloit.edu/%7Epubaff/releases/mindset_2006.html.

Sex and Gender

Sex is biologically assigned at conception. Sex is the physiological characteristic that makes someone male or female. In other words, is someone anatomically male or female? There are particular topics that would be relevant to only one sex or the other. Only men can get prostate cancer. Only women can be physically pregnant. However, there are ways to adapt these topics so that there would be relevant information for each sex in your audience. For example, Jill gave a speech on breast cancer. Although this is a disease that normally only affects those individuals whose sex is female, Jill presented some evidence about male breast cancer as well. In doing so, she was able to make her speech relevant to both sexes in her audience.

Gender is more complicated. Gender is more psychological and emotional than physical, and refers to an identity that is socially constructed throughout an individual's life-span[1]. Research on gender indicates that individuals today can feel masculine in some aspects of their lives, and feminine in other aspects. So although my sex may be female, I may approach relationships in my life with more typically masculine behaviors. In other words, I may be more distant and less emotional. Therefore, simply approaching an all-female audience (sex) and assuming they all approach relationships in the same way, or feel the same way about domestic responsibilities, would be a mistake. The gender differences in this all-female audience would cause them to react very differently to this topic. As a speaker it is important that you are aware of these issues and refrain from alienating certain segments of your audience by stereotyping your audience based on sexual differences.

Geographical Location

The part of the country or world an individual comes from is also part of demographic audience analysis. Individuals are often characterized by certain traits based on where they were born or raised. For example, people from the south are assumed to have a variety of attributes that individuals from other parts of the U.S. are not assumed to possess. Southerners are often thought of as backward, slow-talking, conservative, warm, and friendly, among other characteristics. Simply adapting your speech to a group of southerners based on your stereotyped expectations would be a big mistake. A group of people living or raised in one geographical location are extremely diverse. While it may be safe to assume that individuals who live along the Gulf Coast would be concerned with hurricane safety, it would not be safe to assume they will all vote Republican or are conservative.

Group Affiliation

Group affiliation is another demographic that may inform your presentation preparation. If it is possible to discern what groups your audience members belong to, you will have a better chance of reaching them. Belonging to particular groups may indicate interests or particular positions on topics. For example, you may learn that many of your audience members belong to the American Legion. This is a veteran's organization committed to community service. Membership includes males and females who have served in the U.S. military during wartime. Learning that a large proportion of your audience belongs to the American Legion could be extremely helpful. This is a patriotic organization. It would be safe to assume that most members would not support burning the American flag. This group is also extremely supportive of the military and would be unlikely to support anti-war protests.

Sometimes you get lucky and you are asked to speak to a group that shares an affiliation. Perhaps you are asked to speak to a fraternity on campus. More often than not, though, the individuals who make up your audience will belong to many diverse groups and share little in common in terms of group affiliation. In that case, you have to respect differences and approach your speech in a way that respects diverse views and opinions.

Socioeconomic Factors

Socioeconomic factors include occupation, income, and education. All of these factors can influence the way an audience responds to your message.

If you stop and consider an individual's occupation, it can consume a large portion of their identity. Therefore, it affects the way they think about certain topics and may even determine what types of interests they have. A group of teachers will have different concerns than a group of doctors. Doctors will be interested in how managed care affects their practice, while a group of teachers would likely be concerned how managed care would affect their insurance premiums and the level of care they receive from their physician. Therefore, knowing this information in advance can facilitate the adaptation of your presentation.

The amount of income a particular individual earns can also have an impact on their attitudes, beliefs, and behaviors. Imagine giving a tax-planning seminar to a group of individuals who earn less than $35,000 a year versus a group of individuals who earn over $200,000 a year. This would greatly affect the material you address in your presentation. The amount of income an individual earns would suggest very different topics in terms of tax planning. While someone with a large income may be interested in tax shelters, this type of tax planning would not be appropriate for someone with a lower income.

Knowing the amount of education a particular audience has can also be beneficial in adapting your message to fit their interests. Knowing that most of your audience did not complete college can help you adapt your message. If you were presenting material on saving for your children's college education, there would be certain aspects of the college experience that would need to be explained to this audience. For example, this group may not realize that the cost of textbooks is not included in the cost of tuition. Presenting the same topic to a group of individuals who possess college and advanced degrees would be different. They already know the ins and outs of higher education, and this background information would not be necessary in order for them to understand your message.

As with any other demographic category, it is important that you beware of stereotyping your audience based on their level of education. Just because you are speaking to a group of individuals who hold Ph.D.'s, it is not safe to assume they all enjoy classical music, for example. The reverse is also true. Just because you are speaking to a group of individuals who did not attend college, it is not safe to assume that they do not enjoy and support the arts.

One aspect of demographic audience analysis that cannot be overstated is that you should be extremely careful about stereotyping your audience. Nothing will be more patronizing and alienating to a particular audience if they feel they have been marginalized. So while it is important that you know about demographic audience analysis, use it with caution. Some of the other types of analyses discussed in this chapter will probably prove more useful to you.

> One aspect of demographic audience analysis that cannot be overstated is that you should be extremely careful about stereotyping your audience.

Psychological Audience Analysis

In the previous section of this chapter, we have discussed how you might adapt your presentation based on the demographics of your audience. There is more to audience analysis than simply examining the demographic characteristics of your audience. Understanding why individuals are in your audience and how your audience thinks about your topic, that is, how favorable or unfavorable their reaction to your position, can impact how you prepare your presentation. Understanding how motivated they are by your topic, and the amount of information they already have about your topic, can help you better anticipate and adapt to their interests and needs. In the long run, you will be more successful as a speaker if you engage in a thorough psychological audience analysis.

Attitudes

Sometimes an audience is on your side, and sometimes they just don't see things the way you do. We call audiences who are unfavorable to you or your position hostile audiences. None of us wants to face a hostile audience, but sometimes it is unavoidable. The good news is that research has

shown that individuals perform better when they perceive the audience to be nonsupportive rather than supportive.[2] So even if you do have to face a hostile audience, odds are you will do a good job.

Here are some tips on adapting your presentation to a hostile audience. Stress commonalities between you and your audience, or between your position and the position they hold. Maybe you are trying to persuade the audience to build a community center and they are opposed because of a potential raise in taxes to fund it. You might acknowledge that you all want what is best for the children in the community. It is safe to assume the audience will be in favor of programs that enhance the welfare of young children in your community. The disagreement lies in the approach to take in building these programs. So start from a position that you both agree on. The more similarities the audience perceives between their position and yours, the more likely they will respond favorably to your presentation.

You will also want to take small steps with a hostile audience. You aren't going to persuade an audience who is pro-gun control to donate money to the NRA, but you might get them to listen to your position and at least understand why you believe the right to bear arms is important. As we will discuss in Chapter 9, persuasion is a process. Don't get overly ambitious in one presentation.

Finally, you might acknowledge the differences explicitly between your position and that of your audience. This demonstrates to the audience that you respect and understand their position. This may encourage them to listen fairly to your point of view.

Motivation

Sometimes audiences are very engaged with the material and actively listen to every aspect of a presentation. We call audiences who are engaged motivated audiences. Other times they are less likely to spend a great deal of time elaborating or thinking about the messages you are presenting. We call these types of audiences passive audiences.

The audiences' motivation to process your material is extremely important. It can dictate specific strategies you might use in your actual presentation. Motivation ultimately depends on how involved the audience is with your particular topic. For example, if you are delivering a speech about a proposed increase in Purdue's tuition to an audience of Purdue students, involvement would be extremely high. A change in the curriculum at a local high school in West Lafayette, however, is a topic in which this same audience would have little involvement. The audience is unlikely to be affected by changes in high school curriculum, while they will likely be affected by an increase in tuition at Purdue. Therefore, their motivation to process the material on each of these two topics would be very different.

When topics are highly relevant for an audience, they will be motivated to devote a good deal of mental energy to think about the ideas you present. They will critique arguments more closely and pay attention to the minute details in the presentation. Thus, when dealing with motivated audiences, you must as a speaker be even more attentive to source credibility, timeliness of the material, and the strength of your arguments.

If an audience has low involvement, or is passive, as with the example of curriculum changes in local high schools, they will be less motivated and therefore less likely to a spend large amount of mental energy in processing the material.[5] Rather than spending time thinking about the ideas you present, they will sit back and rely on rules for making decisions. For example, instead of examining the strength of each argument you present, they may only notice the number of arguments or the length of those arguments.

A key factor in determining audiences' motivation for your topic is why they are in the audience. Are they captive or voluntary? Members of a captive audience have to attend your presentation. Such an audience might consist of employees required to attend a training presentation or members of a class. In both of these examples, the audience is there by force. In one case, they could lose their job if they fail to attend, and in the other they could receive a failing grade. Members of a voluntary audience are there on their own free will. They attend a presentation because they are interested in the material you are going to present or are interested in you as a speaker. Understanding the differences in these two types of audiences makes a big difference when planning your presentation.

A captive audience, by definition, is a tougher audience to reach. You have to work harder at capturing their attention and making the presentation relevant to their needs. You must be able to convince this type of audience that you have something that will benefit them. Be explicit; tell them directly how they will benefit from listening to your presentation. Once you have managed to capture their attention, you must work hard to keep it. Using good evidence and strong arguments is essential in maintaining the interest of this type of audience.

A voluntary audience is less daunting. They are attending your presentation because they are interested in your topic or your expertise. Therefore, it will be relatively easy to gain their attention. This audience arrives motivated. It is still important to use good evidence and sound reasoning. However, it will not be as difficult to engage a voluntary audience with your information.

Environmental Audience Analysis

In addition to analyzing the different characteristics of your audience, it is also important to examine the environment that will surround your audience. Where will you be speaking and how will that affect your audience's ability to relate to you?

Physical Setting

Where will you be presenting this presentation? Will your audience be seated in comfortable seating? Will the setting be formal, as in a large lecture hall, or will it be informal, as in a conference room? All of these factors will affect your audience and will require adaptation on your part. Always try and visit the actual place you will be making your presentation. If this is not possible, ask the person who is scheduling or arranging your presentation to describe the accommodations.

If you will be speaking outside, it will be unlikely that you will be able to use audiovisual equipment. PowerPoint slides will not be visible outdoors even if you had the equipment available to you. You will also be competing with the environment. If it is a beautiful spring day after a cold drab winter, it will be hard for your audience to concentrate on what you say. How might you accommodate this? Some type of novelty in your presentation may help you overcome this distraction.

If the room is large, you will need to speak louder so that audience members in the back can hear you. Large rooms also suggest more formality. Speakers are required to be more formal in large settings. Think about your own experiences. Classes conducted in standard classrooms are usually more informal than those conducted in large lecture halls.

If you notice that your audience is uncomfortable due to the room's environment, you will want to shorten your presentation. The attention of an audience sitting in uncomfortable chairs or having to stand in the back of the room will wander. Make accommodations during your presentation if you sense that your audience is uncomfortable.

> The occasion can also affect the need for adaptation on your part as a speaker.

Occasion

The occasion can also affect the need for adaptation on your part as a speaker. Why are you being asked to give this presentation? Is this part of a sales presentation? Are you being asked to reveal changes as part of an organizational restructuring? The occasion will dictate how you will approach the topic as well. For example, organizational restructuring makes employees very nervous. Their jobs are potentially at risk. Therefore, you would approach speaking at this occasion very differently than if you were commemorating the anniversary of the organization. In terms of the occasion, think about what the audience is expecting and feeling and how those expectations can be incorporated into the presentation.

Time of Day

The time of day when you deliver your presentation can also affect your audience. You want to prepare for their reactions and adapt your message to best engage them. If you are asked to deliver a briefing at 11:30 a.m., you can anticipate that your audience will be hungry and looking forward to lunch. You would want to keep your comments brief. If you continued your presentation well after the noon hour, you might lose your audience. They would be distracted and thinking, "When will this presentation be over so I can get some lunch?"

Similarly, speaking right after an audience has returned from lunch can have profound implications on your presentation as well. Audiences are often sleepy after eating a large meal. Therefore, you must plan very engaging and exciting material if you are making a presentation right after the lunch hour. What can you do to get your audience involved? Some type of activity might be necessary when facing this situation.

Audience Adaptation Before the Presentation

Now that you know all the things you need to consider when adapting to your audience, you may be thinking, "How will I get this information? How will I know the demographics of my audience and how motivated they will be to process my presentation?" There are direct and indirect ways of gathering this information.

Direct Methods

One of the best ways to gather information about your audience is through direct methods. These include directly asking your audience who they are and what characteristics they possess. Interviews, focus groups, and surveys are some of the traditional tools used in gathering information directly from your audience.

Interviews are conducted one-on-one with audience members. You should prepare a list of questions in advance that includes both closed-ended and open-ended questions. Closed-ended questions limit responses to a specific range of answers. An example would be, "Do you exercise regularly?" The respondent only has two choices: yes or no. Open-ended questions allow the respondent the freedom to provide any answer they choose. An example would be, "Describe your exercise routine." By including open-ended and closed-ended questions in your interview, you will be able to get better and more varied information about your audience.

The focus group differs from the interview in one substantial way: the number of people involved is much larger. A focus group is a group interview facilitated by one leader. The groups usually range in size from three to twelve individuals. Focus groups are advantageous because the group can often think of ideas or issues that the individual may not think of alone. In comparison to the interview, you are able to collect more information in less time. So from a preparation standpoint, they may be more efficient. However, keep in mind that some individuals may be hesitant to speak up in a group setting.

Surveys or questionnaires are another direct method of collecting information about your audience. Surveys allow you the opportunity to collect a large amount of information in a relatively short amount of time. Polls that political candidates distribute are examples of surveys. You can use the e-mail tool in WebCT to distribute questionnaires to your classmates. This is a quick and easy way for you to collect information on your classroom audience.

While the direct method is the most effective method for gathering information about your audience, it isn't always available to you as a speaker. Direct methods such as those suggested above take time and money. Typically, this type of research is conducted in high-stakes situations such as corporate takeovers, political presentations, and new product launches. If you are unable to gather information directly from your audience, here are some indirect tools to use when analyzing your audience.

Indirect Methods

The best method of collecting information about your audiences is to ask the person who invited you to speak for some information about the group. This person likely knows a great deal about the group and will have a good idea of what the group is expecting from you as a speaker. You can also ask individuals who have spoken to the group before to help you understand the characteristics of the group. They can give you a very good preview of how the audience will likely respond.

I recently delivered a presentation to a large group of students here at Purdue. After speaking with the individual who arranged the presentation, I asked several people who had previously addressed this group to give me some advice about how to approach this audience. All of them gave me some great information, but the most helpful was that they were a rowdy crowd. This enabled me to plan for this possibility. I knew that the style of the presentation would have to be more relaxed and involve the audience from the very beginning. If I had arrived at the speaking engagement and found the audience a bit wild, I would have been unprepared for this outcome. Knowing this information beforehand was extremely helpful.

You can also examine promotional materials associated with the group you will be addressing. If you have been asked to make a presentation to a potential client, you will want to read every newspaper article about that company, visit their corporate website, and read their pamphlets and other materials. Anything you can learn about them will help you adapt to their needs.

Audience Adaptation During the Presentation

It is also important that you continue to adapt to your audience as your make your presentation. Stay tuned to audience feedback. Don't get so engrossed in your presentation that you fail to recognize the subtle messages your audience is sending you. Audiences send a variety of messages to a speaker during a presentation. They can indicate confusion or boredom, or they may even be nodding in agreement.

There are adaptations that you can make during your presentation to help facilitate the effectiveness of your presentation. If your audience seems confused, stop. Go back and explain that part of the presentation again. Try using a different explanatory strategy this time. If they still seem perplexed, ask the audience what seems to be causing difficulty. You may not be able to deliver the presentation as you had expected, but it is much better to ensure that your audience is following you.

If your audience seems bored, try picking up the pace of the presentation. This may mean that you simply speed up the delivery. However, other situations may call for you to cut portions of the presentation. A second strategy is to use more narratives and capitalize on good delivery skills. Stay away from using statistics and facts that are not completely necessary. Make sure you are making good eye contact and using a varied delivery style. You can also try to involve your audience: ask for a show of hands or call on someone directly. This will help you regain your audience's attention.

Conclusion

Audience analysis is fundamental to a successful presentation. As we have discussed in this chapter, there are a variety of methods a speaker can use to adapt a presentation to an audience. A demographic analysis provides a general understanding of an audience and includes items such as age, gender, sex, socioeconomic status, culture, religious background, and sexual orientation. However, demographic audience analyses are limited in nature. You must be careful not to marginalize your audience by stereotyping them. More sophisticated approaches to analyzing your audience include psychological approaches. Understanding what attitudes the audience holds about your message and why they are in your audience is important. By understanding how an audience may process the material you present, you can use various strategies to best reach them and ensure that they elaborate on the material you present. Environmental audience analysis helps you adapt to the situation. There are many methods to collecting the information you will use for your audience analysis. Indirect and direct methods for collecting information can be insightful, so take advantage of both. It is also important to remember that audience analysis isn't only conducted before the presentation. You must also continue to analyze and adapt to their needs during the presentation as well.

Key Terms

Audience Analysis
Captive Audience
Closed-ended Questions
Demographic Analysis

Direct Methods
Focus Groups
Indirect Methods
Interviews

Open-ended Questions
Psychological Analysis
Questionnaires
Voluntary Audience

Notes

1. Ivy, D. K., & Backlund, P. (1994). *Exploring Gender Speak: Personal Effectiveness in Gender Communication*. New York: McGraw-Hill.
2. Butler, J. L., & Baumeister, R. F. (1998). The trouble with friendly faces: Skilled performance with a supportive audience. *Journal of Personality and Social Psychology* 75(5),1213–1230.
3. Petty, R. E., & Cacioppo, J. T. (1986). The elaboration likelihood model of persuasion. In L. Berkowitz (ed.). *Advances in Experimental Social Psychology* (Vol. 19, pp. 123–205). New York: Academic Press.
4. O'Keefe, D. J. (2002). *Persuasion Theory and Research*. Thousand Oaks: Sage.
5. Perloff, R. M. (1993). *The Dynamics of Persuasion*. New Jersey: Lawrence Erlbaum Associates.

CHAPTER 3

Selecting the Topic and Purpose

Chapter Objectives

After reading this chapter, you should be able to:

- Explain the qualities of a good topic.

- Identify methods for choosing a topic.

- Identify differences between the general and specific purpose statements.

- Identify differences between the specific purpose statement and the thesis statement.

- Construct effective general purpose, specific purpose and thesis statements following the criteria outlined in the chapter.

Gino is taking this course and has begun the initial steps of preparing his first presentation. His assignment requires him to pick a topic with which he is familiar and share this material with his audience in an informative presentation. After hours of thinking about the assignment, he still has no topic. When his roommate, Erik, comes home and asks what he is doing, Gino tells him about the assignment and tells him that he cannot find a topic that his audience will find interesting. Erik laughs and says, "You can't find anything exciting and interesting to speak about? You have two part-time jobs, one at the coffee house and the other refereeing intramural athletics on the weekend. There are plenty of interesting topics related to your two jobs alone." After discussing the specifics of his part-time jobs with Erik further, Gino decides to speak on shade grown coffee. This is a special type of coffee he sells in the coffee house.

Gino's situation is not unique. Often the most difficult part of preparing your presentation is choosing your topic. I often hear students say things like, "I have no experiences an audience will find interesting" or "I don't do anything exciting or interesting." I have heard these types of statements from many students. All of them eventually found an exciting topic to deliver to the class and so will you. That being said, choosing the right topic is a difficult process that takes time and effort. This chapter provides steps to assist you in selecting a topic. If you follow these guidelines it will be easier for you to select a topic you are excited about. Following topic selection, we will discuss how to narrow your topic and transform that topic into effective purpose and thesis statements for your presentation.

Let's begin by discussing the elements of a good topic. After that, we will examine the specifics of choosing a topic that will be appropriate to you and your speaking situation.

Qualities of a Good Topic

Interesting to the Speaker

The topics that you choose for your presentations in this course should be interesting and important to you. Because you will spend a good deal of time working on each presentation, the topic you choose needs to be in an area that you find compelling and interesting so that it continues to motivate you throughout the entire speech-planning process. Planning the presentation will be a difficult task to manage if you do not find your topic interesting. In addition to keeping you motivated while you plan the presentation, you must also be able to motivate the audience while you deliver the presentation. If you have little interest in the topic, it will be obvious to your audience. If you have little interest in the topic, your audience will as well. How can you expect to motivate an audience to listen and be excited about a topic that you do not find interesting?

Interesting to the Audience

Your topic must be one that the audience also finds interesting, compelling, and useful. Although you find the topic engaging and interesting, you must find a way to connect that topic with your audience. Audiences are interested in new information that they can use. For example, in this course most of your audience is made up of students who are roughly the same age and in the same situation as you are. Many are hoping to find great jobs after graduation and are preparing for that goal. Therefore, an informative speech on obtaining a summer internship or how to use the job counseling service on your campus would be very useful to your particular audience.

Significant

Your topic should be significant and worthy of being addressed in public. Is it a topic that audiences feel is worthwhile? While you may make the best lasagna in the world, sharing this information with your audience in this particular environment is not extremely significant.

Fits the Time Limits

The topic you choose for your presentation must also fit the time constraints of the situation. In today's frantic pace, we all have limited amounts of time we can devote to messages. The same is true of our audiences. Consequently, we are often constrained in speaking situations by time. More often than not, you will be given a time frame in which your presentation must fit. This time frame may be as small as 4 minutes or as long as several days. You must think about the topic you would like to address and determine whether you can adequately do that topic justice under the time frame you have available. For example, Jodie, a previous student in this course, wanted to explain how a television worked to her audience. She had a 5-minute time frame. The television is a complex machine with many intricacies. After doing initial research, she quickly realized that this was not a topic well suited to the time constraint. In the end, Jodie chose another topic that she could adequately address within the assigned time frame.

Easily Researched

The topic you select for this class should also be easily researched. It should be a topic with a wide availability of resources including traditional print media, such as books, magazines and newspaper articles; personal interviews, etc. If you are having a difficult time generating material for the topic you have chosen, move on to another topic. If the research materials you are finding for your topic are old and do not fit the criteria for the assignment, then the topic may not be novel and informative enough to meet the criteria of the assignment.

Timely

A good topic is also timely. This means it is relatively new or presents new information on an old topic. If you do not have new information to share with an audience, your topic will not be perceived as pertinent or useful. During the research phase of the planning process, make sure that you find new information and developments within the field you are researching. If you are having difficulty finding material that is new and novel for you, perhaps this topic isn't well suited for the presentation. For example, you might find the topic of Alzheimer's disease interesting and

Qualities of a Good Topic

- Is interesting to speaker and audience
- Is significant
- Fits the time limits
- Is easily researched
- Is timely

even know a friend or family member who has suffered from the disease. While most audience members are aware of what the disease is and the symptoms that accompany it, new breakthroughs regarding Alzheimer's are being discovered almost daily. A presentation that focused on the new developments would be timely for your audience. A presentation that simply described the disease would not.

Now that you know the criteria that a topic should meet in order to be considered a good topic, let's examine strategies to help you select a topic.

How to Select a Topic

Although selecting a topic is a large part of the presentation-making process in this course, you will rarely have to pull a topic out of thin air for presentations outside of the classroom. When you are invited to give a presentation or are required to present material as part of a job, for example, your topic will be predetermined for you. That is, you will most likely be invited to speak because of your expertise and your only decision will be how to address the topic in a given situation with a particular audience. In this class, however, you will be required to choose topics to develop into presentations.

Personal Experience

One of the best suggestions for choosing a topic is to select something from your own personal experience. Think about something that you know a lot about. We often feel more comfortable in front of an audience when we know a lot about the topic on which we are presenting. Do you have hobbies or special interests that you could share with the audience that would make a good presentational topic? For example, Shae, a student in this course, was an avid NASCAR fan. He capitalized on his passion and knowledge of racing by tracing the development of the organization for a classroom presentation. Use your areas of expertise to help choose a topic. Perhaps you participated in an internship and you could demonstrate to the class how to get an internship. Do you have a job that could provide interesting material? What about trips you have taken? What are your passions?

Personal Interests

Another good way to choose a topic for this course is to investigate something you have always been interested in. Consider topics that fascinate you that you have never had a chance to pursue. See your assignment as a way to investigate a topic that has always sparked your interest but that you have never had the time to explore. You might think about other courses you are currently taking. Are there issues mentioned in those classes that you would like to know more about?

Current Events

Other good places to look for topics are newspapers, talk radio programs, news magazines, National Public Radio (NPR), and news programs such as *60 Minutes* and *20/20*. Topics presented in the media are usually topics being discussed in society. Therefore, these topics are usually relevant for audiences and are significant and timely. Topics currently being covered in the news are also easy to find, so it may simplify your research process.

Other Sources

Sometimes all we need is a little inspiration to get going. One technique is to brainstorm on ideas related to a topic you have a general interest in. For instance, your general interest in sports might lead you to think about baseball, which leads you to think about the recent threat of another baseball strike, which leads you to wonder whether or not another strike will basically lead to the end of professional baseball. At this point, a possible topic for a persuasive speech is beginning to form. You might also use such tactics as going to the library and looking through the book stacks in areas related to your interest. You will often find interesting books that could form the basis of a presentation. One of the most fruitful ways to brainstorm given current technology is the Internet. Below you will find some examples of brainstorming using subject directories and web portals.

Internet Search

Using an Internet subject directory, such as Yahoo or Google's new web directory, is an easy way to narrow your various interests into more specific topic ideas.

On subject directory sites, web pages are organized by broad subject areas, and then further broken down into more specific sub-subjects. For instance, at Yahoo, your initial screen will feature a standard 14 categories, such as Business & Economy, Entertainment, and Health.

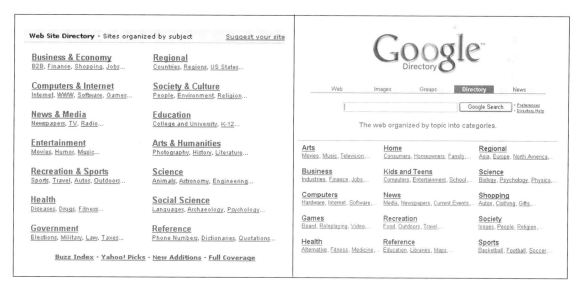

Let's say you have an interest in technology but aren't sure what to give a speech on. You can first click on the category of Computers & Internet. Your next screen will have broken this subject into an additional 48 sub-subjects.

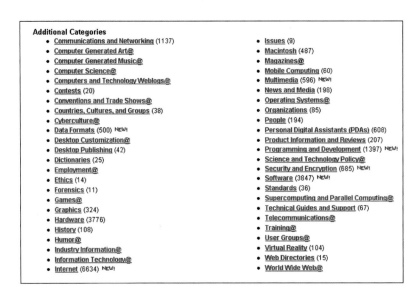

As you peruse these, you notice the category "Personal Digital Assistants." You know a lot of your friends have recently purchased or are thinking about purchasing PDAs, and this might make an interesting speech for a college-age audience. But you still don't know what might be new for your audience.

Clicking on "Personal Digital Assistants" brings you to yet a third screen, which further breaks down the listings for PDAs into 6 more narrow categories. The page also lists the most popular sites for PDA searches, including PDA Buzz, which features news and discussion boards for PDA users and developers. On this site, you notice a news release about the latest uses of PDAs in educational settings. Now you have a topic for your first speech.

Another option for brainstorming topic ideas is the news pages of various web portals, including Yahoo, Google, and members-only sites such as America Online. Most of these portals break the news into various categories for readers. For instance, at http://news.yahoo.com/, in addition to the top national and international news stories, the day's news and news releases are organized by categories such as Sports, Technology, and Science. When you click on a category, such as Technology, not only do the day's top technology stories appear, but you are also provided with nine narrower topics, such as Personal Technology, where you would find information on PDAs and other similar devices.

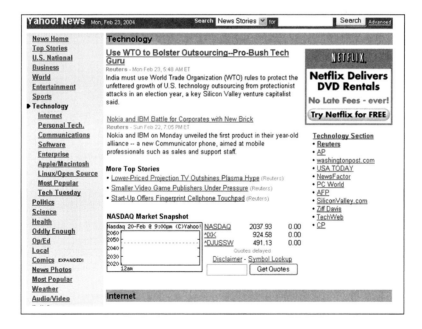

Narrowing the Topic

Once you have selected your topic, you must narrow that topic to fit the situation. A common mistake is attempting to make a presentation on a topic that is too broad. This mistake usually results in a superficial treatment of the topic. There is simply not enough time to address the topic in detail. As a result, the speaker usually only presents information with which the audience is already familiar. Try to avoid this pitfall by focusing in on a particular aspect of the topic that you can develop in detail. Consider the following example: while the history of rock and roll is an interesting topic, you simply cannot adequately address this topic within the 7-minute constraint of an assignment. Sarah, a former student, really had her heart set on pursuing this topic. After determining that she could not adequately address the history of rock and roll in 7 minutes, she found an interesting alternative: The Paul Green School of Rock Music. This is a unique school that teaches children from ages 11 to 18 how to be rock and roll musicians. She was still able to pursue her original interest in rock and roll music, but with a fresh new spin that easily fit within her time constraint.

The General Purpose

After you have selected and narrowed your topic, it is now time to begin thinking about the general purpose or overarching goal of your presentation. As noted in Chapter 1, effective presentations have a strong sense of purpose. Planning your purpose is one of the most important steps in your presentation. Traditionally, the general purpose of a presentation falls into three categories: to inform, to persuade, or to entertain. Because presentations with the goal of entertaining are not

generally a focus of introductory speaking classes, they will not be addressed here. If your general purpose statement is "to inform," you will be providing the audience with new information to create understanding. Informative presentations describe, explain, or demonstrate something. Your role in this type of presentation is that of a teacher. If you do not present new material or if you fail to enhance your audiences' understanding of a topic, you have failed to meet the general purpose of the presentation. Informative presentations are discussed in greater detail in Chapter 8 of this book.

If your general purpose is "to persuade," you will basically act as an advocate or leader in your presentation. Your goal will be to influence the attitudes, beliefs, or behaviors of your audience. You will go beyond presenting information and will actually advocate a particular position or course of action regarding that information. For example, take Gino's topic. Instead of just describing what shade grown coffee is and its benefit of creating a habitat for birds, he might advocate that the audience only consume coffee that was produced in this fashion. Persuasive presentations are discussed further in Chapters 9 and 10 of this book.

Although the framework provided above is useful in getting you started, it is a bit oversimplified. The purpose of a presentation is usually never strictly informative or persuasive. For example, a successful persuasive presentation often has to be entertaining in order to win the audience over. A speech that is persuasive will also contain some informative elements.

One of the primary guiding principles of good or effective presentational speaking is that it should be goal directed. You may have more than one goal in a presentation. However, one of those goals will be the primary goal. What I mean here is while the primary goal may be to persuade your audience to use backpacks that do not cause injury or strain, you may have other goals as well. In order to achieve the primary goal of persuasion, you may have to pursue some secondary goals. For example, you may also want to inform your audience of injury caused by backpacks before you are in a position to persuade them. The general purpose in your presentation is your primary goal. Often times, however, you will also pursue secondary goals in order to achieve your general purpose or goal.

Although the general purpose will be assigned in this course, it is important to remember that in presentations outside of this course, it is your responsibility to determine the purpose of your speech, whether to inform or to persuade. It is also important to note that some complex situations will require that you be both informative and persuasive in order to achieve your general purpose. Sometimes the same topic will be persuasive for one audience and informative for another. It is your role as an effective speaker to determine what the situation calls for and to make the appropriate decisions in those circumstances.

The Specific Purpose

In order to further refine and focus the scope or goal of your presentation, you need to develop your specific purpose statement. The specific purpose statement simply refines your general purpose to make it more narrow. The specific purpose is a statement that conveys what you want your audience to walk away from the presentation knowing or feeling. It expresses exactly what you hope to accomplish in the speech.

- To inform my audience. . . .
- To persuade my audience. . . .

In order to be effective, a specific purpose statement must meet the following guidelines: it must include the audience in the statement, it must be written as a full infinitive phrase, it must be

> The specific purpose statement simply refines your general purpose to make it more narrow. The specific purpose is a statement that conveys what you want your audience to walk away from the presentation knowing or feeling. It expresses exactly what you hope to accomplish in the speech.

written as a declarative statement, it must contain one distinct idea, and it must be written in clear language. Each of these guidelines is discussed below along with some examples.

Qualities of a Well-Written Specific Purpose Statement

Includes the Audience in the Statement   By including the statement my audience in the specific purpose statement, you are more likely to keep the specific attitudes and qualities of your audience in mind as you plan each element of your speech. This will help ensure that each step of your presentation is appropriate for your audience.

Ineffective:	To persuade that nuclear energy is the ideal form of power generation.
Better:	To persuade my audience that nuclear energy is the ideal form of power generation.

By not including the audience in the less effective example, you are more likely to forget about them as you plan your speech. The better example keeps your audience at the forefront, helping to ensure that they are the focus of every aspect of development. An audience of fourth graders is very different from a room full of energy experts. You wouldn't want to use technical language with a fourth-grade audience, but it would be expected with a room full of experts. By structuring your specific purpose in this way, you won't forget who to tailor your message to.

Full infinitive phrase

Ineffective:	Noise pollution and risks.
Better:	To inform my audience about the health risks associated with noise pollution.
Ineffective:	Photomicrography.
Better:	To inform my audience about the origins, techniques, and importance of photomicrography.

The ineffective examples do not adequately address what the presentation hopes to accomplish. While they announce the topic, they do not provide enough detail to indicate the direction of the presentation. Remember, the specific purpose statement guides the direction of your presentation. It is a tool used to refine and focus your presentation. If you cannot identify the exact content of the presentation, the specific purpose is not adequate. An infinitive is composed of the word "to" followed by a verb. In the effective examples, the infinitive announces what the presentation hopes to accomplish. The effective examples provide a clear description of where the presentation is headed.

Phrased as a declarative statement

Ineffective:	What is nanotechnology?
Better:	To inform my audience about the past, present and future of nanotechnology.
Ineffective:	Is a good night's sleep necessary?
Better:	To persuade my audience that a good night's sleep provides many important health benefits.

As you can see, specific purpose statements written in the form of a question do not clearly indicate the goals of the presentation. While they introduce the topic, they do not provide enough information to reveal what the presentation hopes to accomplish. Similarly, specific purpose statements that are expressed as fragments also present problems. They do not give enough information about the direction of the presentation.

One distinct idea

Ineffective:	To inform my audience about shade grown coffee and the plight of endangered bird species.
Better:	To inform my audience about shade grown coffee.
	Or
Better:	To inform my audience about the plight of endangered bird species.
Ineffective:	To persuade my audience to become active in campus organizations and to reside in on-campus housing.
Better:	To persuade my audience to become active in campus organizations.
	Or
Better:	To persuade my audience to reside in on-campus housing.
Ineffective:	To persuade my audience about the benefits of productivity software and the benefits of voice activation software.
Better:	To persuade my audience about the benefits of productivity software.
	Or
Better:	To persuade my audience about the benefits of voice activation software.

While the ineffective examples are written as declarative statements and infinitive phrases, they contain more than one distinct idea. In each of these examples, it would be better to break them into two separate specific purpose statements, one of which could then be chosen as the focus of the presentation.

Clear or Concise Language

Ineffective:	To persuade my audience that something should be done about cheating on college campuses.
Better:	To persuade my audience that an honor code should be adopted at Purdue in order to curtail cheating.
Ineffective:	To inform my audience about diabetes.
Better:	To inform my audience about the causes of and latest treatments for diabetes.
Ineffective:	To inform my audience about hand-held computers.
Better:	To inform my audience about the uses of hand-held computers in the college classroom.

Guidelines for Specific Purpose Statements

When constructing your specific purpose statement, use the following checklist to ensure that your statement will be effective.

- Is it written as a full infinitive phrase?
- Is it written as a declarative sentence?
- Does it contain one distinct idea?
- Is it precise?

The ineffective examples above are too general. The specific purpose statement is a tool that assists you in determining what should and should not be included in your presentation. These examples do not provide guidance in this area. They are too vague and nonspecific. What should be done about cheating? What should we know about diabetes? What it is, who it affects, or its latest treatments? What is interesting about the use of hand-held computers? The history, current uses, new developments, novel uses, or perhaps popularity? The ineffective examples are too broad and do not provide guidance in focusing the presentation. The better examples, however, are appropriate in focus and provide enough detail to assist in the preparation of the presentation.

Thesis Statement

Once you have written a good specific purpose statement that meets all of the criteria outlined above, you are ready to construct your thesis statement. Your thesis statement is a one-sentence summary of the main idea of your presentation. It further refines your purpose for the presentation. The primary difference between the specific purpose statement and the thesis statement is that the specific purpose statement is what you hope to accomplish in your speech. It is the guiding, overarching goal of the presentation. It is a tool for you to use to help ensure that your presentation is focused. It appears on your outline, but you will not actually deliver this statement in your presentation. The thesis statement, on the other hand, is what you will actually say to introduce your topic and main points in the opening of your speech. There are several guidelines that you should use as you prepare your thesis statement. These guidelines are essentially the same as they were for the specific purpose statement.

> The primary difference between the specific purpose statement and the thesis statement is that the specific purpose statement is what you hope to accomplish in your speech.

Guidelines for Thesis Statement

Express as a full declarative sentence   It is important that the thesis statement be expressed in a complete declarative sentence and not as a question.

Ineffective: How does the Food and Drug Administration approve a drug?

Ineffective: Approving a drug.

Better: The process that the Food and Drug Administration uses to approve drugs in this country is complicated and consists of four major stages: the pre-clinical stage, the investigational stage, the license application stage, and the post-licensure stage.

Focus on one main idea   Similar to the specific purpose statement, if your thesis contains more than one distinct idea, the focus of your presentation will be unclear. Remember, you have a very limited amount of time to address your audience. Within your allotted time frame, you simply cannot address more than one main idea sufficiently.

Ineffective: Our lakes are being destroyed by the importation of alien species and our forests are being destroyed by deforestation.

Better: Importation of alien species into our lakes is causing serious environmental and socioeconomic problems.

The ineffective thesis in this example is too broad. Two types of environmental destruction are being covered in this presentation. The presentation will be more effective if the focus centers on only one of these types of destruction.

Use clear and concise language and structure   As will be discussed in Chapter 7, it is more difficult for an audience to follow a verbal message than a written one. It therefore becomes important that your thesis be stated as clearly as possible so that you can enhance your audience's ability to understand the message. This means using simple grammatical structure and avoiding overly complex sentences. It also means using language that is concise and not figurative.

Ineffective: The growing number of bicyclists on our campus makes it necessary to discuss how to purchase a bike that will fit with your body type.

Better: Bicyclists should purchase bikes that fit with their body type to enhance performance, reduce injury, and increase enjoyment.

Ineffective: Ineffective use of a backpack can like crunch the vertebrae in your back if you don't wear it right, pick the right one, or pack it right.

Better: College-age students can protect themselves from backpack injury by choosing the right backpack, packing it correctly, and wearing it correctly.

Be precise   The thesis statement should be very clear. Just as in the specific purpose statement, the thesis should provide guidance in determining what should and should not be included in the presentation. The thesis is the statement that sums up the entire gist of the presentation. If you can't determine the direction of the presentation, then the thesis statement is too vague.

Ineffective: The U.S. Postal Service has many problems and something should be done to fix them.

Better: The U.S. Postal Service is an inefficient monopoly that should be privatized.

Here are several examples that trace the development of a presentation from topic selection to the thesis statement.

Topic:	Backpacks
General Purpose:	To inform
Specific Purpose Statement:	To inform my audience about backpack safety.
Thesis Statement:	College-age students can protect themselves from backpack injury by choosing the right backpack, packing it correctly, and wearing it correctly

Topic:	Drug approval
General Purpose:	To inform
Specific Purpose Statement:	To inform my audience about the Food and Drug Administration's process of approving new drugs.
Thesis Statement:	The process that the Food and Drug Administration uses to approve drugs in this country is complicated and consists of four major stages: the pre-clinical stage, the investigational stage, the license application stage, and the post-licensure stage.

Topic:	Cheating on college campuses
General Purpose:	To persuade
Specific Purpose Statement:	To persuade my audience that an honor code should be adopted at our university in order to curtail cheating.
Thesis Statement:	Solving the problem of academic dishonesty on our campus will require the implementation of an honor code.

Conclusion

This chapter covered the major factors associated with selecting a topic and defining the purpose of the presentation. Many of you are likely struggling with this very issue as you prepare for your class presentations. As indicated earlier, topic selection is not as difficult in professional life as it is in a somewhat artificial classroom environment. However, topics need to be relevant and appropriate regardless of the circumstances. This chapter overviewed qualities of a good topic. It then outlined how to identify and construct the general purpose, specific purpose, and thesis statements that will guide the rest of the presentation's development. By creating these statements, you will be in a better position to identify important resources, conduct research, and organize the information you will use throughout the presentation.

Key Terms

General purpose

Primary goals

Secondary goals

Specific purpose

Thesis statement

CHAPTER 4

Introductions and Conclusions

Chapter Objectives

After reading this chapter, you should be able to:

■ Identify the four components of an effective introduction.

■ Compose an effective introduction.

■ Identify the two components of an effective conclusion.

■ Compose an effective conclusion.

Javier began his presentation with an interesting and humorous anecdote about his brother pulling some teenage pranks. The audience found the story entertaining and was laughing and enjoying the presentation. Javier had done an excellent job capturing the attention of his audience. After telling the story, Javier explained his thesis statement. His presentation was about recidivism rates of state parolees. The audience got very quiet and looked confused. Everyone was trying to figure out what the story of his brother and recidivism rates of parolees had to do with one another. As Javier continued with his introduction, the audience's attention remained focused on how this story was related to the content of the presentation. Rather than concentrating on the material in the introduction, the audience lost focus and missed the important details Javier was trying to explain that set up the rest of his presentation.

Javier made a crucial mistake. He opened his speech with an attention gaining device (the anecdote) that was only tangentially related to his material. This mistake confused his audience and he was never able to regain their attention as he moved through his introduction. This type of mistake is common. Speakers at all levels have difficulty determining how to begin and end their presentations. Like Javier, when faced with making a presentation, many individuals immediately start thinking about how they will begin their presentation. We often get so overcome by how we will start that we neglect some of the important planning aspects of the presentation. We want to come out of the gate running, so to speak, and so we make fundamental errors by focusing on the wrong elements of the presentation.

We have often heard that the beginning and ending of our presentations are the most important elements. I have coached and consulted with many individuals who focus so intently on how to begin the presentation that they do not devote enough attention to the body or the major content of the presentation. This is not to say that the introduction is unimportant. It is extremely important. Yet, you cannot craft an effective introduction unless you have clearly formulated or articulated the body or main ideas of the presentation. After you have a firm grasp on the main ideas you want to share with your audience, you can then begin to design the introduction. If Javier had followed the guidelines presented in this chapter for preparing and delivering his presentation, he would have been far less likely to make the mistake he made with his audience.

A similar mistake is often made with the conclusion. Much like the introduction, many novice speakers immediately focus on the conclusion after they have worked through the introduction. Again, you simply cannot write an effective conclusion until you know what you are going to say in the body of the presentation. The conclusion simply sums up your main ideas. If the main ideas are yet to be formalized, then the conclusion cannot be written. This chapter will also help you formulate effective conclusions.

Introductions

As you recall from earlier chapters, for people to expend significant energy processing your message, two things must be in place: they must be motivated to process the message, and they must be able to process the message. It is in your introduction, the first few moments of your presentation, where listeners make critical assessments about how important and understandable your message will be. If they do not perceive your presentation will be relevant to them and that they will be able to understand or follow your presentation, then they may tune out.

> It is in your introduction, the first few moments of your presentation, where listeners make critical assessments about how important and understandable your message will be.

The introduction in any speech sets the tone for the rest of the presentation. The introduction gains the attention of your audience, introduces the speaker and topic to the audience, and prepares the audience for the rest of the presentation by previewing the main points. All of these elements are vital in an effective presentation. You simply cannot overestimate the impact the introduction will have on your audience.

Components of an Effective Introduction

In order to achieve the goals outlined in the previous section, an effective introduction must contain the following components:

- Attention-gaining device
- Credibility statement
- Relevance statement
- Thesis statement

All of these components must be addressed in the introduction of the presentation in order to be effective. The speaker must also be able to accomplish all of these components or goals within the allotted time frame. A guideline for the length of an introduction is about 10 percent of the total speaking time. For example, if you have been asked to deliver a 7-minute presentation, your introduction should last about 45 seconds in length. Let's examine each of the components of an effective introduction so that you can get a better idea of how they fit together.

Capturing the Attention of Your Audience

One of the most important aspects of any presentation is the first few phrases that a speaker utters. The opening remarks in a presentation set the tone for everything that will follow. Therefore, the attention getter or opening phrase is extremely important. This is the tool a speaker uses to gain immediate attention from an audience. If you are unable to gain the attention of your audience early in the presentation, it is very difficult to regain their focus later.

Regardless of the type of presentation or the situation, whether it is a sales presentation or a classroom presentation, you will always want to begin with an attention getter. There are many devices that you can use to capture attention. We will review several of the most popular.

Questions

Many speakers open with posing a question for their audience. Sometimes this question is purely a rhetorical question, which means that you do not expect a verbal response to the question you have posed. Rather, you only want to get them to think about the question you have raised. Imagine that you are delivering a presentation about the condition of rental properties around campus. You might begin the presentation with questions such as, "Are you tired of paying sky high rents?" "Are you tired of calling your landlord about the leak in the bathroom and the broken toilet week after week with no response?" In this example, the speaker does not expect the audience to answer the questions. The goal with this attention-gaining device is to get the audience to think about the condition of their off-campus housing.

A rhetorical question can also be used when an audience might be interested but will have no way of knowing the answer to the question. For instance, imagine that you are a teacher addressing a group of parents on high school dropout rates. You might start your presentation by asking, "What are the current dropout rates for our district?" While most of the audience members will not know the exact answer, you will get their attention while they wait for you to tell them.

Sometimes we want an answer from the audience. If this is the case, we ask a direct question because we desire a response. The response the audience provides may guide the way we adapt our presentation to that audience. Or perhaps you simply ask the question in order to get the audience actively involved. For example, David, a former student in this course, gave a speech on controlling the wild deer population. He began his speech by asking his audience a direct question: "What animal, reptile, or insect kills more Americans each year?" The audience guessed many responses, from spiders to snakes to dogs. However, the correct answer, as David informed us, was wild deer. According to CNN, deer kill more Americans than any other animal or insect each year. According to the U.S. Department of Transportation, 83 humans were killed in vehicle collisions with deer in 2000. This attention getter was effective because it got the audience involved, and it also revealed their need for this information. He was able to easily demonstrate how uninformed they were, and this functioned to pique their interest in the topic.

Using a direct question can be a little bit risky. What if your audience doesn't respond? Then you have started your presentation off on the wrong foot. You need to make sure that the question is one your audience will feel confident answering. In contrast to a rhetorical question, with a direct question you need to make sure you provide your audience with enough physical or nonverbal cues indicating that you, indeed, are seeking responses from them. Move toward your audience as you ask the question. Scan the audience as if looking for volunteers. Pause to let them know it is time to respond. It is your responsibility as the speaker to provide enough nonverbal cues to indicate that you want a response.

Story/Narrative

One way to build rapport immediately with your audience is to begin with a story or narrative. This is often a great way to personalize your topic and intrigue your audience simultaneously. Audiences are drawn to personal stories.

Here is an example taken from Natalie's informative speech on LASIK eye surgery and the importance of choosing a good surgeon.

> On December 14, 2001, Sandy Keller went in for what she thought would be a "20-Minute Miracle." After her LASIK eye surgery, she would be able to throw away her unwanted glasses and contacts forever. However, things went terribly wrong for Sandy that day. The microkeratome blade used for making the incision in LASIK surgery jammed in her eye leaving a permanent ridge in her eye and a severe infec-

tion. Days after the surgery Sandy saw through a foggy, whitish-haze and became so sensitive to light, it was difficult for her to go outside during the day. She was no longer able to judge distance and had absolutely no depth perception. Sandy's 20-minute miracle turned into two surgeries and a two and a half year nightmare. Although Sandy is now on the road to recovery, she will never regain her pre-surgery vision.

Natalie used this story to immediately involve the audience in the topic. The audience became interested in the plight of Sandy Keller and her traumatic experience and immediately was engaged.

There are a few things to consider when using a story or narrative as an attention-gaining device. First, the story must relate to the topic of the presentation. Secondly, it must also be brief. We often ramble as we tell stories. In a presentation, we do not have that luxury. The story must be succinct and have a clear beginning, middle, and end.

Quotation

Another common way to begin a presentation is by introducing a quotation. If you find a famous quotation or a quotation from a well-known figure that relates to your topic, it can be a clever way to engage your audience. Audiences appreciate comments from individuals they respect. Again, as with a story or narrative, your quotation must relate directly to your material. It should be very clear to your audience why you are using the quotation. If you have to explain the relevance of the quotation to the topic of your presentation, it is probably not the best choice. You also need to avoid obvious clichés. For example, a physician addressing a civic organization was asked to speak about health information on the Internet. He started his speech by saying, "Mark Twain once said, 'Be careful about reading health books. You may die of a misprint.' The same might be said of health sites on the Internet." He then went on to give a presentation on how to evaluate online health information sources. The quote worked well because it was relevant, humorous, from a respected source, and captured the tone of the speech.

Interesting Fact or Statistic

Sometimes the best way to introduce a topic to an audience is to surprise them in some meaningful way. This is often accomplished by sharing some interesting fact or statistic that startles or surprises the audience. A speech on life extension research started this way:

The average life-span for our cohort is 76. So most of us can expect to live to be 76. But, what if I told you that some of you may live to be 150 or even 200 years old? What about ruling out life spans altogether? You might think this sounds like a plot in a science fiction movie, but it isn't as far-fetched as it may seem. A new discovery called the telomere, or tiny pieces of DNA that coat the ends of our chromosomes, may hold the key to human longevity or even immortality.

This was an example from Laura's informative presentation on telomeres. She took an interesting scientific fact and used it to engage and pique the interest of her audience.

> ## Humor is a tricky device to use well.

Humor

One method commonly used to begin a presentation is humor. Humor is a tricky device to use well. There are many pitfalls that can occur when trying to use humor. Some audiences react favorably to humor. Yet others might be offended. So think about your situation, your goals, and your audience before using humor as an attention-gaining device.

If after doing a thorough analysis of the speaking situation you find that humor would be an effective way to engage your audience, you can begin by telling a funny narrative or example, but you still need to make sure the narrative relates to your topic.

You should not begin your speech by telling a joke. This is usually an indication of a novice speaker. Jokes also have the potential of alienating individuals in the audience. What is funny to you may be offensive to someone else. There are more sophisticated and appropriate ways to incorporate humor into the opening of your presentation.

Complimenting the Audience

When you are asked to address an audience outside of the classroom, it is nice if you can draw on some of their previous successes and incorporate those into your opening. It demonstrates that you have done your research about this particular group, thereby enhancing your credibility but also relating their experiences with the topic of your presentation. Consider the following scenario, in which this type of opening is appropriate.

Imagine that you are a fifth-grade teacher addressing a parent's group about an upcoming field trip. One thing you know about the group is they have just completed a very successful fund-raising campaign. It would be nice to compliment the organization on their successful campaign and thank them for all of their hard work. Then you can address your primary goal of presenting information about the field trip by highlighting how the successful fund-raising campaign has provided plenty of funds to cover not only normal classroom expenses, but additional frills as well, such as the upcoming field trip.

Refer to Recent Events

When making a presentation, it is important to remember that speeches never occur in a vacuum. There are many outside events that affect our daily lives. Many times events that are very important to a particular audience have recently occurred. Perhaps their organization has just gone through a big organizational restructuring or has had a change in leadership. If you can relate these events to the presentation topic, it might be important to address them.

Identifying with the Audience

Showing similarity with audience members becomes especially important in persuasive presentations. It is important that the audience see themselves as similar to the speaker in important respects. Those might include factors such as age, political views, or socioeconomic status. If you can highlight some of these similarities, it becomes easier for the audience to identify with you as the speaker and perhaps ultimately, the goal of your presentation.

Bryan, a former student, utilized this device very effectively. He began his presentation by telling the audience that he used to be just like them, college students strapped for cash and working at low-paying dead-end jobs, but that today he is a 21-year-old college student and a successful entrepreneur. He had begun his own neck-tie business and was currently earning $35,000 a year. He went on to give a persuasive presentation that encouraged the audience to become entrepreneurs.

Use Technology (Audio-Visual Aids)

Sometimes the old cliché "a picture is worth a thousand words" is true, and it is possible to grab an audience's interest by demonstrating an important part of your presentation visually. Jeremy, a student at the University of Louisville, was very involved in cheerleading. He delivered a presentation persuading his audience that cheerleading should be considered a sport by the university. He began his presentation by showing a videotape of the national award-winning routine of the University of Louisville co-ed cheerleading squad from the previous year. His audience was dumbfounded. No one in the audience had any idea of the level of athleticism these routines required. The video was one of the most compelling pieces of supporting evidence used in his presentation, and it had an even greater impact by using it as an attention-gaining device.

There are a few guidelines to consider when using a videotape, audiotape, or other multimedia device as an attention getter. First, rather than simply pushing PLAY, you must introduce your visual aid. The audience needs some indication to prepare themselves for whatever it is you want to show them. A frequent mistake made by presenters is to start the media device without

orienting the audience to it. The audience can then end up missing half of the audio-visual presentation. Secondly, cue the video or media to its exact position. It is considered unprofessional to begin the media at the wrong spot. Finally, you must have good working knowledge of the equipment in the room. Orient yourself to the equipment beforehand or arrange to have a knowledgeable person there with whom you have discussed and prac-

ticed your presentation. If you have any doubts about how to run the equipment, choose another attention getter. Your ability to use the equipment must be seamlessly incorporated into your presentation. Anything less is unprofessional. Remember, this is the first thing an audience sees of your presentation. If you have problems right from the start, your credibility will suffer.

Solicit Participation

Another way to get the audience excited about the presentation from the very beginning is to get them involved. You can do this by asking for a show of hands. Asking for a volunteer to participate in some aspect of a demonstration is another way to get the audience directly involved. I was part of an audience where this tactic was used very effectively. The presenter was delivering a speech about long-term care facilities. She asked us to take out a sheet of paper and list the five most important things in our lives. Then she asked us to cross off three of those items. It was a difficult task for the audience to undertake. She then explained that giving up those things most important to us (i.e., our homes, our pets) is exactly what individuals face when entering a long-term care facility such as a nursing home. This attention-gaining device fulfilled two goals for the speaker. First, by getting us involved in the presentation, she got our attention. Second, she aroused empathy for older adults who were facing these life-changing choices, which significantly affected the way we, the audience, reacted to the entire presentation. We were able to take the perspective of the older adult, which was exactly what the speaker wanted us to do.

Considerations in Choosing an Attention Gaining Device

At this point you may be overwhelmed by the choices for beginning your presentation. You may be wondering where you should start and what you should choose. Below are some guidelines that should help you in this phase of the presentation process. These guidelines consider criteria such as tone, time restrictions, your individual strengths, and your audience.

Consider the Tone Your Presentation Is Trying to Establish

If the presentation has a somber tone, humor would not be an appropriate way to begin. You want the attention getter to match the overall tone of your presentation.

Consider Your Time Restrictions

Sometimes we can think of incredible attention getters. However, they take up a large portion of time relative to our entire speaking time. Maybe you have a wonderful narrative that relates well to your subject matter; however, the narrative takes 4 minutes and you can see no way to shorten the story and still achieve the desired effect. It may not be feasible to use the narrative in this case. Remember, your introduction must contain an attention getter, credibility statement, relevance statement, and thesis statement, and preview in order to be effective. This is a good deal of material to cover considering the time constraints and the 10 percent rule (the length of the introduction should be 10 percent of the total speaking time). You do not want your attention getter to take up too much of your speaking time.

Consider Your Strengths as a Speaker

It is also important that you capitalize on your strengths as a speaker in the attention-gaining phase of your presentation. If you have a terrible time using humor, do not use it. If you are a gifted storyteller, use a narrative to engage your audience. Think about what you do best and capitalize on your strengths. Choose an attention-gaining device that is right not only for the topic and presentation, but also for you and your speaking strengths.

Consider the Audience

Always choose an attention-gaining device with your audience in mind. Audience analysis is important at every step in planning your presentation, even when planning the attention-gaining phase. Ask yourself, "How will my audience likely respond to this attention getter?" In order to answer this question, you must also consider your relationship to the audience. Your role in relation to that of the audience is important. Consider this example of a student who did not recognize her relationship to her audience. Mary was in her late 60s, while the rest of the class members were "traditional" college students, aged 18 to 23 years. She was delivering an informative presentation about sex education programs in public schools. In opening the presentation, she told a joke about sex and condoms. Instead of laughing the audience looked horrified. After the presentation, the students in her audience commented that it was almost as if their grandmother had told a dirty joke to their friends. It made them very uncomfortable. Mary had not considered how her relationship with the other students in the class might impact the effect of her attention getter. Although they may have found the same joke funny from another student in the class, and even though they enjoyed and respected Mary as a classmate, her age in relation to theirs changed the impact of the humor.

Consider Your Topic

The attention getter must also contribute to the development of the topic. Many times students find an excellent example or startling statistic that they would like to use as their attention getter, but it is only tangentially related to their topic. If this is the case, do not use it. The attention getter should be the initial step in introducing the topic you will present in your speech. The link between your attention getter and your thesis statement should be extremely clear to your audience. If it is not, you need to consider another opening for your presentation.

Establishing Credibility

Once you have gained the attention of your audience, it is important that you establish your credibility as a speaker on the topic you are addressing. Sometimes the person who invited you to speak will establish your credibility for you in their introduction and you will not have to devote time in your introduction to this step. More often than not, however, you will have to establish your own credibility. Ask yourself what specific experiences, qualifications, or educational background provides you with authority on this particular topic? Whatever those qualifications may be, you need to describe those to your audience. This is the point in the presentation when you really want to sell yourself or the company you represent. You must accomplish this task in a modest manner, since being boastful could offend or insult your audience. However, you do want them to understand why you should be viewed as an expert.

In the classroom, the speaking situation is a little different than presentations made to other groups. Although many of you will choose topics in which you have direct experience and educational credibility, some of you will not. You may choose a topic simply because you are interested in it. Perhaps you will have had no experience with your topic other than the research you did for the presentation. That is perfectly acceptable in this context. Simply tell your audience why you became interested in the topic and what you did in terms of research to prepare for the presentation.

Julie, who gave an informative speech on sleep, relayed her credibility in the following way: "Being a college student myself, and finding myself dozing in my own classes for the first time in my life, I wanted to learn more about sleep deprivation and remedies for this common malady. I began researching the topic through journal articles and books and finally interviewed Dr. Sharon Ward, a leading sleep expert here in our city. I would like to share some of my findings with you today." While Julie has no work or educational experience related to sleep deprivation, she, like many other college students, does experience it on a regular basis. She used her interest in the topic to lead to her credibility.

When providing reasons for why you are credible, you should never explicitly say, "I am credible to talk about this because. . . ." This sounds unprofessional. You must express your credibility implicitly. Let's re-examine the example Julie provided. Alternatively, Julie could have stated, "I am credible to talk to you about sleep deprivation because I researched the topic." While it is true that Julie did complete a good deal of research on the topic, she runs the risk of offending the audience by telling them she is credible rather than allowing them to come to that conclusion on their own.

Instructors have a variety of methods for including the credibility statement in your classroom presentations. Be sure to identify and utilize the guidelines and criteria they have established.

Relating the Material to the Audience

One important factor in motivating your audience to listen to your presentation is demonstrating how the subject relates to them and how they will benefit directly from the information you will impart. We call this the relevance statement. Make these connections for your audience. Do not leave this important step up to them. In order to demonstrate relevance for your audience, try to avoid vague statements such as, "One day you may know someone with this disease or suffer from it yourself." Relate the material to the audience today, right now. You need to answer the question, "What is in this presentation for me?"

For example, a former student used the following relevance statement during a presentation on "Smoke Free Purdue": "Smoking costs each Indiana resident $3,391.00 dollars per year." This gets your audience thinking about the topic in relation to their own pocketbook. For each presentation, you have to spell out to the audience what your message means to them personally or to their organization.

While a relevance statement is important for all types of audiences, it is particularly important for the captive audience. Recall from Chapter 2 that captive audiences attend a presentation

Keys for an Effective Introduction

- Always start with an attention getter.
- Display enthusiasm for your presentation.
- Display a sense of control.
- Do not make apologies.
- Do not make promises your presentation cannot keep.

because they are required to do so. They have no choice. Instead, their attendance is required, perhaps because of a job they hold or due to a course requirement they must fulfill. With a captive audience, you have to work extra hard to motivate them to listen and process your presentation.

Announcing the Topic of the Presentation

As discussed in Chapter 3, the thesis statement encapsulates in a sentence the general message and purpose of the speech. In effect, it announces the topic of your presentation. You will deliver your thesis statement during the introduction of the speech so that you can prepare your audience for what is coming and what they can expect from the body of the presentation.

Previewing the Main Points of the Speech

Although you will state your thesis statement in the introduction of your presentation, you will provide other information as well, which will mentally prepare your audience for the specifics of your presentation. We discussed how organizational structure in an oral presentation is not as apparent as it is in a written presentation. In contrast to a reader of "the printed word," an audience of "the spoken word" does not have the luxury of turning back a few pages in order to follow or review a point you have made. By previewing the main points of the speech, you will be helping the audience to organize the presentation in advance so that they will be prepared to listen when you get there. This repetition helps ensure that your message will be clear and that your audience can follow you. In order to get the audience prepared for the rest of the presentation, you will want to preview your main points. Here is an example of an introduction for a speech, including its specific purpose statement.

Specific Purpose Statement:	To inform my audience about the epidemic of childhood obesity in the U.S.
Attention Getter:	Imagine being the parent of a 6-year-old child attending the first grade at your local elementary school. One day your child brings home a note from the school. You open up the letter, only to discover that the school has determined that your child is obese and has provided some guidelines to help curtail this situation. This is not a plot line out of a bad TV movie of the week. According to a 2001 story reported by the Associated Press, the East Penn School System in

> There is research to suggest that what audiences
> hear last, they remember best.

Pennsylvania and the Citrus County School District in Florida are doing just this. Childhood obesity has become a problem, and reporting to parents in this manner is one way schools are attempting to deal with it.

Credibility Statement: As a Health Promotion and Education major, I am concerned about this issue. Several of my courses and internships have dealt with this concern.

Relevance Statement: Childhood obesity is costing society monetarily as well as physically. Insurance rates are rising due to the increase in obesity-related diseases. These rising costs will affect you directly as premiums for health care plans continue to rise because of obesity-related diseases.

Thesis Statement: Childhood obesity in the U.S. is a severe and rapidly expanding problem with a variety of sociological causes and consequences for our society.

Now that you understand the necessary components for constructing an effective introduction, let's examine how to prepare the final element in a presentation, the conclusion.

The Conclusion

The conclusion is the last thing your audience will hear from you. This is where you will leave your audience with your final thoughts. This will be the last impression you make. There is research to suggest that what audiences hear last, they remember best. This is called the recency effect. Take full advantage of this opportunity to leave your audience with a lasting impression. Many speakers depend on a solid introduction and body to get them through the presentation and pay little attention to the conclusion. These speeches tend to fizzle out. Don't let this happen to you. End your presentation with a bang. The conclusion is the shortest major element in your presentation. It should consist of approximately 5 percent of your total speaking time. Therefore, if your presentation is to last 7 minutes, your conclusion will take 20 to 25 seconds. If there were a motto for the conclusion, it would be "Be clear, brief, and memorable."

There are two components to an effective conclusion. First, you want to restate your thesis statement and review your main points for your audience. And finally, you want to leave your audience with a memorable thought or lasting impression.

Components of an Effective Conclusion

An effective conclusion in any presentation has the following components:

- Restatement of the thesis
- Clincher or memorable thought

Restating the Thesis and Main Points

The conclusion in a presentation "tells the audience what you've told them." That is exactly what you want to do. You want to take advantage of repetition. What you have a chance to repeat during your presentation, your audience will remember. The more the audience can remember about your presentation, the greater your chances for achieving the primary goals of your presentation.

You will want to restate the thesis. You also want the audience to leave your presentation with a clear sense of what you covered. This is where you provide them with that information. This information doesn't have to be stated exactly as it was stated in the introduction. However, the main points of the presentation should be very clear to the audience.

Sometimes, as we deliver a presentation, we are unable to cover all of the material we had hoped to present because of time or other situational constraints. It is important that the conclusion review only material you presented in the body of your presentation. Even those items that may have been previewed in the introduction, but were skipped due to situational constraints, should be omitted from the conclusion.

Ending with a Clincher or Memorable Thought

Just as you should fully engage your audience in the beginning of the speech, you should also seek to hold their attention at the end of your speech. The "clincher" is the final remark that you will make to your audience. It should be as compelling as your attention getter. Give your audience something to think about. Don't let a great presentation fizzle with a weak ending such as "Well, that's about it." There are many ways to end a speech, just as many as there are to begin a speech. Let's review some of the most common approaches.

Referring Back to the Attention Getter

One of the most effective ways to end your speech and provide a sense of closure for your audience is to tie the speech back to your attention getter. For example, if you have opened your presentation with a story, refer back to that story and end with an extension of that narrative. You can see an example of this strategy at the end of the chapter.

Quotation

It also is common to end a speech with a famous quote or a quote from a famous individual. If well chosen, this type of clincher can tie the ideas up nicely. As with using quotes in other parts of the presentation, speakers can benefit from a last additional boost to their credibility through their identification with the source of the quotation.

Keys for an Effective Conclusion

- Continue to make eye contact with your audience for a few seconds after the conclusion of the speech.
- Keep the conclusion brief.
- Refrain from adding new information in the conclusion.
- Stay composed as you return to your seat.

Call to Action

Many times at the end of a persuasive speech on a question of policy, a speaker will call the audience to action. In other words, the speaker will ask the audience to do something at the end of the presentation, such as signing a petition, starting an exercising program, or voting for a proposal. The call to action is a simple statement that makes the goal of the presentation explicit for the audience.

Although you have many options when ending your presentation, clinchers can be tricky. All of the guidelines that apply to attention getters also apply to clinchers. When choosing a clincher make sure to:

- Consider the tone of the presentation
- Consider your time restrictions
- Consider your strengths as a speaker
- Consider your audience
- Consider your topic

An effective conclusion can help maintain the impact of an effective presentation. In order to be successful, the conclusion must restate the thesis of the presentation and provide a sense of closure for your audience. To help clarify how all of these elements come together, let's examine the actual introduction and conclusion of Dayna's informative presentation on a new technological development.

Example Introduction and Conclusion

Specific Purpose: To inform my audience about a new instrument that allows us to detect whether drivers are over the legal blood alcohol limit.

Introduction

Attention Getter: This is a picture of my friend Lucas Dixon when he was 12 years old. In the sixth grade, he was a percussionist in the school band, was a member of his church's bell choir, on the cross-country team, and was that class clown the teacher couldn't get mad at. He was my neighbor and my friend. We had all of the same classes and because of our last names, I sat behind him in every class. On Friday, February 9, 1996, at around 7:00 p.m., his mom, Emma Dixon, was driving him to a rehearsal for a band competition the following morning. His mom had been drinking that night, but she had to drive her son to his practice. Halfway to school, Emma swerved into the opposite lane and hit a station wagon head on. The other driver died, and so did my friend Lucas. He never got older than this picture, and I never saw him again besides in his casket. His mom had an alcohol level of about .10, which was Indiana's legal limit at the time.

Commentary: Dayna tells a very moving and tragic narrative about her friend Lucas. It is an emotional story that engages the audience from the beginning. The detail of her story makes this narrative come to life and the audience is able to empathize with Dayna.

Relevance Statement: According to Mothers Against Drunk Drivers, an average of 59 people per hour, or approximately one person every minute, is injured in alcohol-related crashes. And about two people die every hour in alcohol-related crashes. About three out of every ten Americans will be involved in an alcohol-related car accident sometime in their lives according to MADD.

Commentary: Dayna continues to keep our attention by sharing statistics that show how prevalent drinking and driving are to our society. These statistics make this topic relevant for the audience. It emphasizes that they themselves, or someone they know and care about, will likely be affected by a drinking and driving accident.

Credibility Statement: I have a strong interest in this topic because I have had two very close people to me die from accidents related to drinking and driving. Because of my personal experiences, I stay informed about new developments in this area.

Commentary: Dayna explains to her audience why they should listen to her about this topic. She explains that she developed an interest because of her tragic experiences and has stayed informed of new developments in this area.

Thesis Statement: New instruments that can test the legal blood alcohol limit are now on the market, and it is important that you know what they are, how they work, and the potential benefits of these devices.

Commentary: Dayna announces the topic of the presentation. The audience now understands where she is headed and what they can expect because she has previewed the main points of the presentation.

Conclusion

Review of Thesis: As I have shared with you today, a new instrument has entered the market that can test the legal blood alcohol limit of individuals and may help save lives.

Commentary: At this point, Dayna simply reviews her thesis sentence. This step helps encapsulate the entire presentation for her audience.

Review Statement: I hope you have a better understanding of what this sensor is, how it operates, and some of the benefits and drawbacks of the sensor.

Commentary: Dayna explicitly reminds her audience of her main points.

Clincher: Just think, if this sensor was on the market seven years ago, it may have saved the life of my friend Lucas. He might even be sitting here in this classroom in the desk just ahead of me.

Commentary: Dayna provides a nice sense of closure by tying the attention-gaining devices used in her introduction to the ending of her speech. Not only does this choice add closure, but reminds her audience of the emotional costs of drinking and driving.

Conclusion

Introductions are the first impression a speaker makes on his or her audience. The introduction must capture the attention of your audience, establish your credibility, provide relevance for your audience, announce your topic, and preview your main points.

The conclusion of your presentation is as important as the introduction. According to the recency effect, we remember best what we hear last. Therefore, the conclusion can be a powerful tool in reaching and persuading your audience. In order to be effective, your conclusion must review your thesis and main points, and provide closure for your audience with a clincher or memorable thought. Do not underestimate the power of the clincher. Too many presentations fizzle at this point rather than ending with a bang.

Introductions and conclusions, though brief, are very powerful tools within the overall presentation. They play very valuable roles, and you need to take them seriously. First impressions and last impressions are important. Though introductions and conclusions are relatively short compared to the overall presentation, they can have a big impact on the overall success of your presentation.

Key Terms

Attention getter
Clincher
Conclusion
Credibility statement

Direct question
Introduction
Preview statement
Recency effect

Relevance statement
Rhetorical question
Thesis statement

Organizing the Presentation

Chapter Objectives

After reading this chapter, you should be able to:

- Explain the guidelines for arranging main points.

- Identify the five different types of organizational patterns.

- Explain the four kinds of transitions.

- Discuss the importance of organization.

Organizing the Presentation

Kelly, an agricultural communication student, wanted to give her persuasive speech on how "hydroponic" fruits and vegetables were more beneficial than those grown by traditional methods. She divided her speech into two main points: that "hydroponically grown" fruits and vegetables are healthier for consumers and that "hydroponically grown" fruits and vegetables are better for the environment, and she provided ample evidence for each point. Still after the speech, most of her audience looked confused. It became even more evident to Kelly during the question and answer session that indeed her audience had not followed her. Kelly was certain of her goal and had planned for it consistently throughout her presentation. Why didn't the audience follow her? It was simple: Kelly did not use transitions. Transitions are one of the most important aspects of organization. They help keep your listeners on track. Many times students think transitions are redundant and don't use them. However, transitions along with the other ideas presented in this chapter will help you, and the audience, keep the ideas presented in your speech organized.

Organizing the Body of Your Presentation

The quality of the organization of a speech often makes the difference between an effective presentation and an ineffective one. Research shows that clearly organized material leads to enhanced audience understanding and increased credibility on the part of the speaker.[1] One reason organization becomes so critical in oral presentations is that the audience can't go back and revisit your ideas. Giving a presentation is very different from reading prose on a page. Your audience does not have the luxury of examining the material at their own pace or referring back to material that was already presented. Therefore, clear organization with good use of transitions is vital to a solid presentation. Attention to organization helps ensure that your audience understands your ideas and has been able to process them in the way that you intended. In this chapter, we discuss how to organize the body of your presentation.

Main Points

As mentioned throughout this textbook, there are three main components in a presentation: the introduction, the body, and the conclusion. The body is where you present the "meat" of your presentation. This is where you place the information you are trying to convey to your audience. In order to do this effectively, you divide your material into main points. Here is an example of how one student divided his material into main points:

> Research shows that clearly organized material leads to enhanced audience understanding and increased credibility on the part of the speaker.

Specific Purpose:	To inform my audience about the types of mosquito repellents.
Thesis statement:	There are three types of mosquito repellents: insect-repellent sprays and creams, mosquito sticks and carbon dioxide traps.
Main Points:	I. Insect-repellent sprays or creams containing 35% DEET repel mosquitoes from humans.
	II. Mosquito Sticks repel mosquitoes from small area such as patios.
	III. Carbon dioxide traps repel mosquitoes from large areas such as a backyard area.

These main points form the skeleton of the speech. At this point, we don't know much about the points this student is going to make. After deciding what your main points should be, you go back and provide supporting evidence to each of these main points.

Number of Main Points

So how many main points should you have? In a classroom speech, you will need no more than three main points. Two to three points is a good rule for the amount of time you have to speak in the classroom. Even if you have an unlimited amount of time to address your audience, you will still want to limit your main points. Good presentations will rarely have over four or five main points.

Organization of Main Points

Different topics require different organizational patterns. By *organizational pattern*, we are referring to the nature of the relationship between the main points of your speech. There are some organizational patterns that can strategically facilitate organizing your material. We will discuss each of these patterns, along with suggestions for using them, followed by some examples from student presentations.

Spatial

The spatial pattern is used when you want to demonstrate the relationship between your material geographically or directionally (e.g., top to bottom, inside to outside, left to right, etc.). This pattern can also be used when demonstrating how parts are related to the whole (e.g., parts of the skeleton, parts of the space shuttle).

Specific Purpose:	To inform my audience about new fashion trends around the U.S.
Thesis statement:	There are numerous new fashion trends springing up on the West Coast, the East Coast, and in the Midwest.
Main Points:	I. The most popular trends along the West Coast this winter will be fake fur, purple, and boots.
	II. The most popular trends along the East Coast this winter will be tweed and short skirts.
	III. The most popular trends in the Midwest this winter will include anything leather and vintage t-shirts.

Chronological

The chronological organizational pattern arranges material in an ordered sequence. In other words, it follows a timeline. This pattern is especially well suited for historical topics and instructional presentations (e.g., "how to" presentations).

Specific Purpose:	To inform my audience about the history of the conflict in Kashmir.
Thesis Statement:	The history of the conflict in Kashmir resulted from three major events.
Main Points:	I. On August 15th, 1947, India and Pakistan were liberated from Britain.
	II. On October 27th, 1947, Kashmir became part of India.
	III. In January 1948, the Line of Control was drawn in Kashmir.

Problem-Solution

The problem-solution design is the organizational pattern to use if your material clearly falls into two main points: a problem and a solution. The first main point focuses on demonstrating to the audience that there is a problem and the implications of that problem, while the second main point centers on explaining a workable solution to the problem. While problem-solution speeches can be used in either informative or persuasive situations, they are primarily used in persuasive presentations. Chapter 9 in your textbook provides more information on the problem-solution speech design.

Specific Purpose Statement:	To persuade my audience to reduce plastic bag usage and waste.
Thesis Statement:	Discarded plastic bags create major problems for our environment and with some simple strategies, we can eliminate some of these issues.
Main Points:	I. There are two major problems with the use of plastic bags: they are non-biodegradable and they negatively affect the ecosystem.
	II. There are three simple solutions we can employ to reduce our plastic bag waste.

Here is another example from another student on a speech about noise pollution.

Specific Purpose Statement:	To persuade my audience to protect themselves from the dangers of noise pollution.
Thesis statement:	Noise pollution leads to three primary problems but by following a few easy guidelines, we can reduce our exposure.
Main Points:	I. Noise pollution leads to three problems: annoyance, speech interference, and hearing loss.
	II. Noise pollution can be prevented if we adhere to three easy guidelines.

Causal Pattern:

Speeches using the causal design seek to establish a cause-effect relationship between two variables or events. Presentations arranged in this format have two main points. The first main point centers on the causes, while the second main point addresses the effects. It is important to understand that speeches of cause and effect can be arranged in either two ways: cause, then effect or effect, followed by cause. Here are examples:

Main Points:
    I. Strong storms on the surface of the sun called solar flares release large amounts of magnetic energy toward the Earth.

    II. Solar flares are so powerful they can damage satellites, cause power outages, and disrupt other electronic and magnetic equipment.

Or

Main Points:
    I. The history of life on the planet Earth has been characterized by a series of major extinctions.

    II. The cause of many of these extinctions has been traced to the impact of larger meteors or comets.

Topical

Presentations that do not fall into one of the other organizational patterns described (spatial, chronological, problem-solution, or causal) usually fit within the topical pattern. The topic is subdivided into smaller parts or subtopics that then become the main points of the speech. The key to using the topical pattern successfully is ensuring that your topic divides into a set of main points that are logical and consistent.

Consider the following topic that Nathan pursued last semester: controversies in men's professional golf.

Specific Purpose: To inform my audience of the major controversies that have recently occurred in men's professional golf.

Thesis Statement: Recently, men's professional golf has experienced controversies regarding race, disability and sex.

Main Points:
    I. Professional golf has experienced controversies regarding race.

    II. Professional golf has experienced controversies regarding disabilities.

    II. Professional golf has experienced controversies regarding gender.

Heather gave an informative speech on the process of parents selecting the gender of their offspring.

Specific Purpose: To inform my audience about the methods of gender selection.

Thesis statement: The two methods used for gender selection today are MicroSort and the timing method.

Main Points:	I.	MicroSort is the process of sorting the x and y chromosomes through a cytometer.
	II.	The timing method is the process of using the woman's natural cycle to enhance the likelihood of conceiving a male or female child.

Characteristics of Good Main Points

Main Points Should Be Balanced

Balance is an extremely important characteristic of main points. When you select material for your main points you are saying that these items are essentially equal in importance. If that is true, you should spend roughly the same amount of time addressing each main point. If after examining your outline you notice that your speech breaks down like this:

MPI:	75%
MPII:	20%
MPIII:	5%

then you can determine one of two things: first, you may not have developed points two and three like they should have been developed. Perhaps you have focused too much energy and planning on the first main point. Second, perhaps you only have one main point. In this case, go back and look at your material and see if you can break it down differently. You may not have initially divided the material in the most effective way.

Your time allocation for each main point does not have to be equal. Spending roughly the same amount of time on each main point is sufficient. Here are a few breakdowns that give you an idea of how much time you might spend on each of your main points:

MPI:	30%	MPI:	30%
MPII:	45%	MPII:	30%
MPIII:	25%	MPIII:	40%

Try to Use Parallel Wording

It is easier for an audience to follow your speech if you use parallel wording for your main points. What this means is using the same phrasing for your main points. For example, the following sets of main points demonstrate the difference between main points that are parallel in structure and those that are not. While both sets of points get the same ideas across, the first set of points will be easier for your audience to follow.

MPI:	A good night's sleep helps promote healthy glucose processing.
MPII:	A good night's sleep helps regulate a healthy weight.
MPIII:	A good night's sleep helps promote cognitive health.

MPI:	Glucose is converted to insulin more efficiently after a productive sleep period.
MPII:	Leptin, a hormone that regulates feelings of fullness and therefore regulates weight, is produced after a good night's rest.
MPIII:	Lack of sleep is associated with shrinkage in the right temporal lobe of the brain.

Of course, all materials will not allow themselves to be so easily organized into parallel structure.

Supporting Evidence

The main points are just the skeletons of your presentation. The supporting evidence you provide for each of your main points will flesh out the body of your speech. One important aspect that beginning speakers often overlook is that the supporting material within each main point should also be organized into subpoints. This means that you should have an organizational pattern within each main point. So while your overall pattern may be topical, one main point and its supporting material or subpoints may be organized chronologically or spatially. Examine the organization of the main points and subpoints in following excerpt. As you can see, the subpoints of main point one are arranged topically, while the subpoints of main point two are arranged spatially.

MPI:	Dangerous traffic signs are characterized by one of the following attributes.
	A. Sign lettering is illegible.
	B. Sign is obstructed.
	C. Sign is missing.
MPII:	West Lafayette has many dangerous signs and some of the most hazardous can be found at the following locations.
	A. At the intersection of 3rd and Main, there are three illegible street signs.
	B. In the older New Chauncey neighborhood, there are many obstructed signs.
	C. On roads adjacent to Purdue's on-campus housing, there are many missing signs.

(Although not noted here, the student then provided statistics and other documentation to further support this material.)

Another key to remember is to make sure that all of your main points are supported. Sometimes you will find that your material only supports a couple of your main points. That leaves some of your arguments completely unsupported. Although the material you have collected is related to your topic, it does not directly support all of your arguments. At this point, you may have to discard some of your research and go back to the library to collect more supporting material. One trip to the library or one massive search for supporting material is rarely enough.

Another mistake students commonly make is dividing their material incorrectly. There is a tendency to have too many main points and not enough supporting evidence or subpoints. Many times, the extra main points can be collapsed into subpoints that support two or three main points. Examine the following example:

MP 1:	The media portray hackers incorrectly.
MP2:	The media describe hackers as males who lack social skills.

MP3:   The media define hackers as overweight and unattractive.

MP4:   The media describe hackers as inherently evil.

Although each of these main points supports the speaker's ultimate goal, to persuade the audience that the media misrepresents hackers, they do not stand alone. They can be collapsed into a more concise organizational pattern. It would make more sense to combine the speech the following way:

MPI: The media portray hackers incorrectly.

    A. The media describe hackers as those who lack social skills.

    B. The media define hackers as overweight and unattractive.

    C. The media describe hackers as inherently evil.

Transitions

Transitions are the elements that help your speech flow and allow listeners to follow you easily. Research suggests that the skillful use of transitions is essential to audience understanding.[2] Students often work very hard to organize their main points and supporting material but still feel something is missing that could aid their audience in understanding their message. Just like Kelly in the opening story, usually, that key is transitions. There are four types of transitions: directional transitions, signposts, internal previews, and internal summaries. Transitions can be sentences, phrases and in some cases a single word. Let's discuss each of these types of transitions and strategies for using them effectively in your presentations.

Directional Transitions

Directional transitions let audiences know that you are moving from one idea to another. They contain two parts. First, they restate the information you are leaving and, second, preview the information that is coming. **You must use a directional transition between each of your main points.** Below you will find some examples of directional transitions.

Now that you understand the causes of poverty, *let's examine the effect* on our nation's youth.

As you can see, internships are an important step in attaining future employment, *so* the university has implemented a process to aid in the search of finding these opportunities.

After examining some of the problems associated with e-waste, it is important that *we explore* some possible solutions.

The key to using directional transitions effectively is to remind the audience of what they have just heard and then preview the upcoming point. Directional transitions are primarily used between the major sections of the speech (e.g., the introduction, body, and conclusion) and between each of the main points. While it is necessary to include a directional transition between the major elements of a presentation and between each main point, it can also be necessary to use directional transitions within main points.

Signposts

Signposts are transitions that mark the exact location in the speech. They tell the audience where they are within the presentation. Here are some commonly used signposts:

> The first point. . .
>
> The second cause. . .
>
> In conclusion. . .
>
> The most important point. . .

Signposts are extremely helpful for the audience. They help organize the material in a way that is easy to follow. Students often overlook the importance of signposting. This is one of the easiest ways to assist your audience in following the information in your presentation.

Internal Previews

Internal previews are just that, they preview material but within the body of the presentation or even within a main point. Internal previews are not always necessary. However, if your material is lengthy and contains many small components and subpoints, or is complicated, an internal preview will enhance your audience's ability to follow your message. Here is an example taken from a student presentation:

> In examining the effects of e-waste there are two problems: the use of landfills and the use hazardous materials.

Sometimes you can combine a directional transition with an internal preview. Here is an example of how that might look:

> After understanding how DNA profiling works, let's move on to the techniques of DNA profiling (directional transition). I will examine two types of DNA profiling—PCR analysis and STR analysis (internal preview).

Internal Summaries

Internal summaries are similar to internal previews except they remind the audience of what was just covered. Like internal previews, they should be used when the material you just presented was complicated, lengthy, or important. Here is an example:

> As you have seen, there are many reasons plastic bags have become a problem for our environment. They are dispersed in large quantities, are disposed of carelessly,

and are cheaper and hold less than paper or cloth bags, therefore increasing our consumption.

Internal summaries are an excellent way to assist audiences in remembering your ideas. By restating key material, you are able to reinforce the main ideas of the presentation.

Just as you can combine a directional transition and internal preview, you can also combine an internal summary with other transitions. Here is an example:

> To reiterate, there are several problems with environmental tobacco smoke (internal summary). First (signpost), it has been proven to cause cancer. Second (signpost), it increases heart rate and blood pressure. Third (signpost), it increases the likelihood of Sudden Infant Death Syndrome among babies. Now that you have a thorough understanding of the problem, let's examine some possible solutions (directional transition).

Conclusion

Organization is vital to a successful presentation. Using the right organizational pattern (spatial, chronological, problem-solution, causal, or topical) is extremely important; not only does organization affect your audience's ability to process your information, it also has implications for the credibility of the speaker. The number of main points, the way they are worded, and the skillful use of transitions are all important elements of effective organization. Don't overlook the importance of organization. Your audience will appreciate it and your presentation will be more successful.

Key Terms

Main points
Spatial Pattern
Chronological Pattern
Problem-Solution Pattern
Causal Pattern

Topical Pattern
Balance
Parallel wording
Transitions
Directional transitions

Internal summaries
Internal previews
Signposts

Notes

1. Thompson, E. C. (1960). An experimental investigation of the relative effectiveness of organizational structure in oral communication. *Southern Speech Journal* 26, 59–69.
   Sharp, H. J., & McClung, T. (1966). Effects of the organization on the speaker's ethos. *Speech Monographs* 33, 182–183.
2. Rowan, K. E. (2003). Informing and explaining skills: Theory and research on informative communication. In J. O. Greene & B. R. Burleson (Eds.), *The handbook of communication and social interaction skills* (pp. 10–81). Mahwah, NJ: Erlbaum.

CHAPTER 6

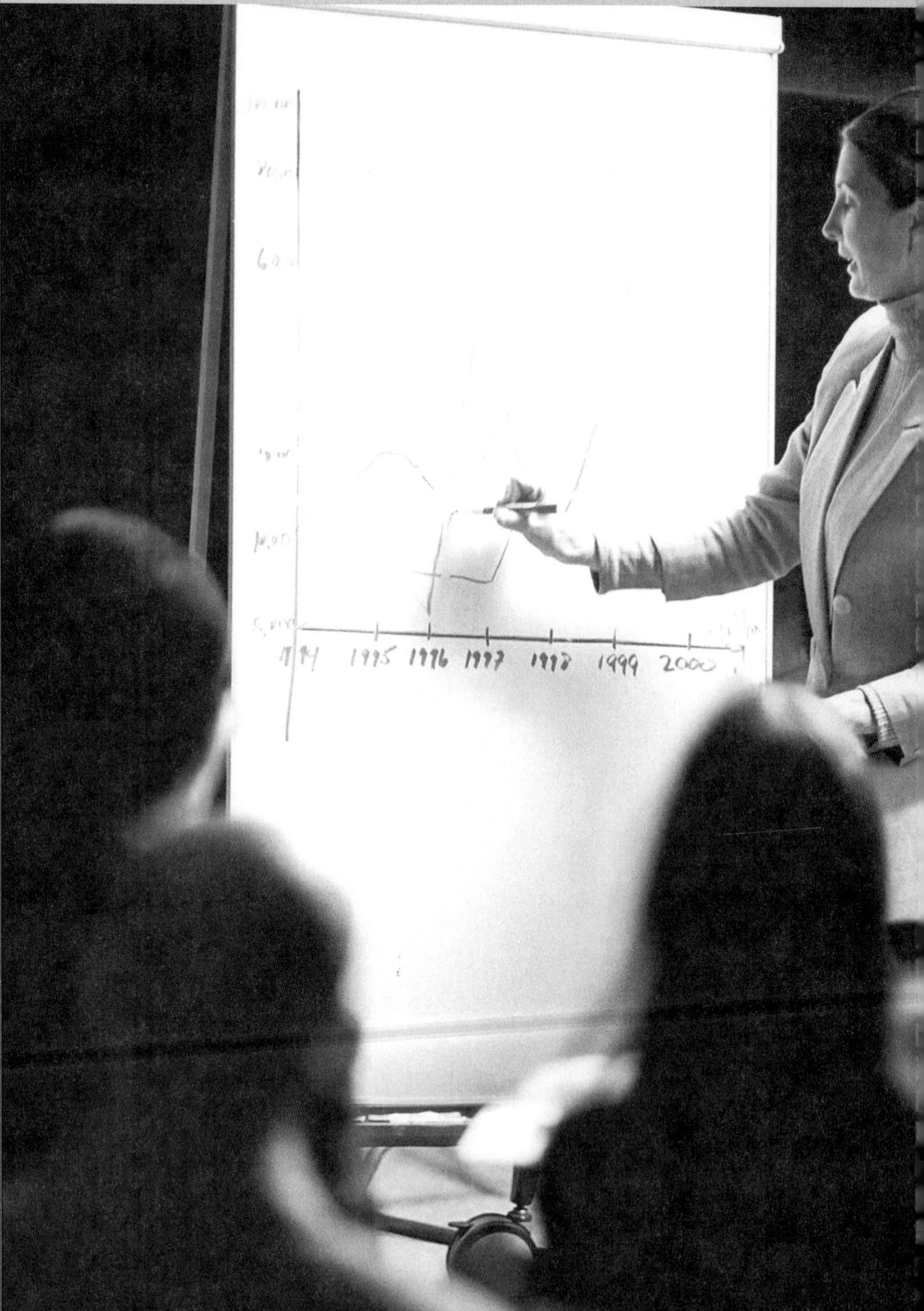

Supporting Evidence and Research

Chapter Objectives

After reading this chapter, you should be able to:

- ■ Explain why speakers need strong evidence.

- ■ Identify types of supporting materials.

- ■ Distinguish among types of examples.

- ■ Distinguish between types of testimony.

- ■ Understand how to evaluate supporting material.

- ■ Identify sources for finding supporting evidence.

Supporting Evidence and Research

A former student, Carol, came to me very excited about the topic for her persuasive speech. Her roommate had been a Peace Corps volunteer, and Carol said she had wonderful stories to share about the people she helped and the rewarding work that the Peace Corps did. Carol wanted to give a speech encouraging her classmates to visit with the Peace Corps during an upcoming on-campus recruiting trip. On the day of her speech, Carol reported that:

> "In its 40 years, more than 170,000 Peace Corps volunteers have helped people have a better life in more than 136 countries."

She continued with numerous statistics about the number of schools and hospitals built, acres planted, etc., that Peace Corps volunteers had helped achieve. After the speech was over, Carol came to me and said she didn't think her speech delivered the emotional impact she had hoped, despite the fact that she had opened with strong statistics to back up her point that the Peace Corps was a worthwhile organization. I asked Carol to recall her conversations with her roommate and decide just what it was that convinced her that the Peace Corps was a worthy organization. "Well, her stories about the people she helped," Carol said.

If it was the stories she heard that convinced Carol that the Peace Corps was a worthy organization, chances are those stories would have had the same impact on her audience of peers. The stories of real people might have been more persuasive to her audience than the numbers she chose to provide. Narratives make strong emotional appeals to audiences that have little knowledge about a subject matter, such as poverty in third-world countries.

The material or evidence you use to support your main points is actually the heart of your presentation. Without it, your thesis statement and all of your claims are just uninformed opinions. Depending on the presentation, you will need to use different types of supporting material in varying degrees to provide evidence for your main points or arguments. How much and what type of supporting material will depend on a variety of factors, including: audience knowledge of the topic (novice/ or expert), your own credibility with the topic (novice/ or expert), and the purpose of the speech (informative/ or persuasive).

For example, if you were a scientist giving a presentation on the formation of the solar system to other scientists in the field, the nature of the facts you discuss would most likely be the results of your own scientific studies. If the same expert was invited to give this same talk to a lay audience, he or she would likely avoid this type of supporting material and focus more on providing supporting material related to the general beliefs of scientists regarding the age of the solar system and why it is important to understand this subject in the first place. If a novice were to speak on this topic, it would be important for them to systematically document what specific experts in the field believe about the age of the solar system. This would bolster their own credibility as speakers on the subject and demonstrate that they are basically summarizing and explaining the research and thoughts of experts on this topic. Each of these presentations would look very different, primarily because they used different types of supporting evidence to make different claims about the topic. It is the supporting evidence, ultimately, that makes the difference between a believable and interesting presentation and one that is ultimately uninformative or unimportant to the audience.

This chapter is designed to give you an overview of the types of supporting evidence you will likely use as you begin to construct your presentation. It will also provide you with information on where to find supporting material and how to evaluate it.

Types of Supporting Materials

Statistics

Statistics are an extremely powerful type of supporting evidence. In our world today, we are bombarded by statistics. Just think about the number of statistics you read or hear every day: Reports indicate that 15% of U.S. children between the ages of 6 to 19 are severely overweight; the film "American Wedding" opened at number one at the box office, earning $34.3 million; 75 percent of American high school students report getting along well, if not very well, with their parents. We feel secure using numbers. Statistics are especially useful in demonstrating trends, explaining relationships, and quantifying information. By using statistics, you can summarize a large amount of material in a very concise manner.

Using statistics as supporting evidence in your presentations can be very compelling for an audience. Consider the following two statements:

Americans are throwing away large amounts of trash each day.

Or

According to the Environmental Defense Fund, Americans go through 2.5 million plastic bottles every hour. American consumers and industries throw away enough aluminum to rebuild our entire commercial air fleet every three months.

The second statement is much more compelling. It clarifies the point and adds strength to the argument. We have a much better idea of just how much trash Americans are disposing each day. By adding statistics to bolster the argument, audiences will more likely be persuaded.

Tips for Using Statistics

Make Sure Statistics Are Representative   One common flaw in the use of statistical evidence is that the data can be collected in unscientific ways. Every time you hear statistics you should ask yourself the following questions: How was the data collected? How large was the sample size? Who were the participants in the study? Was the sample representative of the population it claims to represent? Who conducted the survey? When was it conducted?

Let us assume that you survey your classmates in COM 114 and then claim that 50% of Purdue students are dissatisfied with food services on campus. This is not a compelling statistic. The twenty-eight students in your class are not a good sample. Using the criteria above, we can see that this statistic is problematic. First of all, the sample size is too small to be representative. Additionally, because the individuals are all drawn from the same class, there are likely peculiar characteristics of your audience sample that would not apply to the larger student body at Purdue. For example, they come from a restrictive set of majors and they are primarily freshmen or sophomores. As an ethical speaker, it is up to you to ensure that your statistics truly represent what you claim.

Understand What the Statistics Mean

It is important when using statistics that you have a reasonable understanding of what statistics are appropriate for making which type of claims. For example, if you have a relatively small sample size, a single outlier will influence the mean of the group more than it will the median. The mean and median are all different ways of describing average tendencies within a set of data. They are often confused with each other. They both have their advantages and disadvantages, depending on the nature of the data being reported.

The mean is the arithmetic average of a collection of numbers, computed by adding them up and dividing by the number of cases in your sample. For example, if you survey ten people and find that one of them makes a million dollars a year but the other nine make around fifty-thousand dollars a year, the mean salary will suggest that, on average, the sample makes one hundred and forty five thousand per year. This statistic, while technically accurate, would lead audience members to conclude that the sample makes a whole lot more money than they really do. The median, on the other hand, represents the middle value in a series of numbers. It is found by arranging a set of values in order and then selecting the one in the middle. (If the total number of values in the sample is even, then the median is the average of the two middle numbers.) In our example, the median income would be $50,000. This would provide a statistic that would show a much lower value than the mean and would give the audience a better picture of the earnings of this sample.

Explain the Statistics

It is extremely important that you explain what the statistics mean to your audience. In other words, you need to relate them to your audience and put them in particular context for your audience. One of the easiest ways to accomplish explaining statistics is through visual aids. It is hard for audiences to visualize large numbers. However, if you can relate the information to something that is easy to visualize, they will have a much easier time following your arguments. For example, "40 million U.S. adults have only rudimentary reading and writing skills."[1] This figure is equal to the populations of Illinois, Indiana, Ohio, and Michigan combined. By making this comparison for your audience, you have provided them with a much better understanding of exactly how many people 40 million is. Sometimes, when numbers get very large, audiences have difficulty conceptualizing them.

Limit Your Use of Statistics

Long lists of statistics get very tiresome for audiences to follow. Nothing will bore an audience faster than being bombarded with a list of statistics. Be strategic. Use statistics when you really need the added impact or the type of audience you will be addressing demands it.

Round Off Statistics

Processing large amounts of numerical data is taxing on an audience. One way to simplify large amounts of data is to round off your statistics; unless it is extremely important that your numbers be exact, round them off.

Examples

Examples are another type of supporting evidence. They give life to your presentation. They are powerful tools that personalize or put a "face" on your message and your ideas. They help your audience see your ideas and they add vividness to the entire presentation. Often your message is abstract and by using examples, you make the concept more relatable to your audience. For example, poverty is a difficult topic to grasp without the aid of an example. Statistics alone cannot create a personal tie with your audience. The concept becomes more real when we hear the story of a family similar to ours who was separated due to homelessness and hunger. There are three different kinds of examples that you can use to add support to your presentation.

Brief Examples

Brief examples are specific instances. They are cases used to briefly illustrate an idea. Here are a couple of examples from student speeches:

> A new revolutionary AbioCor heart transplant system has given Robert Tools back his life. Tools was suffering from diabetes, kidney failure, and congestive hear failure. But within a month of his transplant, he could take trips outside of the hospital and is able to converse with others as he had not done in months.

> Some fabrics protect from UV light better than others. For example, blue jeans provide more protection than cotton knits.

Extended Examples

Extended examples are longer stories or narratives. This is an excellent way to generate audience interest in your topic. Consider the example below from a recent student speech:

> Hugo Paulino was a UN peacekeeper who wanted to make a difference in the world. He was one of hundreds of Portuguese peacekeepers that were sent to Kosovo. In their time off, the peacekeepers bathed in the river, ate the local fruit, and wandered around the town that had been heavily bombed during the Kosovo War. At age 21, Hugo returned to Portugal on February 12, 2000. He came home complaining of headaches, nausea, and flu-like symptoms. Ten days later, Hugo had a major seizure, and was rushed to the military hospital where he remained until March 9, when Hugo died of leukemia. His case of leukemia was caused by exposure to radiation in Kosovo from the depleted uranium shells that were used previously during the war. Scientists predict that there will be 10,000 deaths among local residents, aid workers, and peacekeepers due to the use of depleted uranium in Serbia.[2]

The speaker could have easily said that many peacekeepers in Kosovo experienced exposure to high levels of radiation. However, her story makes the presentation more compelling and adds a human component that the audience would not otherwise have experienced.

You don't have to know of the example firsthand. Many magazines and newspapers have these types of examples that you can use. As long as you cite your source, feel free to use the examples you find in the media.

Hypothetical Examples

Sometimes, the examples you use will be true or factual like the ones you have just read and sometimes, they will be hypothetical or imaginary. Hypothetical examples allow your audience to identify with the situation you are describing. Here is an example a student used in her speech on power blackouts:

It's 3:00 a.m. and you are sitting in front of your computer putting the finishing touches on your final paper for your English composition course. Suddenly, you hear a buzzing sound and your power goes out. Your screen goes black. You can't remember the last time you saved your work. You start to panic as the power comes back on and you frantically wait to see just how much work you have lost.

By using this example, the speaker is able to draw her audience into her presentation. In a classroom presentation, most of her audience members are going to be able to identify with the scenario she has depicted. The example would have been even more powerful if the speaker had added statistics indicating how often power blackouts occur. It's a good idea to add facts or testimony to demonstrate that a hypothetical example is realistic.

One mistake speakers make is using outrageous hypothetical examples. You cannot ask an audience of college-aged students to picture themselves as 80-year-old men who have just lost their partner of 60 years. They simply will not be able to identify.

Tips for Using Examples

Make Examples Vivid   Detail makes examples come to life. You want to paint a mental picture for your audience. Include details that help your audience envision the scenario you are describing. One way to enhance vividness is through the characters in your story. Make sure you mention the names of your characters. It is much easier to envision Mary, a Purdue freshman, than if you had just said a female student. These small details give your examples texture that helps your audience relate to them.

Make Sure Extended Examples Have a Beginning, Middle, and End   Anytime you tell a story you want to ensure it has a beginning, middle, and end. You want your examples, especially extended examples, to be fully developed. Most of the time, you will not want to leave your audience hanging. Even if the final outcome of your story isn't essential, your audience will appreciate closure.

Practice Delivering Extended Examples   Not all of us are born storytellers. Some of us are naturally better at telling stories than others. So practice telling your examples. You would never want to read an extended example to your audience. You should maintain good eye contact and use delivery cues that will add impact to your story. You simply cannot accomplish this if you read to them.

By practicing you can also determine how long your story will be when delivered orally. I have seen many students spend so much time telling a narrative that they run out of speaking time and fail to complete the entire presentation. Don't let this happen to you. Practice your extended examples so that they achieve your desired impact.

Testimony

The third type of supporting evidence is testimony. Testimony is a quotation or paraphrase from an expert or knowledgeable source used to support an idea or point you are making in a presentation. Testimony can be very persuasive. Think about the following scenario: you have a sore tooth and are talking to your friend about it. You explain that you are not from Lafayette and so you don't have a dentist in the area. Your friend tells you that she has been seeing Dr. Browne, a local dentist, and finds him to be gentle, professional, and affordable. Based on your friend's recommendation, you schedule an appointment with Dr. Browne. You have been persuaded from the testimony of your friend.

Audiences are often swayed by testimony of individuals they respect. Within the course of a presentation, you can use testimony to add strength to your claims. There are three types of testimony: expert testimony, peer testimony, and prestige testimony.

Expert Testimony

Expert testimony is from people who have the experience or education to be recognized as authorities in their field. Since you will rarely be speaking on topics on which you are an expert in this class, expert testimony is a way to enhance your own credibility. By borrowing the ethos or credibility of an expert, you can add support to the claims you are making within your presentation.

In trying to persuade the class that DNA evidence is reliable, Jessie used the following testimony:

> According to Dr. Ian Findlay, a scientist involved in the human genome project at Queensland University, it is impossible to not leave behind traces of blood, semen, hair, or skin cells at crime scenes. He stated that someone would have to wear a spacesuit to avoid leaving DNA evidence at a crime scene.

Although Jessie is studying health sciences and has even worked in a crime lab, her credibility is greatly enhanced by providing the opinion of an expert.

Peer Testimony

Another type of testimony is peer testimony. These are opinions from ordinary people, not experts, who have experienced the topic at hand. This type of evidence is compelling because it capitalizes on average experience that your audience can easily relate to.

If you were delivering a speech on parking issues here at Purdue, it would be important that you share statements of opinion from students here at Purdue who actually have a car. Without hearing about their experiences, the speech would not have the impact you would want it to.

Prestige Testimony

Prestige testimony is the paraphrase or quotation of the opinion of a celebrity or famous individual. The individuals are not experts on the topic, but they carry a great deal of respect, and audiences often solicit their opinions. For example, millions of Americans tune in to hear Oprah

Winfrey's opinions on fashion, literature, and a host of other topics. While she is not an expert on literature, as someone who has earned a Ph.D. or written best-selling novels, she does carry immense credibility. Millions of Americans buy books on her recommended reading list. Prestige testimony can be a strong source of evidence if you recognize the differences between it and expert testimony.

Tips for Using Testimony

Quote or paraphrase accurately
Make sure that you quote or paraphrase your sources accurately. So many times, individuals are misquoted. Often their statements are abbreviated so that we don't hear their entire statements, or their comments are taken out of context. It is your responsibility as an ethical speaker to ensure that you have used their words as your sources intended.

Use testimony from unbiased sources
Make sure that the testimony you are citing is from an unbiased source. I once read an article that claimed that canned vegetables were healthier than either frozen or fresh vegetables. After further investigation, I discovered the research presented in the article was conducted by the aluminum can industry, hardly an unbiased source. For all I know the information in the article and the conclusions of the study may have been right on target. However, given the biased nature of the source, I had my suspicions. Your audience will as well. Make sure your testimony is from credible, competent, and objective experts.

Cite the credentials of your sources
When you introduce testimony, identify your source. Here are a couple of examples of how you would introduce this information within your presentation:

> Beth, a Purdue freshman and nursing major, had this to say about the Grand Prix. . . .

> Dr. Browne, a cardiologist at M. D. Anderson Hospital in Houston, warns that obesity. . . .

You owe it to your audience to let them know what the qualifications of your experts are. Your audience should be able to judge for themselves whether or not they find your expert credible.

General Tips on Using Supporting Material

Use a Variety of Types of Supporting Material
As you begin to prepare your presentation, it will be important for you to include a variety of different types of supporting materials. As discussed in Chapter 2 of the textbook, certain audiences are more likely to be interested and persuaded by different types of evidence. It is important that you use a variety of materials so that you can appeal to different members of your audience.

Use a Variety of Sources for Supporting Material
Even if you use a variety of types of supporting material, your audience may question your motives or your level of research if you use a limited number of sources for your support. By using different

sources (newspapers, journal, interviews, etc.) and different types of material, you will enhance your own credibility, and, at the same time, increase the believability of your information.

Use Consistent and Complimentary Supporting Material

Your supporting material is not a set of independent observations. They are all parts of a larger whole. They should work together to build a case or make a point. Ask yourself, "Does this evidence enhance the overall presentation?" Or, "How does this evidence or supporting material relate to other supporting material I am providing?" Often, novice speakers string together miscellaneous bits of information that do not, in totality, work together in meaningful ways.

Where to Find Supporting Evidence

Students often cringe at the thought of going to the library to collect research. Many of you are unfamiliar with the library and don't know where to go to get started. One of the best pieces of advice I can give you is to ask a reference librarian for help. That's what they are there for. You will find them extremely helpful and you can find what you need in less time if you just ask for help when you need it.

The undergraduate library provides an on-line tutorial called CORE (Comprehensive On-line Research Education). This tutorial is extremely helpful in getting you started on the research process. The undergraduate library at Purdue also offers a 15-minute audio tour. You can check out the equipment at the circulation desk and find out where everything is. Both of these are excellent resources and I encourage you to use them to become familiar with the material at the library.

There are many places to go in the library to find supporting material. You can visit the libraries at Purdue by going to their homepage at *http://www.lib.purdue.edu*. We have several libraries at Purdue and you may have to visit several of them to locate all the materials you need.

Even with access to excellent libraries, libraries are not the only source for information. You may have to go elsewhere for information. For instance, you may need to actually interview experts, conduct polls, go to museums, visit organizations, or use other methods to get the information and supporting material necessary for your presentation. The library represents only the most common source for gathering information, but your speech may require that you use more than the library to locate information.

Sources of Supporting Material

Books

Books are a good place to begin your research for your presentations. They usually provide a thorough treatment of the topic that they address and, therefore, provide a substantial amount of material on a given topic. The primary limitation with books is that they become outdated rather quickly. It takes a book a good deal of time to reach the shelf, from the moment it is written to the time it is published, so even books with very recent copyright dates may have dated material. This may not be important for every topic but for those topics where information is changing quickly, such as technological or scientific advancements, books may not be the best source of supporting evidence.

Reference Works

Sometimes you need to check a quick fact when putting together your presentation. For example, you may need to know the date of an important historical event, the Gross National Product of a country, or the population of a particular geographical region. Answers to these questions can be found in a variety of common and respected reference resources. These may include encyclopedias, dictionaries, atlases, yearbooks, almanacs, and biographical aids, just to name a few. Look for the most current version of these materials; they, too, can become dated very quickly and are often updated yearly. Online versions of these publications may be the most beneficial because they are continuously updated. While reference works are good places to find quick facts, they will not provide ample material for your presentation.

Magazines and Newspapers

Articles from magazines and newspapers will provide some of the best supporting materials for your presentations. These periodicals are published often (daily, weekly, or monthly), so they usually provide current and up-to-date material. One limitation with magazines and newspapers is that the authors are usually journalists and not experts on the topic on which they are writing. It is important that you keep this in mind as you evaluate the material you consult for the presentation.

One of the best indexes to help you search these materials efficiently is LexisNexis. This index is an invaluable source for finding information. The Purdue library offers this database on-line. You can access it from any computer on campus or even from home. All of the articles it indexes are in full-text. This means the entire content of every article indexed is provided within the data base, not just the abstract, so you can do some of your research from the comfort of your own home.

Newspaper Source is another database you can use to easily locate newspapers. This database provides full-text articles for over 240 U.S. and international newspapers, newswires, and other sources. This collection includes major newspapers such as *The Christian Science Monitor, The Chicago Tribune*, and international papers such as the *Hong Kong Standard*. Visit the Purdue libraries' home page for information on finding both of these databases.

Government Documents

Government documents are generated by federal, state, and local governments. The purpose of these documents is keeping records and statistics. They are also key in helping keep the public informed on government activity and policy. You can visit the Purdue libraries for a list of many websites that can facilitate the search of government documents. The following site will give you more information on what is available to Purdue students and it is sorted by subject: *http://www.lib.purdue.edu/govdocs/subjguides.html*.

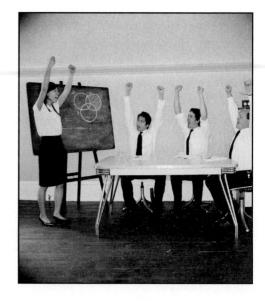

Academic Journals

Academic journals are written for scholars or individuals who do research in a particular area. They distribute original research to a particular scientific or scholarly community.

They contain the latest developments in the field. Sometimes they are difficult for students to decipher because they are full of technical jargon particular to a specific subject area. However, they are a highly credible source of information.

A good place to search for academic journals is Academic Search Elite. This database indexes over 1,850 academic journals in the social sciences, humanities, general sciences, and in education. Proquest Research Library is another database suited for finding academic publications. This database indexes over 2,600 magazines, academic journals, and newspaper articles in many different subject areas. Some are even available in full-text versions.

Evaluating Supporting Materials

Is it Relevant?

Sometimes we can find fascinating material that is only tangentially related to our topic. Perhaps you have found an interesting statistic that you would like to include just because you think your audience might find it fascinating. If it isn't directly related to the goal of your presentation, do not include the material. Only include that information that directly helps you achieve the goal of your presentation. Doing otherwise may distract your audience.

Is it Credible?

As an ethical speaker, you owe it to your audience to find information that comes from sources that are credible. Many times as a speaker you will be asking your audience to make changes that may affect their lives. Asking them to base their decisions on material that is less than reliable is unethical. Your supporting material should come from respected sources.

Is it Current?

In addition to being credible, your supporting material should be current. We are living during a time when scientific advancements are being made daily. So, how current is current? Well, it depends on your topic. Some subject areas are experiencing changes in knowledge daily, while others have had little advancement in several years. For most topics, you will need to consult the most recently published evidence.

Have You Consulted a Variety of Resources?

Ethical speakers consult a variety of resources hoping to validate their research in multiple places. Make sure you look at a variety of types of information, ranging from scholarly journals to newspapers. Each publication has its own strengths and weaknesses. By drawing supporting materials from a variety of sources, you will compensate for any weakness a particular source may have.

Citing Your Evidence During the Presentation

As you will read in Chapter 9 in your textbook, citing your sources within your speech will enhance your credibility as a speaker and can even make your presentation more persuasive. As an ethical speaker, it is also important that you cite your sources to avoid plagiarism. The following examples demonstrate methods for citing sources orally during your presentation.

Books

When citing a book, you need to cite the author, his or her credentials (if it will enhance your credibility), the title of the book, and the date it was published. Here is an example:

> In his 1988 book, "Influence: Science and Practice," Robert Cialdini, a professor of psychology at the University of Arizona, says that there are seven weapons of influence.

Journal or Magazine Articles

You should include the name and date of the publication. You may also want to include the name of the author or the article.

> According to an August 3rd, 2003 article in *Time Magazine,* urban cities, or centers, "not only endure bad weather, they help create it."

> Jeffrey Kluger, writes in an August 3rd, 2003 article in *Time Magazine* titled, "How Cities Make Their Own Weather," that urban cities, or centers, "not only endure bad weather, they help create it."

Newspapers

For newspaper articles, include the name of the newspaper and the date of the article.

> According to an August 6th, 2003 article in the *New York Times,* hotels in New York City are charging less for rooms than they did last summer.

Interviews

To cite information from an interview that you conducted, cite the person's name, their credentials, and when the interview took place.

> In a November 23rd, 2003 interview, Dr. Steven R. Wilson, a family violence researcher at Purdue University, stated, "Child abuse is an interactional phenomenon; that is, parents do not strike their children at random moments, but rather at predictable times that grow out of larger daily interactions."

Conclusion

The use of supporting evidence is crucial to an effective presentation. Without supporting material, your information is just your opinion. There are a variety of types of materials that you can use to bolster your assertions and arguments. These include statistics, examples, and testimony. Each of these types of supporting evidence has strengths and weaknesses. You should evaluate your speaking situation thoroughly in order to determine what evidence is best suited to your particular needs. Regardless of what you choose, using a variety of types of supporting material that are cited effectively will help ensure that your presentation is successful.

Notes

1. Campbell, A., Kirsche, I. S., & Kolstad, A. (1992). *Assessing literacy. The framework for the national adult literacy survey* (NCES No. 92113). Washington, DC: U. S. National Center for Education Statistics.
2. Goncalves, E. (2002). The secret nuclear war. *The ecologist 29, 2.*

CHAPTER 7

Outlining the Presentation

Chapter Objectives

After reading this chapter, you should be able to:

- Explain why outlining is important to an effective presentation.

- Explain the differences between a preparation outline and a speaking outline.

- Construct a preparation outline following the guidelines presented in this chapter.

- Construct a speaking outline following the guidelines presented in this chapter.

One complaint students often make about speech preparation is the process of writing the outline. Students often find this step challenging and time consuming. This chapter is designed to walk you through each of the steps of preparing both your preparation outline and your speaking outline. After reading this chapter and working through the guidelines, you will find that outlining is not as difficult as you may have initially thought.

The outline is the blueprint of your entire presentation and is the tool that ensures your decisions in the planning process have been adequate. The outline lays the foundation for everything you want to accomplish during the speech. If something is wrong in this initial design, your presentation will likely suffer. Zach, a former student in one of my public speaking courses, realized this lesson the hard way.

Zach, who took this class a few years ago, landed a fabulous job at ESPN after graduation. Within a couple of months at the broadcasting network, he was asked to deliver a presentation to some clients. Zach had done well in this class and felt confident in his ability to speak effectively. After preparing a slick PowerPoint slide show, which included digitized video, and conducting numerous interviews with leading authorities on his subject, Zach thought he was thoroughly prepared.

After the big event, Zach was very disappointed with the way the presentation had gone. He felt the speech was flat, and it was obvious to him from the questions the audience asked that they didn't understand and follow all of the points in his presentation. His audience seemed confused and unable to follow the main ideas in his presentation. The organization of the presentation had not been clear, and Zach felt embarrassed and humiliated.

After processing what went wrong during the presentation and not being able to discern where he had lost his audience, he became frustrated and decided to seek advice. Zach called me, and I agreed to meet with him to talk about the presentation. I asked him to bring in all of the materials he used to prepare and deliver the talk. As we started to go through the material, I asked him if I could see his outline. Zach replied that he didn't write one because he thought he had passed that stage and didn't need to do that anymore. There was Zach's fundamental error. The outline is the tool speakers of all levels use to envision and critique their entire presentation. It helps ensure that the organization of the presentation is clear and balanced, that transitions are natural and smooth, that the flow is logical and progressive, that content is supported by evidence from credible sources, that the amount of material reflects the time you will have, and that you will be able to adapt flexibly to the moment if so required. This was the one crucial mistake Zach made in preparing his presentation and explains why his audience was unable to follow the presentation. Without a blueprint, Zach's presentation inherently lacked a structure and his audience became lost.

Zach learned the hard way about the importance of the outline. The outlining stage of the speech preparation process is crucial. Without drafting a blueprint, it is hard to envision a speech, which can lead to things going unexpectedly. As we will discuss in this chapter, the outline stage determines if all the decisions you have made thus far in the presentation will work together.

Why Outlining Is Important

Once you have selected your topic, purpose, and thesis, determined your main ideas, conducted your research, and begun crafting the introduction and conclusion of your presentation, you are ready to test this plan by examining the design through a preparation outline. The outline is the initial representation of your content. It allows you the first opportunity to adapt the presentation to the audience. If you skip this step, you will have missed a vital opportunity to analyze your speech in terms of the audience. Through the outline, you will organize what you will say in the presentation, how you will introduce the material, how you will arrange main points, how you will support those points, and how you will conclude the presentation. It can be best thought of as a tool to determine whether the choices you have made thus far in the planning process are effective and whether you will need to resolve any problem areas.

Ensures Organization

One of the most important functions of the outline is to ensure clear organization. By examining the way the main points and supporting material work together, you can determine whether the organizational pattern you have selected is the most appropriate for the material, the audience, and the goal of your presentation. Clear organization often characterizes a well-received presentation, since audiences perceive organized speakers as more credible and become frustrated by those presentations that lack organization.

Balances Presentation

The preparation outline is a mechanism that ensures balance. In other words, it in effect prompts you to make sure all your main points completely portray the phenomenon you are presenting and whether they are adequately developed. Each main point should be covered in approximately the same amount of detail. For example, you would want to avoid a lengthy explanation of main point number one and cursory coverage of main point number two. From a preparation outline, even a brief glance will provide basic visual clues about how balanced your presentation will be. If your second main point fills up half a page and your third main point runs just two sentences, you quickly will have identified a problem with balance.

From your outline, you can also measure the length of your introduction and conclusion relative to the body of the speech. A commonly used guideline is that introductions should take up about 10 percent of the presentation time, while conclusions take about 5 percent.

Identifies Evidence

The outline also provides an opportunity for you to check and see whether each point has been supported with appropriate research material. If your main points do not have research supporting the claims you make, you will lose credibility and find it difficult to achieve the goals of your presentation. The outline also allows you to ensure that your research has been adequately cited within the presentation. A good guideline is that every point or subpoint should have at least one type of supporting evidence.

Assesses Quantity

One of the most restrictive factors of the presentational situation is the time constraint to which the speech must adhere. The outline can roughly indicate how much material you have and how long it will take you to cover it. With experience, you will be able to use the outline as a very precise gauge of how long your presentation will run. It is important to note here that it is a speaker's ethical obligation to understand how much time they have to speak and to fill that time appropriately. Audiences place a high value on their own time and expect to get their "money's worth" when listening to a speaker. They may become resentful when speakers take advantage of the situation by speaking longer or shorter than expected.

Allows for Flexibility

One of the most important benefits to speaking from an outline rather than a manuscript or memorized presentation is the flexibility an outline provides. When the presentation isn't committed to an exact stream of words, sentences, and paragraphs, it affords you the agility needed to make adjustments during the presentation. This flexible nature of an outline gives you the ability to adapt to the specific needs of the audience and the situation.

Now that you know the importance of the presentational outline, let's examine its format and features.

Formatting the Preparation Outline

The preparation outline is a very detailed representation of a speech. It is carefully constructed and has a variety of features. The following sections identify each of the features that need to be included in your presentation outline.

Specific Purpose and Thesis Statements

It is important to include your specific purpose statement and your thesis statement at the top of your outline. After all, these are the overarching goals of your speech. Every decision that you make about what to include in the presentation should enhance these goals. So when thinking about including a point or a piece of supporting material, refer back to the specific purpose and thesis statements. If the material will assist in achieving these goals include it; if not, leave it out.

Full Sentences

The preparation outline is written in full sentences. Every aspect of the outline is written in complete sentences: main points, subpoints, sub-subpoints, and transitions. This forces you to be specific about the claims you will make in your speech and ensures that your presentation will be more focused and to the point. One maxim worth heeding in this situation is, "If you can't say it, you don't know it." In other words, if you have trouble articulating your ideas in your outline, it will be impossible to do so in the presentation. If you can't outline it, you simply do not have a solid grip on your material. The point is not to write out the entire speech word for word, but to clearly state your main ideas. Let's look at an example:

Ineffective:	I.	Sleeping habits
Effective:	I.	Sleep is being widely neglected among individuals aged 18 to 35 in today's society.

The ineffective main point doesn't tell us much. What about sleeping habits? Whose sleeping habits? This main point doesn't have focus or direction. It has not been clearly articulated.

The more effective example has been expressed as a complete sentence. Notice the difference in clarity from the ineffective example. The direction of this main point is clear and more precise. The complete sentence tells us exactly what direction the main point is heading. The ineffective version would likely result in a rambling, imprecise speech. Writing your outline in complete sentences will help alleviate this problem.

Appropriate Symbolization

The format for the outline follows the common alphanumeric system. You will designate main points with Roman numerals (I., II., III.), supporting points with capital letters (A., B., C.), sub-points with Arabic (regular) numbers (1., 2., 3.), and sub-subpoints (a., b., c.) with lowercase letters. In most cases, you will proceed from the most important ideas to the least important. The structure for the body of the presentation looks something like this:

I. Main Point One

    A. Supporting Point

        1. Subpoint

        2. Subpoint

    B. Supporting Point

II. Main Point Two

    A. Supporting Point

        1. Subpoint

            a. Sub-subpoint

            b. Sub-subpoint

        2. Subpoint

    B. Supporting Point

    C. Supporting Point

        1. Subpoint

        2. Subpoint

Effective Subordination

One of the primary reasons for preparing the outline is to examine and critique the relationship between your claims and your supporting evidence. This makes sure that you have sound reasoning and helps the audience follow your presentation. Each claim you make should be supported by evidence. Simply stated, the idea of subordination means that all the first level points, or main points, are supported by supporting points. These supporting points are further supported or followed by subpoints. And subpoints are supported by sub-subpoints so that each subordinate point supports the idea under which it is indented. Basically, it is a method of physically indenting material so that the relationship among ideas becomes clear and becomes visually apparent. Let's examine the example below.

I. Childhood obesity is an epidemic in the United States (The Morning Call, March 3, 2002).

   A. According to a December 12, 2001 article in the Journal of the American Medical Association, "Being overweight is the most common health problem facing US Children" (pg. 2845).

   B. The study found that 14% of U.S. children are overweight.

   C. Obesity in children has increased for all age, race and sex groups since 1970.

      1. The biggest increase in obesity, however, is among African American and Hispanic children, up 120%.

      2. There was a 50% increase in obesity among white children.

   D. Not only did the number of children who were overweight increase, but also the severity of the obesity increased as well.

As is demonstrated in this excerpt of a sample outline, each of the subpoints serves to support or further illuminate or explain the point above. Take, for example, subpoint C. This statement supports and further explains the obesity epidemic for children in the U.S. It provides further clarification by explaining that this is an epidemic for all age and race groups. Subpoint C is further supported by sub-subpoint 1 by the explanation that this statistic has increased most for African-American and Hispanic children.

Coordinated Points

In addition to subordination, it is important that your outline follow the rules for coordination. Coordination means that the ideas at the same level of importance should use the same series of symbols. Consider the following example:

 I. Violence on television is increasing each year.

 II. Children who watch a lot of television are becoming more violent.

You can see that both main point one and two are equal in terms of importance. This particular example utilizes the cause/effect organizational pattern. The first main point establishes the cause, and the second main point establishes the effect. If we add supporting material to each of these main points, it is important that we insert it at the appropriate level.

 I. Violence on television is increasing each year.

   A. The average number of murders depicted on television is increasing.

   B. The average number of scenes of domestic violence is increasing.

 II. Children who watch a lot of television are becoming more violent.

   A. Children who watch high levels of television are more likely to be bullies.

   B. Children who watch high levels of television are more likely to throw tantrums.

Transitions

Transitions are the elements that make your speech flow and enable your audience to follow your presentation. Directional transitions are used between main points to let the audience know that you are moving from one idea to another (i.e., Now that we have discussed the causes of eating disorders, let's examine some of the treatments.). Signposts mark the exact place in the speech by alerting the audience to their exact location in the presentation (e.g., The first cause . . ., The most important point . . ., In summary . . .). Internal previews are transitions used within main points and alert listeners of what lies ahead (e.g., There are many different causes of eating disorders: media representations, concern with body image, and issues of self-esteem. Let's begin by focusing on media representations). Internal reviews are also located within main points and simply restate the main ideas of a main point (e.g., We have examined three causes of eating disorders: media representations, concern with body image, and self-esteem). Remember, internal previews and reviews are only necessary when a main point is extremely complex or there are a lot of ideas for the audience to keep up with. It is important to include all transitions, regardless of type, in your preparation outline. You are more likely to include your transitions in your actual presentation when they are part of your outline.

Bibliography and Citations

A bibliography composed of the sources you consulted to construct the outline makes the preparation outline complete. Citations are the mentions of those sources at appropriate points during your presentation.

The bibliography will include any books, magazine articles, newspaper articles, pamphlets and brochures, personal interviews, and web resources that you used. (Check with your instructor to see if web pages are appropriate supporting material.) You may use a variety of citation styles to construct your bibliography. (For this class, use APA [American Psychological Association] style or MLA [Modern Language Association] style). Regardless of which style you choose to use to format your bibliography, it is important that the citations are complete and consistent. You can go to the Purdue Online Writing Lab for an example of how to use MLA or APA formatting: http://owl.english.purdue.edu/handouts/research/index.html/. A complete example of a bibliography is provided at the end of the chapter.

Citations are the verbal references to the dates and sources of the material you consulted to write the presentation. Citations are distributed throughout the presentation to demonstrate and bolster your credibility. The source you verbally cite within your presentation will be less detailed than the bibliographic entry. Chapter 6 provides examples of appropriate verbal citations.

Putting the Outline Together

The next few paragraphs will walk you step by step through the process of creating an outline that fits the appropriate format.

Step One: Start by writing your specific purpose statement and your thesis statement at the top of your outline. It will look something like this:

Specific Purpose Statement: To inform my audience about the origins and techniques of photomicrography.

Thesis Statement: Photomicrography is an intriguing type of photography with interesting origins and unusual techniques.

Step Two: Begin by labeling your introduction, body, and conclusion. This ensures that each of these components will be included in your presentation.

Introduction

Body

Conclusion

Step Three: Go back and add Roman numerals for all of the components of each of these elements (introduction, body, conclusion).

Introduction

I. Attention Getter

II. Credibility Statement

III. Thesis Statement

IV. Relate topic to audience

Body

I. Main Point One

II. Main Point Two

III. Main Point Three

Conclusion

I. Restatement of Thesis

II. Clincher

Step Four: Next, go back and outline the body of the presentation. The body should always be constructed before the introduction or conclusion, since your introduction and conclusion will reflect the body of the presentation, once you are certain of it.

Begin by adding the appropriate subpoints to your main points. Use capital letters to insert the subpoints. Recall that a subpoint is content that supports a main point. Sometimes it may also be necessary to add sub-subpoints in a presentation. If you need this extra level of detail, simply add Arabic numbers (1., 2., 3.). It is important that you recognize that at this step you are dividing your main points into subpoints. The rule is, if you divide, you need at least two parts. Therefore, you cannot have an A without a B. If you have a 1, you must have a 2 too!

Tips/Checklist for an Effective Preparation Outline

- Use full sentences
- Use a consistent indentation and symbolization system
- Include transitions
- Include internal citations
- Include a complete bibliography in APA or MLA format.

Step Five: Add transitions between each of your main points. If you have internal transitions, such as internal previews or reviews, mark those as well. Adding the transitions to the preparation outline increases the likelihood that you will use them during the presentation.

Step Six: Once you have arranged your main points and transitions in the outline, you are ready to go back and add your verbal citations. This ensures that you cite appropriately during your presentation.

Step Seven: Outline your introduction and conclusion. Once the body has been finalized, you will be in good shape to finish these important elements. Simply insert the material into the appropriate place in the outline.

Step Eight: Create your bibliography. Recall that the bibliography completes the outline. Use a consistent style of citation. For this class you may use either the MLA or APA styles.

Step Nine: Once you have completed your outline, you are ready to finalize the entire presentation. Check for each of the following components:

- Audience Analysis-Relevance
- Balance
- External Sources/Supporting Material
- Requirements of the assignment

Step Ten: If you are asked to provide a title for your presentation, do this last. You probably won't need one for classroom presentations. Titles often are important if your presentation will be listed in a program or announced in some way. Titles should be brief, yet encapsulate the major idea of your presentation.

The Speaking Outline

After finalizing your preparation outline, you are ready to begin constructing the speaking outline. The speaking outline consists of the notes you will actually use to deliver your speech. It is important to remember that the speaking outline is merely a tool to jog your memory. By the time of

> The speaking outline consists of the notes you will actually use to deliver your speech. It is important to remember that the speaking outline is merely a tool to jog your memory.

your presentation, you will have rehearsed your speech so many times that you will know the material cold. The speaking outline will function primarily as a memory aid and as a gauge to remind you of where you are during the presentation.

At this point, you are probably wondering exactly what you should include in your speaking outline and what it should look like. Speaking outlines are very idiosyncratic. Each individual has certain items they like to include, and those they prefer to omit. As you gain more experience making presentations, you will develop a style that works best for you. Until you gain this experience, here are some guidelines that will help you get started.

Guidelines for the Speaking Outline

Be Brief

In order to maintain extemporaneous delivery, it is important to keep the speaking outline brief. Unlike the preparation outline, the speaking outline consists of key words, phrases, and abbreviations. If your notes are too detailed, you will have trouble making eye contact and, therefore, connections with your audience. Most beginning speakers use too many notes, leaning on them as a psychological crutch that ends up interfering with the delivery of the presentation. However, if you have practiced the speech adequately, you will only need the memory cues contained in a well-written speaking outline to get you through the presentation.

Follow Structure of the Preparation Outline

For the speaking outline, it is important to use the same outline style used in your preparation outline, which means you will want to use the same exact symbols and indentation as you used in the preparation outline. However, because the speaking outline must be brief, you will want to replicate only a brief version of the presentation outline. The example at the end of the chapter on pages 101–102 demonstrates these guidelines.

Include Supporting Materials

You will also want to include any references you will need to cite during the presentation. This will enhance your credibility as a speaker and dispel any hint of plagiarism. Also consider adding on your note cards any direct quotations you plan to present. Lengthy quotations and statistics should be written out verbatim so that you can cite them completely and accurately.

Be Legible

One of the most important aspects of the speaking outline is making sure that you can read it while you are delivering your presentation. Write or type in large letters so that you can see them

Tips for an Effective Speaking Outline

- Be brief
- Print large enough for you to read
- Write legibly
- Write out quotations and statistics
- Number your cards or pages
- Write on only one side of the note card or paper
- Unless you are using a lectern, use index cards

easily during your presentation. Write on only one side of the note card and number each one. If the stack of cards falls on the floor, you will want to be able to recover quickly and easily!

Provide Delivery Cues

Delivery cues are the stage directions that add emphasis to your presentation. Dramatic pauses, repetition, rate, and volume are all examples of important delivery aspects. A well-polished and effective presentation depends not only on what you say, but how you say it. Including delivery cues in your speaking outline will remind you to use these types of special features to add impact.

Delivery cues can be added to the speaking outline in a variety of ways. Perhaps you would like to highlight certain portions of the speech or maybe you want to write in specific directions. Whatever choice you make, insert your delivery cues clearly and legibly so that they do not interfere with your ability to read the outline. Here are some example cues you might add to your speaking outline:

- slow down
- pause
- make eye contact
- move from the podium
- walk to the other side of the room

Usually Use Note Cards

One common question that speakers often ask is whether they should write their speaking outline on note cards or a sheet of paper. Most experts agree that note cards are sturdier and more adaptable. For example, note cards work with either a lectern or without one. They also tend to be less distracting and easier to rearrange. One guideline regarding this question is simple: if you do not have access to a lectern, use note cards. They will be less distracting than sheets of paper. Regardless of which you decide to use, it is important to write on only one side of the card or paper. Additionally, you should number each of your cards or sheets of paper.

Conclusion

Outlines are extremely important. Even experienced speakers cannot afford to take shortcuts at this step in the process. A great outline increases the likelihood of a successful speech, and a flawed outline translates into a flawed presentation every single time. This chapter presented two different types of outlines that play different roles during different parts of the preparation of the presentation.

The preparation outline is the major outline you prepare that enables you to see your entire presentation in a highly structured and detailed way. It affords you the opportunity to critique your presentation's organization, level of detail, use of evidence, etc. The speaking outline is what you actually use during the presentation. It prompts you to cover your main points, to read exact quotes, to express transitions and to gauge your timing, as well as to include other vital information during the presentation. However, the overall level of detail is considerably less than the presentation outline.

By taking the information in this chapter seriously, you can learn from Zach's mistake. Snazzy PowerPoints might look good and help make a point, but they do not constitute adequate preparation for a presentation. And they cannot compensate for a weak outline. Outlining is fundamental.

Key Terms

APA Style	Directional transitions	Signpost
Balance	Internal preview	Speaking outline
Bibliography	Internal review	Subordination
Coordination	MLA style	Subpoint
Delivery cues	Preparation outline	Transitions

Uncovering the Solace of Sleep

Specific Purpose: To inform my audience about the role of sleep in our everyday lives.

Thesis Statement: In order to understand the role of sleep in our daily lives, it is important to recognize the effects of sleep on health, typical sleep profiles of Americans, and factors that interfere with our ability to get enough sleep.

INTRODUCTION

I. **Attention Getter:** In 2001, the National Highway Traffic Safety Administration estimated that more than 100,000 automobile accidents are related to driver fatigue. In fact, 1,500 deaths and tens of thousands of injuries and disabilities are related to drowsy driving. This problem impacts drivers age 25 and younger more than any other age group. (National Highway Traffic Safety Administration, 2002)

II. **Credibility Statement:** After falling asleep at the wheel many times myself, I became curious about sleep's role in our day-to-day activities and would like to share some of the interesting information I have uncovered.

III. **Relating to the Audience:** As college students, we all know how precious time is and sleep is one of the first things we cut from our schedules.

IV. **Thesis Statement:** In order to understand the role of sleep in our daily lives, it is important to recognize the effects of sleep on health, typical sleep profiles of Americans, and factors that interfere with our ability to get enough sleep.

Transition: First, I'll discuss the effects of sleep on health.

BODY

I. Generally, sleep is necessary for our health.

A. First, sleep is necessary for physical health.

1. According to the 2001 *Chicago Tribune* article, "Waking Up to the Danger of Sleep Deprivation" by Ronald Kotulak, when people do not get enough sleep, their insulin has a harder time converting glucose from food into energy. (Kotulak, 2001)

a. As a result, the body produces 2 to 3 times the normal amount of glucose, which is called insulin resistance.

b. This puts a person at a much higher risk of getting diabetes and/or suffering from obesity.

2. The lack of sleep influences production of leptin, a hormone that tells the brain you are full or no longer hungry.

a. The less you sleep, the less leptin is produced in your body.

b. People who do not sleep enough may eat more because they do not feel full due to the lack of leptin, which can put them at risk for gaining weight.

B. Second, sleep is necessary for cognitive health.

   1. The lack of sleep influences levels of learning.

       a. A 2001 *Chicago Tribune* article by Ronald Kotulak cites an experiment done by Robert Stickgold of Harvard University showing a connection between sleep, learning, and retaining information. (Kotulak, 2001)

       b. The results indicate that the ability for people to learn and retain information is best if they had received an adequate amount of sleep.

   2. The lack of sleep also influences the structure of the brain.

       a. A study by Kwangwook Cho published in the June 2001 *Nature Neuroscience* concludes that sleep deprivation due to intense traveling and regular jet lag can change the structure of the brain. (Cho, 2001)

       b. Brain scans done in this research showed that part of the patients' brains, specifically the right temporal lobe, had shrunk due to the lack of sleep.

Transition: Now that you know the effects of sleep on our health, next I will discuss the typical sleep profiles of Americans.

II. The sleep profiles of Americans indicate that they do not get the recommended amount of sleep.

A. According to the 2002 National Sleep Foundation brochure, "When You Can't Sleep: ABCs of ZZZs," the majority of healthy adults need an average of eight hours of sleep per night. (National Sleep Foundation, 2002)

B. In 2001, the National Sleep Foundation published a "Sleep in America Poll," an opinion poll involving telephone interviews with 1,004 adults that examines the sleep profiles of Americans. (National Sleep Foundation, 2001)

C. The results of this poll indicates Americans' sleep profiles differ based on age, gender, region of residency, family status, and weight status.

   1. Age influences the sleep patterns of Americans.

       a. 18 to 29 year olds report getting an average of 7.1 hours of sleep on weekdays and 65% have driven while drowsy.

       b. 30 to 64 year olds report getting an average of 7.0 hours of sleep on weekdays and 51% have driven while drowsy.

   2. Gender influences the sleep patterns of Americans.

       a. Males get an average of 6.9 hours of sleep a night.

       b. Females get an average of 7.1 hours of sleep a night.

   3. Region of residency influences the sleep patterns of Americans.

       a. Individuals from the Midwest get an average of 6.8 hours of sleep.

   b. Individuals from the Northeast get an average of 7.1 hours of sleep.

   c. Individuals from the West get an average of 7.2 hours of sleep.

4. Family status influences the sleep patterns of Americans.

   a. Individuals married with children get an average of 6.7 hours of sleep.

   b. Individuals married without children get an average of 7.2 hours of sleep.

   c. Individuals single without children get an average of 7.1 hours of sleep.

5. Weight status influences the sleep patterns of Americans.

   a. Individuals who are overweight get an average of 6.9 hours of sleep.

   b. Individuals who are underweight get an average of 7.1 hours of sleep.

Transition: Now that you know the sleep profiles of Americans, finally I'll tell you about factors that interfere with our ability to get enough sleep.

III. According to the 2002 National Sleep Foundation brochure titled "When You Can't Sleep: ABCs of ZZZs," there are various "sleep stealers" that make it difficult to get the recommended eight hours of sleep a night. (National Sleep Foundation, 2002)

   A. First, factors related to stress serve as sleep stealers.

   1. Stress is the number one cause of short-term sleeping difficulties.

   2. Stressful situations that trigger sleep problems include school or job pressures, family or marriage problems, and a serious illness or death in the family.

   3. In most cases, sleep problems disappear when the stressful situation disappears, but if not managed correctly the problems may persist.

   B. Second, lifestyle behaviors serve as sleep stealers.

   1. Things that may interfere with a good night's sleep include drinking alcoholic beverages in the afternoon or evening, having an irregular morning and nighttime schedule, and doing mentally intense activities before or after getting into bed.

   2. In a 2001 *Sunday Times (London)* article, Helen Kirwan-Taylor argues exercising near bedtime, eating spicy foods, and drinking carbonated or caffeine beverages anytime after 4:00 p.m. makes it difficult to fall asleep. (Kirwan-Taylor, 2001)

   C. Finally, physical factors serve as sleep stealers.

   1. Physical conditions that cause pain, backache, or discomfort, such as arthritis, make it hard to sleep comfortably.

   2. Sleep apnea, a condition involving snoring and interrupted breathing, causes brief awakenings and excessive daytime sleepiness.

   3. Disorders that cause involuntary limb movement interrupt normal sleep patterns, such as Restless Leg Syndrome.

4. Women can experience physical factors that intrude on normal sleep patterns, such as pregnancy, hormonal shifts, premenstrual syndrome (PMS), or menopause.

Transition: In closing, I have shared with you the important role sleep plays in our everyday lives.

CONCLUSION

I. **Restate Thesis:** Specifically, I have discussed the effects of sleep on health, typical sleep profiles of Americans, and factors that interfere with our ability to get enough sleep.

II. **Closing Statement:** Thousands of automobile deaths each year aren't "just random;" rather, they occur because we fail to recognize the power of a fundamental part of human life we almost never think about—the solace that is sleep.

BIBLIOGRAPHY

Cho, K. (2001, June). Chronic 'jet lag' produces temporal lobe atrophy and spatial cognitive deficits. *Nature Neuroscience*, 4, 567–568.

Kirwan-Taylor, H. (2001, May 13). Snooze control. *Sunday Times (London)*, p. A12.

Kotulak, R. (2001, June 12). Waking up to the danger of sleep deprivation. *Chicago Tribune*, p. A4.

National Highway Traffic Safety Administration. (2002). *Drowsy driving and automobile crashes* [Brochure]. Washington, DC: Author.

National Sleep Foundation. (2001, January). *Sleep in America Poll*. Washington, DC: Author.

National Sleep Foundation. (2002). *When you can't sleep: The ABCs of ZZZs* (2nd ed.) [Brochure]. Washington, DC: Author.

Sample Speaking Outline

The following note cards provide a speaking outline for the introduction, conclusion, and main point one for the sample outline.

1

INTRO   ***Make Eye Contact!!!!!!***

I. 2001, NHTSA est. more than 100,000 auto, 1500 deaths, 10s of 1000s injuries, drivers 25 & ↓

II. Falling asleep myself . . .

III. Sleep first thing cut

IV. Preview, effect on health /// sleep profiles /// factors that interfere

Transition: *First, discuss effects of sleep on health*

2

I. Sleep necessary for health

  A. First, physical health

    1. 2001 Chic Tribune—Kotulak

       Waking up Dangers of Sleep Depr.

       Insulin harder convert glucose

      a. 2 to 3 more glucose

      b. diabetes/obesity

    2. Production of leptin

      a. less sleep = less leptin

      b. eat more-gain weight

3

B. Second, cognitive health

   1. Levels of learning

      a. Previous Kotulak article Stickgold—Harvard—connect sleep, learning, retain info

      b. retain info if enough sleep

   2. Structure of Brain

      a. Cho 6/01 Nature Neuroscience Jet lag change structure brain

      b. scan show rite temporal lobe shrinkage

7

Transition: In closing share importance of sleep

CONCLUSION

  I. Specifically, effects on health//sleep profiles//factors that interfere

  II. 1000 accidents not random, rather occur fail to recognize fund part of life—solace of sleep.

Notes

1. Sharp, H., Jr. & McClung, T. (1966). Effects of organization on the speaker's ethos. Speech Monographs, 33, 182ff.

CHAPTER 8

Informative Speaking

Chapter Objectives

After reading this chapter, you should be able to:

- Explain the differences between informatory and explanatory presentations.

- Understand and explain the states of instructional presentations.

- Understand the strategies for explaining information.

Our ability to explain information to an audience is extremely important. While students enrolled in this course readily see the benefits of persuasive speaking and look forward to those presentations all semester, they overlook the importance of the informative presentation. Providing information to an audience, however, is one of the most important skills you can develop as an effective speaker. The ability to share information effectively and increase audience understanding has extreme consequences. Just consider this recent example where confusion led to a costly mistake.

In 1999, the Mars Polar Orbiter was deployed to Mars to collect information on the planet's climate and atmosphere. The orbiter was never able to collect this information because it disintegrated in the Martian atmosphere because of a communication error.[1] Lockheed engineers in Colorado transmitted the orbiter's final course and velocity to JPL Mission Control in Pasadena using the English term of pounds per second of force. Almost all space scientists and engineers always use the metric system. Therefore, their computers used the metric term newtons, or grams per second of force, to send final course and velocity commands to the orbiter. This mistake caused the orbiter to fly too close to Mars and disintegrate. This small communication error cost $125 million dollars.

While poor informative skills can be costly and dangerous, as you have just seen, the good news is that there is a good deal of research on how to present information effectively so that our audiences can understand us. This chapter will present some of the latest theories and research to help you excel at this important communicative skill.

There are two types of informative speaking that we will address in this course. The first is called informatory and the second, explanatory. The remainder of this chapter discusses these two types of informative presentations, their differences, and strategies for using each effectively.

Differences Between Informatory and Explanatory Speaking

Informatory speaking seeks to create awareness on the part of an audience regarding a specific issue. This type of speaking assumes that there is a need for new information on a topic for a specific audience. For example, we know that animals are being trained to help in the fight against terrorism. Dogs are used to detect bombs and other potentially hazardous situations. A student from a past semester took this same topic and put a spin on it using new information. He delivered a presentation informing his audience that bees are now being trained to detect bombs. He described the program and its components. This was a fascinating presentation. The topic was novel and almost every audience member was interested in hearing new developments related to detecting and, therefore, preventing terrorism.

Explanatory speaking, on the other hand, takes the presentation a step further. This type of speaking assumes that an audience has some knowledge of the topic, but lacks sufficient understanding of the process. Therefore, the goal of this type of presentation is to deepen an audience's understanding[2] of a specific issue. For example, a former student in this course gave an explanatory presentation explaining how banks process our checks. While many of us have some awareness of this process, we don't know all the details and specifics that occur. Another student explained the process the FDA uses to approve drugs. Each of these presentations went beyond presenting new information and actually deepened our level of understanding of the phenomena under question.

Informatory Presentations

There are basically two types of informatory presentations: news and instructional. Each of these presentations enhances an audience's awareness of a topic. Primarily, informatory presentations are delivered when an audience is interested in the latest information on a particular issue (news), or desires the necessary steps to complete a task (instructions).

News Presentations

News presentations present interesting information to an audience on a new topic or a topic that they are already familiar with and interested in. The goal of a news presentation is to create awareness of the latest information on the topic. The speaker may provide an update on the information, present a progress report, describe an unpredictable recent event, or share completely new information. Another key component in news presentations is that they need to be relevant to the audience. It would be senseless to deliver a presentation on developments in the technology used in treating diabetes when no one in the audience had the disease or any experience with the disease. While they might find the topic interesting, the topic has little relevance to this audience and their everyday lives.

According to research in this area,[3] news presentations should have the following components: surprise value, factuality, and comprehensiveness. *Surprise value* is the amount of novel or new information relative to the information already known by the audience. Since the goal of the presentation is to make your audience aware of "news" in this area, most of the information you present should be new to your audience. You want to spend very little time describing elements of the topic that the audience is already aware of—spend your time on the new information.

Factuality is the extent to which the material presented in the speech actually corresponds to the research in this area. Here, it is important that you verify your information through several different sources and make sure that you report this information accurately to your audience. As an ethical speaker, it is your responsibility to make sure your information is true and presented in a straightforward manner.

Comprehensiveness simply refers to the thoroughness or completeness of the information in your presentation. As an ethical speaker, you want to ensure that you adequately address the information in your presentation. You will need to consider your time constraints and may only be able to address a small portion of the latest developments thoroughly. The key here is to make sure that you present enough detail on the topic so that your audience has adequate information on which to base decisions regarding the material in your presentation.

While all three components (surprise value, factuality, and comprehensiveness) are extremely important to an effective news presentation, the real motivation for audience involvement comes from the surprise value. So you really want to highlight this aspect of the presentation. Since this is what will be most captivating for your audience, you don't want to save the surprise value for the end of the presentation. Present this information early so you can get your audience involved right away.

In order to plan an effective news presentation, there are three major skills you should keep in mind. First, you must have a clear understanding of your audience and what types of information are likely to both surprise and be relevant to your audience. Second, you must also be a good researcher and have the skills necessary to verify the factuality of that information. Finally, you must present the information in such a way as to provide your audience with a contextual frame

> ## Instructional presentations are concerned with giving audiences directions on performing a particular task.

with which to interpret the information. What this means is that you have to present the big picture for your audience. For example, suppose you deliver new information on diabetes to an audience of individuals who suffer from this disease. You must contextualize or answer for the audience how this information changes how they cope with the illness. Should they change their eating habits based on these new developments? Should they alter their exercise routines? You must answer these questions for the audience in order to achieve all of the goals of a news presentation. There is an example of a News Presentation Outline on the course WebCT page.

Instructional Presentations

Instructional presentations are concerned with giving audiences directions on performing a particular task. Sometimes these types of presentations are called "how to" presentations, or demonstration presentations. In this type of presentation, your goal is to move an audience from their current level of knowledge (wanting to build a PC) to a desired state of knowledge (having the ability to build a PC).

According to the research on instructional or demonstration presentations, there are four states that must be addressed. First, you must explain to your audience the *desired state*. What is the goal you are hoping they will be able to accomplish? Perhaps it is registering for classes online. In this example, you must explain to your audience exactly what you want them to be able to achieve at the end of your presentation. Secondly, you must address any *prerequisite states*. What do they need to have or need to have completed so that they can achieve this desired goal? Continuing with our example, if you are explaining to your audience how to register for classes

online, you should explain all of the things necessary to begin that process. First, they need to know their career account ID and password. They must have paid all fees and currently have a zero balance in their university account. And finally, they will need to have met with their counselor to discuss their degree plan and received their special registration code.

Once all the prerequisites have been explained,

you can begin to address the process of registering online. This is called the *interim state*. These are simply the steps we move through as we proceed toward our goal. In our example, these steps may include first, to locate a computer with Internet access and, second, to locate a web browser (such as Internet Explorer). Type the following URL: *http://purdue.registrar.edu*. These directions would continue until you had walked your audience through each of the steps necessary to get enrolled electronically.

The final state that must be addressed is *unwanted states*. These are states you want the audience to avoid. These would include errors that could impede their ability to effectively register online. For example, you will notice on the URL used to locate the registration site that there is no "www." You might want to point this out to your audience. Many are accustomed to supplying this information when typing in a web address in their browser. Simply telling them that they should type in the address without the www should help them avoid ending up at the wrong website. By including each of these four states, you have a better chance of reaching your audience and ensuring they are able to perform the task you are trying to explain.

So how should you organize this type of presentation? Historically, we have told students to use a chronological or spatial pattern. However, simply placing your material in this type of pattern overlooks some of the important states that we have discussed earlier. While you may be able to effectively use one of these two patterns, you should examine the complexity of the states you need to address and choose a pattern that will best address your informational needs.

Explanatory Presentations

The focus of this section of the chapter is on developing strategies for making explanatory presentations. Essentially, an explanatory presentation is a type of informative speaking that deepens the audience's understanding. The explanatory presentation requires that you go beyond simply making the audience aware of a particular phenomena and actually create understanding on the part of your audience. For example, a speech on how to fax a document creates awareness, whereas, a speech on how that fax machine works increases an audience's understanding. For help choosing a topic for this assignment, ask yourself, "Why?" or "What does that mean?" Answers to these questions make good challenging or explanatory topics.

Explanatory presentations introduce unique problems for the speaker. Not only must you deal with the issues of organization and support, but it also presents special challenges in terms of audience analysis. As mentioned in other chapters in this book, all good presentations require thorough audience analysis. However, when faced with presenting difficult information, we must step back and analyze our audience in different ways. We must ask the following questions:

- What type of educational background does this particular audience bring to this situation that may enhance or impede their ability to process the material?
- What obstacles (e.g., previously held ideas) may interfere with this audience's ability to process this information?
- What are the challenges inherent in this information that might make it difficult for an audience to understand (e.g., vocabulary, amount of material, etc.)?

In order to be an effective speaker in this complex situation, you must have a thorough understanding of just what it is about the information you are presenting that may make it difficult for an audience to understand it. The goal for you when presenting an explanation is to anticipate what difficulties it may present for your audience and then to design a presentation that overcomes those obstacles.

There are several obstacles that may interfere with an audience's ability to understand a difficult presentation. These difficulties are inherent in the material itself. Audiences experience difficulty understanding ideas or topics for three reasons:

1. Difficulty understanding the use of a concept or term.

For example, your audience may be unfamiliar with the idea of nanotechnology. What does this concept mean, and how is it used? Other problems in understanding the use of a concept or term may surround the misuse of terminology. For example, many people outside of the world of information technology do not understand the difference between a server, an ISP, and the internet. We often misuse these terms to describe our activities on the computer.

2. Difficulty understanding a phenomenon, structure, or process.

Some presentations are difficult to understand because they describe processes or structures that are hard for an audience to envision. Either the amount of the material is difficult to process, or the relationship between elements in the presentation is hard for the audience to see. For example, audiences may have difficulty understanding how food is genetically engineered. This is a complicated process with many facets. Picturing and following all of the components in this process is difficult for an audience with limited understanding of genetic engineering. Therefore, laying this presentation out in such a way that the audience can follow and grasp the essential parts in the process is imperative.

3. Difficulty understanding particular phenomena that are hard to believe.

Sometimes information is hard to understand because the ideas surrounding the information are counter-intuitive to our experiences. Audiences may have trouble understanding that the Earth is weightless or how forest fires could be good for a forest.

Each of these three difficulties or obstacles has unique strategies that can help illuminate your ideas for an audience. The remaining portion of this chapter will discuss in more detail each of the three difficulties followed by a discussion of the specific strategies that will help increase audience understanding.

Difficulty Understanding the Use of a Concept or Term

Sometimes the difficulty in understanding information comes in understanding the concepts or the definitions that surround a particular phenomena. We often misuse certain terminology in ways that make it difficult for us to understand larger issues. For example, imagine that you are planning to present material concerning schizophrenia, a type of mental illness. Schizophrenia is a very complex disease of the brain that is misunderstood by a large majority of society. After conducting your research, you have decided that your audience's primary obstacle in understanding your presentation will surround their ideas about what schizophrenia is and what it is not. Now that you understand what obstacle your audience may face in thoroughly understanding your topic, you can plan to overcome this hurdle.

Research has shown that in order for audiences to understand content in which concepts or definitions may be difficult, it is best to use an **elucidating explanation.** Elucidating explanations simply explain a concept's meaning or use. It is helpful if you can explain to the audience what is essential in the definition and what is not essential. Let's consider the example of schizophrenia. Many people think individuals suffering from schizophrenia are dangerous, psychotic individuals.[4] In fact, the media perpetuates images of violent and dangerous serial killers suffering from schizophrenia. Schizophrenia, however, is defined as a brain disorder accompanied by some or all of the following symptoms: hallucinations, delusions, thought disorder, altered sense of self, depression, lack of motivation, and social withdrawal.[5] So as you can see, violence and aggression are not essential elements of the definition. Although in very rare circumstances a person with schizophrenia may become violent, it is more common for the person to withdraw socially. Therefore, being violent and dangerous are nonessential elements of schizophrenia.

When making a presentation that uses the elucidating explanation, it is best to follow these steps.

Step One: Provide a Definition of the Concept

Provide the audience with a definition that lists all of the essential characteristics and essential features of the definition. Let's examine the following example of dietary fiber. "The term dietary fiber refers to the parts of plants that pass through the human stomach and small intestine undigested—ranging from the brittle husks of whole wheat, to the stringy pods of green beans, to the gummy flesh of barley grains."[6] This definition becomes very clear for the audience. We know exactly what is dietary fiber, the part of a plant that passes through the stomach undigested. The essential characteristics of the definition are made clear.

Sometimes concepts have associated meanings that make truly understanding the definition difficult. For example, members of an audience often consider radiation dangerous. However, all radiation is not harmful. Radiation is simply the process of emitting radiant energy in the form of waves or particles. The term radiation refers to the electromagnetic radiation that includes radio waves, x-rays and even the energy from sunlight, light bulbs and candles. By addressing the associated meaning—dangerous—along with providing a definition, the audience gets a much better understanding of the concept radiation.

Step Two: Provide Examples

While it may seem obvious to provide an example of the definition you are presenting, research on explaining information suggests that you should provide several examples. Continuing with the example on fiber, the speaker should also provide us with the following examples that further illuminate the definition. Apples, carrots, oranges, bran, oats, whole wheat, peas, kidney beans, and lentils are all examples of dietary fiber.

Step Three: Provide Non-examples

Your audience's understanding will be further enhanced by using varied examples and non-examples of the concepts you are explaining. Often your audience may have difficulty deciding what examples fit the definition of your concept. By presenting examples and commonly held non-examples you can enhance understanding. Non-examples resemble the concept by sharing some aspects of the criteria but fall short of having all of the criteria. By presenting some of these non-examples to the audience, they will clearly understand the difference. Continuing with the fiber example, you may explain the following non-example, "It is a common belief that tough meat is also a good source of dietary fiber. However, as previously explained in our definition, animal protein is not a source of fiber because only plant materials are classified as fiber."

Understanding Complex Structures or Processes

Often, what makes a particular topic difficult is the structure or the processes inherent in the topic. It is, therefore, difficult for an audience to picture the phenomena in question. For example, individuals have difficulty picturing genetic mutation, understanding why butterfly wings dissipate heat effectively, or how bar codes work. In each of these examples, the audience struggles

to envision the processes or structures that accompany these processes. Complex structures or processes can best be explained using **quasi-scientific explanations.** Effective quasi-scientific explanations have two important characteristics. First, they help audiences attune to important features of the message. Secondly, they help organize the information so that audiences see relationships in the material.

One of the best ways to organize the information for your audience is to use an organizing analogy. Take the material and relate it to something with which the audience is already familiar. Here is an example that recently appeared in a magazine article that explained weather patterns by comparing them to a dance.

The atmosphere and the ocean are partners in a dance. But who leads? Which initiates the eastward surge of warm water that ends La Nina and starts El Nino? Though intimately coupled, the ocean and the atmosphere do not form a perfectly symmetrical pair. Whereas the atmosphere is quick and agile and responds numbly to

> ## People develop lay theories around events and experiences that are familiar to them.

hints from the ocean, the ocean is ponderous and cumbersome and takes a long time to adjust to a change in the winds. The atmosphere responds to the altered sea surface temperature patterns within a matter of days or weeks. The ocean has far more inertia and takes months to reach a new equilibrium.[7]

Another example used by a former student in this course explained the way the body processed cholesterol by comparing the body to a factory. He continued using this analogy throughout his entire presentation. Because his audience was familiar with the working of a factory, the analogy made the explanation of the process more clear.

Diagramming the process for your audience is also an effective tool. Diagrams, charts, and visual representations aid audiences in processing this information. Research shows that when the types of devices just discussed (organizing analogies and diagrams) are used, audiences are better able to envision the processes discussed and their problem-solving abilities regarding the material are improved.[8]

Hard to Believe Phenomena

Occasionally, a topic is difficult for an audience to understand because the theories or ideas that encompass that topic are hard for an audience to believe. The difficulty with the material isn't related to any particular term, or a complex collection of information, but rather the idea itself is counter-intuitive to a particular audience.

People develop lay theories around events and experiences that are familiar to them. They do not develop lay theories around phenomena that do not hold personal importance. Thus, people do not hold lay theories about new findings regarding galaxies and spiral arms. They do hold lay theories about household safety, disease management, and nutrition.

Lay audiences struggle to understand how the Earth could be weightless, or why getting a chill doesn't cause a cold. With each of these ideas, we have developed lay theories that we use to explain our world. Some of these theories are passed down from generation to generation, so they are deeply ingrained. In many cases, these lay theories are wrong. In fact, these nonscientific or lay theories are the source of our confusion and often lead to dangerous consequences. If you believe the material you are presenting to your audience is hard to understand due to some preconceived notion or lay theory the audience holds, you will want to use a **transformative explanation.**

An effective transformative explanation contains four elements. First, the explanation should contain a statement of the lay theory to which the audience currently subscribes. Secondly, the strengths or reasonableness of the lay theory are acknowledged in the explanation. Thirdly, transformative presentations create dissatisfaction with the current lay theory by explaining its weaknesses. Finally, the scientific explanation is presented and a justification is provided as to why it better explains the phenomena under question. Each of these steps is further explained along with an illustrative example about hypothermia.

Step One:	State the Lay Theory

At this step, present the lay theory that the audience holds or currently believes to be true. Here is an example, "Usually, we think of hypothermia as something that happens to people outdoors in extremely cold temperatures." The speaker simply states what the audience currently believes regarding hypothermia.

Step Two:	Acknowledge the Reasonableness of the Lay View

At this step, you want to show that the current view does have some merit for explaining the current situation. Continuing with our hypothermia example, one might say, "Sometimes this is true. However, hypothermia is defined as a sudden loss of the core temperature of your body to below 96°F. This is just a two-degree drop in temperature." Here the speaker acknowledges that yes, normally, things must be very cold, but sometimes this may not be the case.

Step Three:	Show Dissatisfaction with the Current View

Here you want to show them what is wrong with their current view. For example, you might state, "Did you know that some older adults have had a dangerous drop in body temperature while sitting inside their own homes? As people age, they may lose their ability to keep themselves warm in the cold, but even a young healthy individual can suffer hypothermia in temperatures as warm as 60°F. Bill Wately, an experienced hiker, took off for a run in the foothills of Southern California. He left wearing a T-shirt and shorts due to the 65°F day. After about an hour, a group of hikers found Bill sitting down along the trail. His complexion was pale and he was complaining of being dizzy. They called for medical assistance only to learn that Bill was suffering from hypothermia."

These two examples have demonstrated that people can get hypothermia inside of their homes and in temperatures as high as 60°F. Problems with the nonscientific or lay view have been pointed out to the audience.

Step Four:	Explain the Scientific Theory or Position

Here you must lay out the true explanation for the audience and provide them with the evidence that will help them accept the orthodox notion. Continuing with the example, "According to health officials, heavy exertion (such as running), wet clothes, and wind exposure can easily lead to hypothermia, even in 60°F weather in a healthy person. Body temperature in mammals is maintained by both the heat energy individuals generate within their bodies and the environmental conditions they experience. Wind and wetness lead to heat loss." Here you have explained why individuals can get hypothermia even in moderate temperatures. By providing your audience with this information, you may have prevented them from experiencing this condition because of their erroneously held beliefs.

One important factor related to transformative explanations is that the steps do not have to be presented in order within your presentation. As long as all four steps are present and adequate, your presentation will be effective.

Conclusion

Informative speaking is a vital skill for you to develop. As this chapter has demonstrated, informative speaking is just as important, and can be as challenging for the speaker, as persuasive speaking is. Informative speaking consists of both informatory speaking and explanatory speaking. Each of these two types of presentations contains its own set of challenges and recommendations for overcoming those challenges.

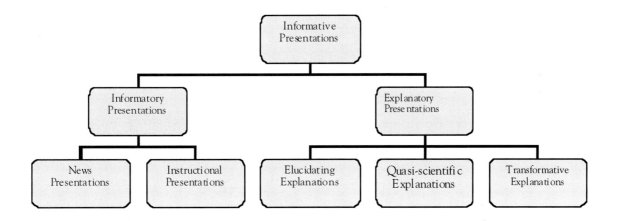

Key Terms

Comprehensiveness
Desired state
Elucidating explanation
Explanatory Speaking
Factuality

Informative Speaking
Informatory Speaking
Instructional presentations
Interim state
News presentations

Prerequisite states
Quasi-scientific explanation
Surprise value
Transformative explanation

Notes

1 Perlman, D. (1999, Oct. 1). Simple error doomed Mars Polar Orbiter: Computer confused pounds, grams when determining its course. *San Francisco Chronicle*, p. 1.
2. Rowan, K. (2003). Informing and explaining skills: Theory and research on informative communication. *The handbook of communication and social interaction skills* (eds.,) John Greene & Brant Burleson, Mahwah, NJ: Erlbaum.
3. Kinneavy, J. L. (1971). *A theory of discourse*. New York: W. W. Norton.
4. NIMH (2001).
5. Canada Health (2001).
6. Murray, M. (1990). Confused about fiber? *Reader's Digest*, p. 76.
7. Philander, S. G. (1999). El Nino: A predictable climate fluctuation. *Phi Kappa Ph* 79, 11–14.
8. Rowan, K. E. (1992). Strategies for enhancing the comprehension of science. In B. V. Lewenstein (ed.) *When science meets the public* (pg. 131–143). Washington, D.C. American Association for the Advancement of Science.

CHAPTER 9

The Persuasive Process

Chapter Objectives

After reading this chapter, you should be able to:

- Explain the differences between informative and persuasive speaking.

- Explain persuasion as a process and its implications for delivering a presentation.

- Clarify the differences between beliefs, attitudes, and behaviors.

- Differentiate between the different types of persuasive speaking.

- Discuss additional persuasive factors such as speaker and message characteristics.

Each day we deliver numerous persuasive messages to our friends, family, and acquaintances. We may try to convince friends to see the movie we want to see or eat at our favorite restaurant. We may try to convince a professor to give the class an extension on the class project. We usually have to convince a boss of the need for time off to study for an exam or to travel out of town.

All of us engage in numerous persuasive attempts like those above each and every day. Some of these attempts at persuasion are successful, and some don't turn out as well as we might have liked. Persuasion is one of the most important skills you can develop as a communicator. To help ensure success in this arena, it is imperative that you have a firm understanding of the persuasive process and its underlying principles. Persuasion, however, is a difficult task. When crafting a persuasive message, there are many things to consider and employ. This chapter is designed to lay out some of the basic issues of the persuasion process so that this task may seem a bit more manageable.

Before we discuss persuasive strategies and theories, it is important that you have a firm grasp of the differences between informative and persuasive speaking. This will enable you to choose the best set of strategies for your speaking situation.

Differences Between Informative and Persuasive Presentations

As we have mentioned in Chapter 3, in order to achieve their goal, presentations often contain elements of both informative and persuasive speaking. However, the situation will dictate a primary goal, either informative or persuasive, that will dominate the approach. In order to make the best strategic choices when delivering a persuasive presentation, it is important to understand the differences between informative and persuasive speaking.

Persuasive Speaking Asks the Audience to Choose between Two or More Alternatives

As was mentioned earlier in the text, in an informative speech a speaker acts as a teacher. As a teacher, a presenter simply explains a particular point of view or presents information on a topic. In persuasive speaking, the task becomes more complex. In addition to illuminating the topic, the presenter must also act as a leader. You are asking your audience to do more than just learn and understand issues on a specific topic; you are also asking them to adopt a position on the issue. For example, there isn't much controversy on a speech about the history of reproductive rights in the U.S. However, a speech advocating human cloning as a choice for reproduction is highly volatile. In this example, a persuasive speaker's primary goal is to convince the audience to agree with his or her position.

Persuasive Speaking Demands More Thorough Audience Analysis

Because persuasion relies so much on attitudes, beliefs, and behaviors, it is imperative that a persuasive speaker know as much about how a particular audience feels about an issue as possible. If you are a sales representative for Microsoft pitching your proposal on incorporating a new computing system into an organization, you need to know what types of attitudes and beliefs the organization holds about Microsoft prior to the presentation. If the company had invested substantial time and money in a competitor's products, then the presentation should have a different focus than if it had had experience with Microsoft products. This might further be complicated by how positive or negative those experiences had been. Persuasive speakers simply must know their audience well and prepare their presentation accordingly.

Persuasive Speaking Makes More Demands of an Audience

Whereas informative presentations ask audiences to understand something, persuasive presentations go a step further. The persuasive speech asks audiences to do or change something as a function of that understanding. This is more difficult. People are often skeptical and resistant to change. They often do not see reasons to change their behavior or beliefs. Because of this, they have to process your information more carefully, evaluating the arguments and appeals in your message against the information and beliefs they hold. As you recall from Chapter 2, while audiences often take shortcuts to evaluating a message, they are also highly motivated to believe or do the right things. When it becomes apparent that your goal is to change their beliefs, they will need to take more time evaluating your message than otherwise.

Persuasive Speaking Has a Higher Ethical Threshold

When asking the audience to change a behavior or to support a particular position, you are assuming an important responsibility. If you encourage your audience to vote for a particular candidate for student government, you must really know that this candidate will be the best person for the job. Another part of your responsibility is to ensure that your supporting evidence is of the highest quality. Are your experts qualified? Are your statistics up to date? Have you verified your information in more than just one source? Asking your audiences to make changes or commitments based on questionable evidence is unethical. As an ethical speaker, it is your responsibility to ensure that the appeals you make are reasonable and in the best interest of your audience.

Now that you have a firm grasp of the characteristics of persuasive speaking, let's examine the process of persuasion and how you can apply it to your speech.

What Is Persuasion?

In order to be successful at persuasive speaking, it is important to examine the definition of persuasion itself. For the purposes in this course, persuasion can be defined as the process of changing, creating, or reinforcing an attitude, belief, or behavior.

> One of the most important aspects of this definition is
> that persuasion is a process.

The Process of Persuasion

One of the most important aspects of this definition is that persuasion is a process. People are rarely persuaded in one shot. It usually takes multiple messages and multiple exposures to a message in order to persuade a particular audience. The following example will illuminate this feature of the definition.[1]

Imagine that you are a sales representative making a pitch to an important client. A sales rep rarely has only one shot at persuading the client. Usually, your company will make multiple presentations, send backup documents, and engage in multiple conversations with key players within that organization before a decision is reached. Each of these communication efforts with the client is a persuasive attempt. While we will focus on the persuasive presentation itself, it is important for you as a speaker to recognize that this presentation is just one of many tools you or your organization will be using to persuade the client. This realization can help you develop strategies for creating a more effective presentation. Realizing that you don't have to cover everything in one shot ensures that the presentation can be more targeted and strategic.

Targets of Persuasion

One of the most important elements to consider when constructing a persuasive message or presentation is your target. Just exactly what do you want the audience to think, feel, or do? As a speaker, you must decide if your persuasive presentation will target your audience's beliefs, attitudes, or behaviors. Each of these targets interacts with each other in complex ways. In order to increase the likelihood of achieving your persuasive goal, it is important to understand how these three relate to each other. Let's examine each of these targets in more detail.

Beliefs

A belief is a cognition held by an individual concerning the truth or falsity of a claim or the existence or reality of something.[2] For example, some individuals in the medical community believe a series of vaccinations given in early childhood is leading to an increase in autism. On the other hand, there are many individuals in the medical community who think this claim is false. There is evidence that can be presented for both sides of this claim.

One important feature about beliefs is that they cannot be proven or disproven for certain. There is always a degree of uncertainty associated with beliefs. Other points of view are possible

> A belief is a cognition held by an individual concerning the truth or
> falsity of a claim or the existence or reality of something.

Attitudes attach a positive or negative connotation to a belief.

and defendable. Consider this claim: Violent video games are causing our country's youth to become more violent. There is evidence that could be presented both for and against this claim. Some experts think that the increased violence in these games affects the behavior of children and has led to events like the Columbine shootings. Other experts say these games have a minimal effect. Each of these respective experts has research to back up the claim. An audience's belief concerning this claim will rest with the side they find most convincing. Here are some examples of beliefs:

- The Atkins Diet will help you lose weight.
- Aliens from outer space visit Earth on a regular basis.
- Listening to Mozart's music will make you smarter.

Beliefs are usually well-established and difficult to change. In order to change an audience's belief on any particular topic, you will have to present convincing evidence.[3]

Attitudes

Attitudes are learned and enduring evaluations of things that affect our behavior. People are highly motivated to act in ways that are consistent with their attitudes toward those things. Because people want their attitude toward something to be consistent with their behavior, they will change their attitude to accommodate the behavior.[4] Here are some statements that reflect attitudes:

- The Atkins Diet is a good diet.
- Space aliens are dangerous to the human species.
- Mozart is the best composer of the Classical Period.

As you can see, attitudes attach a positive or negative connotation to a belief. While we are ambivalent toward some beliefs, others are extremely important to us. For instance, while most people may prefer to drink either Coke or Pepsi, they will often drink the other if their favorite is unavailable. However, most people are not so lackadaisical about their attitude toward an issue like abortion. When persuading people to change their evaluation of something, speakers need to factor in how important or strongly held an audience's existing attitudes are. Also, people do not always behave in ways that are consistent with attitudes. For instance, a person may hold the attitude that Mercedes automobiles are the best cars to own, yet only be able to afford a Hyundai.

Behaviors

Behaviors are observable actions. The behaviors we choose to enact are largely based on the beliefs and attitudes we hold. There is a strong link between beliefs, attitudes, and behaviors. We try not to engage in behaviors that we do not value or that are in opposition to the beliefs and attitudes we hold.

Behaviors are observable actions.

Most of our persuasive attempts target behavior. We are bombarded by messages that attempt to persuade us to alter our behavior, for example, to buy a particular product or vote for a specific candidate. The daily attempts you make at persuasion are primarily targeted toward behaviors. You might try to persuade your parents to buy you a car or persuade your roommate to go on a blind date.

Although your primary goal may be to achieve some behavioral outcome, you may not be able to achieve this goal in a single persuasive presentation. Sometimes we have to focus on one of the underlying beliefs or attitudes first, and incrementally build toward a behavioral change in an audience. As a speaker, you cannot underestimate the important relationship between our beliefs, attitudes, and behaviors.

Goals of Persuasion

Once you have selected a target for your persuasive presentation, you must decide on the best goal for your particular needs. There are three primary goals you can have in a persuasive message: you can seek to create, reinforce, or change an attitude, belief, or behavior. Let's further examine each of these goals so that you can get a better understanding of the process.

Creating

Sometimes an audience will have no established beliefs, attitudes, or behaviors regarding a particular issue. For example, Americans had few attitudes or behaviors concerning terrorism on U.S. soil before September 11, 2001. However, after that day, President Bush worked diligently to create attitudes and behaviors consistent with his plan for increased homeland security. Today, American's attitudes, beliefs, and behaviors toward security are much stronger and more sophisticated than in the past.

The goal of many advertising campaigns usually involves creating new beliefs, attitudes, and behaviors. Several years ago, Procter & Gamble introduced the Swiffer mop. Initially, I had no beliefs, attitudes, or behaviors concerning this new product. After watching commercial after commercial, being bombarded with coupons, and overhearing people in the grocery store talk about how great this new product worked, I bought a Swiffer and all of the supplies necessary to make it work. The advertisers had been successful. They capitalized on beliefs I already had, such as "My home should be clean." They convinced me that their product would help achieve a cleaner home and thus created a new behavior.

Reinforcing

Sometimes it is important that we reinforce the beliefs, attitudes, and behaviors that people already hold. Consider Sunday sermons. The purpose of these messages is usually not to change or create, but to make the audience more devout and to strengthen those beliefs, attitudes, and behaviors they already hold. You have likely heard of the phrase "Preaching to the choir." Politicians are well aware of this phenomenon. Every rally and fundraising event they hold is primarily concerned with reinforcing their followers' commitment. This particular goal highlights the incremental nature of persuasion. Audiences are rarely persuaded in one single attempt. They have to be exposed to the persuasive attempt again and again before persuasion occurs.

Changing

Changing a persuasive target is usually what we associate with persuasion: getting PC computer users to switch to Macintosh computers, getting Republicans to vote Democrat, getting pro-lifers to become pro-choice.

When I teach this course, students always get excited about the persuasive assignment because they want to change the way the audience thinks or behaves. While changing persuasive targets is important, it is not always realistic. Some beliefs and attitudes are held very strongly by individuals and they are very resistant to change. After conducting a thorough audience analysis (see Chapter 2 for these methods), you will be able to determine your audience's attitudes, beliefs, and behaviors. You may even be able to discern how strongly they hold these attitudes and beliefs. Given this information, you may be able to determine how much latitude a particular audience has for movement in the direction you are advocating.

Any of the goals discussed above are appropriate for your classroom presentations. You need to be cognizant of your situation and your audience, and choose those goals that you might be able to accomplish in the amount of time allotted for your presentation. These types of situational constraints should influence the decisions you make about targets and goals.

Now that we understand all of this theory surrounding persuasion, we'll discuss how to take these ideas and turn them into meaningful presentations.

Organizing the Persuasive Speech

This section is designed to help you organize your persuasive presentation. It presents each of the three types of persuasive speeches and discusses the appropriate way to organize each type.

Presentations Concerning Questions of Fact

If you decide to deliver a speech targeting an audience's beliefs, you will be giving a speech regarding a question of fact. Persuasive speeches regarding questions of fact are concerned with what is true or false, what happened or did not happen, or what exists or does not exist. If you think about it for a moment, there are very few questions for which we have definitive answers. We know for example, that it is 190 miles from West Lafayette, Indiana to Louisville, Kentucky. We know that Ford makes the Explorer SUV. These are simple questions to which we have concrete answers. Everyone would agree that these are true. There are other questions of fact, however, that are not so easily answered but are often debated. Consider the following examples:

- Do other intelligent life forms exist?
- Did Lee Harvey Oswald act alone?
- Was Princess Diana's death an accident?
- Does eating a low-calorie diet lengthen the lifespan?

We have no definitive answers to any of the questions listed above. There are many experts who believe that Lee Harvey Oswald acted alone in shooting President John F. Kennedy, and many

> Persuasive speeches regarding questions of fact are concerned
> with what is true or false, what happened or did not happen,
> or what exists or does not exist.

experts who believe that he did not. We have no definitive answer to this question. We might have a definitive answer at some point in the future, but right now we do not know for certain. Questions of fact surround a controversy. It is important to remember that if there is no controversy surrounding your claim, you are not delivering a persuasive presentation concerning a question of fact.

Organizing the Presentation

The speech regarding a question of fact can be organized in many different ways. The most common way is the topical design. Another design that is appropriate for presentations concerning questions of fact is the *causal pattern*. This particular pattern is most appropriate for those speeches where you are trying to establish a causal relationship between two variables.

Here is an example thesis statement that would follow the causal pattern of organization:

Specific Purpose Statement:	To persuade my audience that television causes Attention Deficit Disorder in young children.
Thesis Statement:	Television viewing by young children affects neurological development and leads to attention deficit disorder in later years.

In this presentation, the speaker would need to argue that early exposure to television (the cause) leads to changes in brain chemistry that trigger Attention Deficit Disorder (the effect).

I. **Main Point One:**	Early exposure to television causes changes in brain chemistry.
II. **Main Point Two:**	These changes in brain chemistry lead to disorders such as Attention Deficit Disorder.

Another type of pattern to use when making a presentation regarding a question of fact is the *refutative pattern*. While the topical and causal design patterns are appropriate for informative speaking as well, the refutative pattern is unique to persuasive speaking.

The refutative pattern seeks to accomplish two goals: to deflate the opposition's arguments and to bolster your own. In order to accomplish this task, you must point out flaws in the opponent's argument. They may have weak evidence or problems in reasoning. The key to using this design successfully is a clear understanding of the opponent's position. You must have a thorough understanding of their purpose, arguments, and evidence.

The refutative pattern is particularly effective when addressing an audience that is hostile or unfavorable to your position. The design works with hostile audiences because you acknowledge your opponent's arguments first and then show the weaknesses in those arguments before presenting your own position.

There are four steps in the refutation pattern:

Step One: State the argument you are going to refute.

Step Two: State and list the errors of the opposing argument. At this step you must present facts, figures, examples, and/or testimony to support your refutation.

Step Three: State and deliver evidence to support your alternative argument. Again, at this step you must present evidence that the audience will find credible and persuasive in order to support your position.

Step Four: Explain how your argument or position disputes that of the opposition.

These steps can be arranged in many different ways within the body of your presentation. Let's look at one way a student organized her arguments for a classroom presentation.

Main Point I: According to the Atkins Center, high-protein diets contribute to weight loss and therefore to good health and disease prevention.

A. Individuals who follow these diet plans do lose weight in the short term by eating high-protein foods, which lowers their caloric intake. (Explain the basics of the diet.)

B. While individuals will lose weight in the short term, they are unlikely to continue with these diets for the long term and quickly return to unhealthy eating patterns.

C. A diet high in protein and low in fruits and carbohydrates is risky even in the short term, and recent research shows it can lead to diseases such as diabetes, heart disease, and kidney disease. (Cite some of the recent studies.)

D. When we examine the recent research in healthy eating, it becomes obvious that high-protein diets will not lead to good health or disease prevention.

Main Point II: In order to reach optimum health through healthy eating, one must make lifestyle changes.

A. Lifestyle changes, not high-protein diets, lead to prolonged weight loss. (Cite some of the recent research.)

    B. Fruits, vegetables, and whole grains are the optimal base for a healthy diet and have been shown to lead to a decrease in diseases such as diabetes and heart problems. (Again, cite some of the research.)

    C. As you can see, adopting and maintaining a healthy lifestyle change by eating a well-balanced diet is the road to better nutrition.

In this design the student combined steps one and two in the first main point and steps three and four in the second main point. She addressed the opposition's arguments and showed why they are flawed. There are other combinations that could have worked. You could take each of the four steps and make each a main point. There is flexibility in how you arrange the four steps. As long as all the steps are included for all of the arguments you are refuting, you will be in good shape. One key element to remember is that if you are refuting more than one of your opponent's arguments in your presentation, attack the weakest argument first.

Presentations Concerning Questions of Value

The persuasive presentation concerning a question of value involves the audience's attitudes on a particular topic. Questions of value argue that positions are good or bad, ethical or unethical, moral or immoral, or right or wrong. Here are some examples of questions of value:

- Is hunting unethical?
- Is bullfighting inhumane?
- Is solar energy the ideal form of power?
- Is the space program a good use of taxpayer money?

One important key to handling a question of value effectively is to remember that questions of value are not opinions. Simply stating, "I think solar power is wonderful," is an opinion. This is your opinion, and no one will question you about it. You do not have to supply supporting evidence for your opinion. If, however, you make the claim, "Solar power is the ideal form of power," you have gone beyond stating your personal opinion and are now making a claim about a question of value.

When you go beyond personal opinion, you must justify your claim through the use of supporting evidence. You must build a case for your position. One way to build the case for your position is set the standards for the claim you are making. What makes an ideal power source? Define those standards first. Then show how your claim meets those standards.

Organizing the Presentation

Persuasive presentations on questions of value are usually organized topically. If you have a topic that requires you to set a standard against which to judge your argument, you will want to begin by laying out your standards. The second main point demonstrates how your argument measures

> The persuasive presentation concerning a question of value involves the audience's attitudes on a particular topic.

up against the standards you have set. The following is an example of a speech positing that solar power is the ideal form of power:

Specific Purpose Statement: To persuade my audience that solar energy is the ideal form of power.

Thesis Statement: Solar power is the ideal form of power because it is clean, cost effective, and sustainable.

Main Point I: An ideal form of power should meet the following criteria:
A. It should be dean.
B. It should be cost effective.
C. It should be sustainable.

Main Point II: Solar energy meets all of these criteria for an ideal form of power.
A. Solar energy produces no by-products that pollute the environment, making it the cleanest form of power currently available.
B. Current advancements in solar panel construction have radically increased their efficiency, making them more cost effective than they have been in the past.
C. Unlike other fuels, solar power relies on a source of energy that will not be exhausted over time and through use.

You do not always have to follow the guidelines of setting up your criteria in the first main point and using the second main point to demonstrate how your claim meets the criteria. The following is another way you might organize a speech of value.

Specific Purpose Statement: To persuade my audience that spanking children is morally wrong.

Thesis statement: Spanking children is morally wrong because it demeans our children and devalues human integrity.

Main Point I: Spanking our children is an immoral practice that demeans our youngest citizens. (Speaker provides supporting evidence.)

Main Point II: Spanking young individuals devalues the worth of human beings. (Speaker provides supporting evidence.)

It is important to keep in mind that speeches of value may often be the catalyst that moves people to action. If someone becomes moved by your presentation on the unethical nature of hunting to get involved in an organization such as People for the Ethical Treatment of Animals (PETA), it is just the end result of your speech. Presentations on questions of value only argue the right and wrong of a particular issue. They do not concern themselves with what should or should not be done. Once you ask your audience to do something, you have targeted a behavior and crossed the line between questions of value and policy. Make sure that if your assignment asks you to make a persuasive presentation on a question of value, you stick to that goal. Do not make the

> The persuasive presentation concerning a question of policy targets behaviors or what we should or should not be doing—as an individual, a community, or even a nation.

mistake of asking your audience to take action. The action step moves you into questions of policy, which we will discuss next.

Presentations Concerning Questions of Policy

The persuasive presentation concerning a question of policy targets behaviors or what we should or should not be doing—as an individual, a community, or even a nation. Here are some examples of questions of policy:

- Should we ban smoking in all public buildings including restaurants and bars?
- Should physical education be mandatory at every grade level in our nation's schools?
- Should our community engage in curbside recycling?
- Should the United States change its immigration policies?

When you think about making a persuasive presentation, most of us think about speeches on questions of policy. We usually want to persuade someone or a group of people to do something related to some policy. We might want them to vote for our candidate for homecoming court, protest a recent Purdue administration decision, or take up exercising. If you are trying to get your audience to do something, you are talking about a question of policy.

It is important to note that questions of policy almost always include questions of fact or value. While the question of policy would be the primary goal of the presentation, secondary attention would have to be paid to questions of fact or value. Questions of policy, however, always go beyond questions of fact and value, and advocate that something should or should not be done.

When making a speech concerning a question of policy, careful attention must be paid to the need, plan, and practicality of the proposals being presented.[5] First of all, you must demonstrate to your audience that there is a problem or a need for your proposed policy. Why should we ban smoking in all public buildings in our community? You must present evidence to show that smoking in public buildings is a problem for individuals in your community. The evidence you present must be compelling enough to convince your audience that some change in policy should be adopted.

Sometimes you are trying to change a policy and other times you might be arguing that some policy should remain the same. Consider the following topic: The U.S. should not change its immigration policies. In this speech you would argue that changing the current policies would cause more harm than good, and advocate that the U.S. continue doing what it is already doing. You are still advocating a course of action.

In addition to convincing your audience that a problem or need exists, you must also demonstrate that you have a clear plan that will address the cause or causes of the problem. You must convince your audience that your solution will be able to alleviate the problem.

Once you have established a need to change current policy and presented your plan or solution, you must demonstrate that your plan is practical. Although you may have done an incredible job convincing your audience that there is a problem with current policy, unless you can also persuade them that your solution for alleviating the problem is feasible, you will be unsuccessful. The bottom line is that the audience wants to believe your plan is workable. They must believe that your plan will alleviate problems without causing new ones. While you may propose a wonderful plan to clean up the Wabash River, the price tag associated with your proposal may be too much for the community to absorb. The expense of the proposal would create problems in other areas for the community, perhaps increases in taxes and cutbacks in other community-funded programs.

Sometimes when speaking on a question of policy, a speakers' only goal is to get an audience to agree that, indeed, a change in policy does need to be made. However, the speaker may not be asking anything else from the audience. In this case, the speaker is seeking passive agreement.

Sometimes a speaker is seeking more than just passive agreement. That is, a speaker is asking for more than just an agreement that the proposed policy change should be made. The speaker seeks what we call active agreement. In this case, the speaker needs the audience to get involved in order to achieve the change in policy. Perhaps the speaker asks the audience to sign a petition, buy a raffle ticket, vote for a proposition in an upcoming election, or sign a donor registration card. Regardless of the behavior the speaker advocates, the audience is being asked for more than just agreement. The audience has to become actively involved in order to achieve the ultimate goal of the presentation.

Organizing the Presentation

There are many ways to organize presentations concerning questions of policy. The problem-solution and the problem-cause-solution designs are organizational schemes for the presentation regarding the speech of policy. The following is an example of the problem-solution speech structure.

Specific Purpose: To persuade my audience that action is needed to deal with the problems created by ineffective design and placement of street and road signs in Lafayette.

Thesis Statement: Ineffective design and placement of street signs in Lafayette causes many traffic problems in our city, and there are steps we can take to improve the situation.

Main Point I: The ineffective design and placement of street and road signs in Lafayette is very dangerous for pedestrians, bicyclists, and vehicle passengers. (This is the problem.)

    A. It is estimated that nearly one third to one half of all street signs in Lafayette are missing.

    B. More than one half of the street signs in Lafayette are not clearly legible.

    C. Many local accidents are a result of mistakes drivers make due to ineffective or absent signs.

Main Point II: The problem with our road signs can be solved in a three-step process. (This is the solution.)

   A. First, all of the road signs in Lafayette must be replaced with signs that meet national safety recommendations.

   B. Second, the road signs must be relocated to appropriate locations within intersections.

   C. Finally, missing signs must be replaced.

The problem-cause-solution design simply adds a third step. After outlining the problem, you add a second main point, which lays out the causes of the problem. The final or third main point in this design is the solution. The design looks like this: Main point one, the problem; main point two, the causes of the problem; and main point three, the solution. I have found that when speakers use the problem-cause-solution design, their solutions are often more practical. Addressing the causes helps insure that you propose a solution that is more feasible. This arrangement usually results in a tighter overall argument. The following is a brief example of an outline using the problem-cause-solution design.

Specific Purpose Statement: To persuade the audience that they should recycle as a way of combating the waste disposal problem in our area.

Thesis statement: If we don't want garbage to overcome us and our community, we must make the habit of recycling the norm rather than the exception.

Main Point I: Waste disposal is a significant problem. (This is the problem.)

Main Point II: Since most of us realize that waste disposal is a serious problem and recycling can be an effective solution, why aren't we better about recycling? (This is the underlying cause or causes.)

   A. One reason has to do with ignorance about recycling.

   B. Another reason has to do with the inconvenience of recycling.

Main Point III: I propose a three-step solution that will make recycling both easier and more convenient. (This is the solution.)

   A. We need to implement promotional campaigns that clarify proper recycling procedures.

   B. Public restaurants should be required to have clearly labeled recycling bins wherever they have trash containers.

   C. City sanitation departments must be expanded to provide curbside pickup.[6]

In addition to these options is Monroe's motivated sequence, an adapted version of the problem-solution design. It was created at Purdue University by Professor Alan Monroe in the 1930s and is still prominently used in marketing and advertising today. Monroe's motivated sequence is primarily used when a speaker wants to move an audience to immediate action. While all of the

> **The motivated sequence provides a design to organize the entire presentation.**

other organizational patterns presented in your textbook have provided ways to organize the main points of a presentation, the motivated sequence provides a design to organize the entire presentation.[7] There are five steps in this pattern: attention, need, satisfaction, visualization, and action.

Step One: Attention

This step is exactly like the first step in any other presentation you make. You must gain the audience's attention. You can accomplish this through a variety of strategies.

Step Two: Need

Once you have grabbed your audience's attention, you then must convince the audience that there is a need for change. You must persuade them that the current product, policy, or candidate (for example) is problematic. You establish this need through the use of evidence. It is important that you have conducted a thorough audience analysis so that you can use the type of evidence that will convince your target audience that a need exists.

Step Three: Satisfaction

Now that you have generated a sense of need in your audience, you provide them with your solution, or satisfaction, to this need. Explain your plan. Remember, it is important at this point in the presentation that you demonstrate to your audience that the plan you are proposing is practical.

Step Four: Visualization

At this point, ask your audience to visualize your plan. You want to paint a mental picture of the solution. You must be able to demonstrate to your audience how they will benefit from your proposed solution.

Step Five: Action

Once you have convinced your audience that there is a need and you have proposed a workable solution, it is time to call them to action. Tell the audience exactly what they need to do and how to do it in order to ensure the activation of your plan. If you want them to send an e-mail to their representative, provide the e-mail address. If you want them to write a letter to the city commissioner, provide the address. If you want them to vote in the upcoming election, give details about where and when to vote. The clearer and easier you make the action step, the more likely your audience will respond to your call for action. End the speech with a resounding appeal to action that will motivate your audience to get involved.

Here is an example of a speech that utilizes Monroe's motivated sequence.

Introduction:
I. Attention: Have you ever dreamed about being a hero or heroine? Have you ever wished you could do something great, something that would really make a difference in our world? I'm here to tell you, you can, if you're willing to give just three hours a week.

Body:
II. Need: Our community needs volunteers to help children who are lonely and neglected. Big Sisters and Big Brothers of Lafayette have a program for these children, but only volunteers can make the program work. The program needs at least 80 volunteers to work. At this point we only have 58.
III. Satisfaction: Volunteering to be a Big Brother or Big Sister will help to ensure that this worthwhile program continues and flourishes. Being involved in this program will also make you a hero or heroine in the eyes of a child.
IV. Visualization: Maybe you can have an experience that will be as rewarding as mine has been. Last year I worked with 7-year-old Keneka two afternoons each week. She needed help with her homework because her grades were marginal. I tutored her in reading and math. But more than that help, she needed someone to be her friend and to know that someone cared about her. Keneka's grades went from Cs and Ds to Bs. This program was remarkable. Not only was I able to help Keneka improve her grades and gain self-esteem, but I was able to feel like a hero. I think I got more out of participating in the program than she did.

Conclusion:
V. Call for Action: Won't you join me and become one of the unsung heroines or heroes in a young boy or girl's life? You can make a difference in just one or two afternoons each week. I've got the applications with me and will be waiting for you to sign up after class. You can make a difference.[8]

Additional Persuasive Factors

In addition to the ways of organizing your persuasive presentation, there are additional strategies that may enable you to achieve your goal more successfully. In the final section of this chapter, we will examine some of the research related to speaker and message characteristics that will help you further refine your persuasive speaking skills.

Speaker Credibility

So far, we have talked about the goals you may have for your persuasive message and about the target and the organization of your message. However, we know from the discussion of message processing that the characteristics of a particular speaker are very important to your success in a persuasive attempt. For instance, speakers who are likeable and perceived as similar to the audience are generally more persuasive than those who are not as likeable or similar. One factor that has received a lot of research is the notion of speaker credibility.

As is discussed in Chapter 10, credibility is how competent the audience finds the speaker. The audience asks themselves, "Can I believe this individual?" For most audiences, credibility comes down to two issues: how much expertise does this individual have, and how trustworthy is he or she? We may feel that a car salesman is competent in his or her knowledge of the vehicle they are trying to sell us, but at the same time we may question the trustworthiness of the individual. Have they disclosed everything about this vehicle? Both of these issues in combination are used by audiences to determine the credibility of a speaker.

One way an audience assesses speaker credibility is through an introduction. As was discussed in Chapter 4, when you are invited to speak to an organization, someone in the organization will usually introduce you. This introduction will likely include some reference to your educational background, your current or past occupations, and your experience. All of these factors combined help the audience determine how qualified they believe you are to present this particular information.

As mentioned in Chapter 4, sometimes you will not receive an introduction and you must establish your credibility for yourself. If this is the case, you will have to include a credibility statement early in your introduction.

A second factor that plays a big role in perceived speaker credibility is the use of nonfluencies, or unplanned vocal pauses (see Chapter 11). These pauses in the flow of delivery and vocalizations ("ums," "uhs," "you knows," and the like) go a long way in reducing your credibility. It becomes even more important that you practice presentations so that you are able to eliminate these potential problems from your presentational style.

Citing sources is an area that can bolster your credibility. Research has shown that when speakers cited sources within their persuasive arguments, they are more likely to be persuasive. Simply stating that "research has shown" or "studies conclude" is not effective. Rather, a speaker must refer to specific studies. Follow the guidelines outlined on WebCT for citing sources in presentations, and you will be able to take advantage of the added credibility that results from citation of evidence.

Message Characteristics

In addition to focusing on characteristics of the speaker, there are also certain message features that may enable a speaker to be more effective. We will discuss two of these factors: order of arguments and explicitly spelling out the conclusion.

Order of Arguments

One of the most common questions students ask is which argument should be put first and which last? Should I spring my strongest argument on my audience first (primacy effect), or wait until the very end to use my strongest evidence (recency effect)? The research at this time is inconclusive. One thing is for certain, never sandwich your best or strongest piece of evidence in the middle of your presentation. It is better to end or begin with a bang.

One aspect to consider is the situation in which you are speaking. If you know that you are likely to run out of time during the presentation, do not save your best argument for the end of the presentation because you may not get to it. In a situation where time is limited and you are worried about your ability to finish the presentation, use your strongest evidence or argument first, so that you can adequately explain and present that material. However, if you know that you will have plenty of time to address all of the points of your presentation, you may be able to build to your strongest piece of evidence. You will also want to think about how motivated your audience is to process the arguments you will present. If they are less motivated, their attention may wane as the presentation continues, so you may want to present your strongest argument first. As with every stage in the process of developing a presentation, you must consider the situation and audience when making these types of decisions.

Message Directness

Sometimes students feel that spelling out a conclusion for an audience is demeaning or condescending. They feel that they are working with an intelligent audience that will be able to draw a conclusion from the evidence that was just presented to them. However, research has shown that a message or presentation is more likely to be persuasive when the conclusion is explicitly stated for the audience. Suppose you are delivering a presentation on the importance of voting. Your entire presentation has consisted of arguments on why individuals should vote. At the end of your presentation you may conclude that your audience understands that you are asking them to vote in the next election. However, you should make this call to your audience directly. Do not assume that they will automatically draw the conclusion you have envisioned for the presentation. As demonstrated in Monroe's motivated sequence, you want to directly call them to action. Spell out for your audience what you want them to believe, feel, or do. This may increase the likelihood that you have persuaded your audience.[9]

Conclusion

Although persuasion is something that we engage in every day, it is a very complex process. Persuasive presentations ask the audience to choose between two or more alternatives; demand a thorough analysis of the audience; make more demands of the audience; and have a higher ethical threshold than informative speaking.

In order to be effective, the persuasive speech must have a strong sense of purpose. The persuasive process begins with an understanding of what you are going to target in a persuasive attempt—attitude, belief, or behavior—and what your goal is, whether changing, creating, or reinforcing that target. Once this decision has been made, you must determine whether your presentation concerns a question of fact, value, or policy and organize it accordingly. Additionally, you will want to consider additional persuasive factors such as speaker credibility and message characteristics.

Key Terms

Active Agreement
Attitude
Behavior
Belief
Causal Pattern
Change
Create
Goals of Persuasion
Monroe's Motivated
  Sequence

Need
Passive Agreement
Persuasion
Plan
Practicality
Primacy Effect
Problem-cause-solution
  design

Questions of Fact
Questions of Policy
Questions of Value
Recency Effect
Refutative Design
Reinforce
Targets

Notes

1. Miller, G. R. (1972). Persuasion. In C. R. Berger & S. H. Chaffee (Eds.), *Handbook of communication science* (pp. 446–483). Newbury Park, CA: Sage.
2. Perloff, R. M. (1993). *The dynamics of persuasion*. Hillsdale, NJ: Lawrence Erlbaum.
3. Fishbein, M. (1967). A consideration of beliefs, and their role in attitude measurement. In M. Fishbein (ed.), *Readings in attitude theory and measurement* (pp. 257–266). New York: John Wiley.
4. Eagly, A. H., & Chaiken, S. (1993). *The psychology of attitudes*. Orlando, FL: Harcourt.
5. Lucas, S. (2001). *The art of public speaking*. New York: McGraw-Hill.
6. Sellnow, D. (2002). *Public speaking: A process approach*. Fort Worth, TX: Harcourt.
7. Devito, J. A. (2000). *The elements of public speaking*. 7th edition. New York: Addison Wesley Longman.
8. Adapted from: Osborn, M., & Osborn, S. (1994). *Public speaking* (3rd ed.). Boston: Houghton Mifflin Company.
9. O'Keefe, D. J. (2002). *Persuasion: Theory & research*. Thousand Oaks, CA: Sage.

Strategies for Persuasive Presentations

Chapter Objectives

After reading this chapter, you should be able to:

- Explain the role of ethos, logos, and pathos in presentational speaking.

- Define the differences between initial credibility, derived credibility, and terminal credibility.

- Define reasoning from induction and explain tips for using it effectively.

- Define reasoning from deduction and explain tips for using it effectively.

- Define casual reasoning and explain guidelines for using it effectively.

- Define analogical reasoning and explain guidelines for using it effectively.

- Discuss ethical considerations of using emotional appeals.

Students often ask me what the key to successful persuasion is. They always seem to be looking for a magic bullet that will ensure their persuasive attempts are successful. There is no easy solution. Persuasion is a process. However, the strategies discussed in this chapter play a big part in that process. Solid reasoning, emotion, and credibility can make the difference between an effective persuasive attempt and an ineffective attempt. Appeals alone aren't magic bullets, but they may be the thing to push your presentation to the next level. This chapter discusses the art of using appeals and strategies for implementing them successfully.

Ethos, Logos, and Pathos

The strategies of reasoning rely on three appeals. According to Greek philosopher Aristotle, in his book, *The Rhetoric*, these appeals include: appeals to ethos or credibility, logos or logic, and pathos or emotion. Although Aristotle lived in another time far removed from the society we live in today, these three appeals continue to guide the communication strategies we use in the modern world. We use these three appeals in all types of speaking, but they become even more important when delivering persuasive presentations. In this chapter we will examine each of these three types of appeals.

Using Ethos in your Presentation

According to Aristotle, ethos refers to your credibility as a speaker. As discussed in other chapters, the credibility your audience feels that you have on a particular topic can greatly affect how they react to your presentation. Will they listen attentively or will they take what you have to say with a grain of salt? Your perceived credibility can have a profound impact on how your audience approaches your presentation.

It is important to keep in mind that credibility can vary from situation to situation and from audience to audience. Credibility is an attitude an audience holds and so it will vary greatly depending on the situation. You may have great credibility with your classroom audience as a speaker on nanotechnology. After all, you are an undergraduate engineering student working in the lab of a professor involved in cutting-edge research on the topic. If you delivered a similar presentation to an audience made up of professors pursuing lines of research in the area of nanotechnology, your credibility would be questionable.

Similarly, while you may be extremely qualified and competent to deliver a presentation on one topic, you would not be qualified to deliver a presentation on another topic. For example, Peter Jennings, a well-respected national news anchor, is well qualified to deliver a presentation to an audience on the media coverage of Iraq. We would be less likely to find Peter Jennings competent to deliver a presentation on gracious entertaining; however, we would find Martha Stewart competent to deliver that presentation.

> Credibility is an attitude an audience holds and so it will vary greatly depending on the situation.

> It is essential that your audience perceive you to be credible as well as honest, trustworthy, and sincere.

As you have seen, credibility changes from topic to topic and audience to audience, but it also changes during a presentation. There are three types of credibility that help describe the changes to a speaker's credibility during a presentation. **Initial credibility** refers to the credibility a speaker has before he or she begins the presentation. This information may be publicized by posters listing your credentials. If you are introduced by someone, they will usually list your qualifications. You can also explain your own competence in the introduction of your presentation (see Chapter 4). So, before you even begin your presentation, your audience has already formed an attitude about how credible you will be on the topic you will address.

Derived credibility results from the actual messages you send during your presentation. What you say or do during the presentation has a great impact on your credibility. While you may have had extremely high initial credibility, you can do things during the actual presentation that erode your credibility. The good news is that you can start a presentation with low initial credibility and through high derived credibility, develop an overall credible perception during your presentation.

Terminal credibility refers to the credibility of the speaker at the end of the presentation. If you have applied the strategies discussed in this section successfully, you may arrive at the end of your presentation with even more credibility than when you began. Don't underestimate the importance of your credibility. It can have a dramatic effect on the success of a presentation. Terminal credibility is important because it establishes the credibility you have going into future presentations. In other words, the terminal credibility in one presentation affects the initial credibility in your next presentation. Thus, giving a poor presentation affects your credibility as a whole.

While the discussion concerning ethos to this point has centered on competence or credibility, there is another component of this appeal: character. It is essential that your audience perceive you to be honest, trustworthy, and sincere as well as credible. Having perceived credibility without character will not achieve the results you are pursuing with your audience. Think of the stereotypical used car salesman as an example. He has credibility. He knows a great deal about all of the cars on his lot, but is he being honest in his dealings with you as a customer? We are not always sure. He has a conflict of interest, in that his primary goal is to get you to buy a car. Therefore, we are skeptical about all of the information he presents. You don't want your audience to feel this way. An audience must feel a speaker has high credibility and character if they are going to be persuaded.

Tips for Enhancing Ethos

How can you establish credibility during your presentation? First and foremost, use strong evidence. You want to use evidence from respected sources. Supporting evidence from less than legitimate sources won't do much to bolster your credibility. Analyze your audience and ask yourself, what type of sources will this particular audience respect? Use those sources. You may have to vary supporting material depending on the particular audience you are addressing. You also want to

ensure that your supporting evidence is timely. Outdated evidence will limit your ability to achieve your goals.

Secondly, you want to establish common ground with your audience. As we discussed in Chapter 2, you never want to alienate an audience. If you start off by attacking the position your audience holds, you won't get very far. Begin by showing similarities between you and your audience and then move to areas where you may experience controversy. You want to demonstrate respect for your audience. This enhances liking for the speaker and goes a long way toward enhancing your character as a speaker.

Finally, using an appropriate delivery style will also enhance audience perception of your competence. Using fluent vocal delivery is extremely important. Make sure your vocal style is free from any vocal nonfluencies. Vocal pauses such as "ums," "uhs," "you knows," and the like cause the credibility of a speaker to diminish.[1] Wearing appropriate attire can also affect your credibility. Review the guidelines on dressing appropriately in Chapter 11.

Using Logos in your Presentation

Logos refers to logic and appeals to an individual's intelligence. You incorporate logos into your presentations by using arguments or reasoning. We build strong arguments by gathering supporting evidence, organizing solid arguments, and using reasoning to explain how that evidence supports the claims we are making. In order to be effective, you must ask yourself, "How does this piece of evidence support my main point?" "How can I make this connection evident to my audience?" Answering these questions is essentially reasoning.

This chapter will discuss four types of reasoning: deductive reasoning, inductive reasoning, analogical reasoning, and causal reasoning. You will choose the type of reasoning that best fits the evidence you have collected. Most presentations use more than one type of reasoning.

Deductive Reasoning

Deductive reasoning is moving from a widely accepted principle to a specific case. Deductive reasoning takes the form of a syllogism. Most of you have probably heard the famous syllogism:

Major Premise: All persons are mortal.

Minor Premise: Socrates is a person.

Conclusion: Therefore, Socrates is mortal.

Syllogisms, or deductive arguments, consist of three parts: a major premise, a minor premise, and a conclusion. The major premise is a general statement that is widely accepted. The minor premise is a specific observation about a case and demonstrates that it fits within the general principle. The conclusion simply states that the general principle applies to your specific observation or minor premise.

Major Premise: Presidential candidates spend a good deal of time in New Hampshire.

Minor Premise: Dick Gebhardt is running for president.

Conclusion: Therefore, Dick Gebhardt spends a good deal of time in New Hampshire.

Tips for Using Deductive Arguments Deductive arguments are very powerful. If the major and minor premise are true, then the conclusion will naturally follow. Therefore it is an extremely strong type of argument. As a speaker, you have to determine how powerful your major and minor premises are. Will your audience accept them? If not, you will have to present evidence to persuade them. Your argument will only be successful if your audience buys your major and minor premises. If they fail to accept them, you will not convince your audience.

Inductive Reasoning

Inductive reasoning is the opposite of deductive reasoning. Instead of starting with a widely accepted principle, you start with individual cases and draw a conclusion that applies to all of the cases you examined.

Horse number one has hooves.

Horse number two has hooves.

Horse number three has hooves.

Horse number ten has hooves.

Conclusion: All horses have hooves.

We typically use induction when we cannot examine every case that exists, but we want to make a conclusion about an entire category. For example, while at Purdue you won't have every teaching assistant as an instructor; but you may have experiences with several. Based on your experiences you might draw a conclusion about all teaching assistants at Purdue. We make decisions based on inductive reasoning all the time. Think about how you choose the courses you take. You ask several people who have taken a course for their assessments. Based on their comments, you draw a conclusion about the course. Then you decide if you will take it or not.

Harris delivered a speech on the healing power of tea. He offered several examples of studies that had been conducted that indicated tea was healthy. He used these examples to support his conclusion that tea is a healthy beverage.

According to a 2002 Dutch study of 4,807 individuals, those who drank 13 ounces or more of tea a day cut their risk of heart attack in half. In another study conducted in the same year in Boston, researchers found that heart patients who drank two or more cups of tea a day were 44% less likely to die over the next four years. Other studies show that tea can lower bad cholesterol. So, as you can see, tea has many health benefits.

Tips for Using Induction   Inductive arguments can be persuasive if you use them well. First, you must make sure you have enough examples of specific cases to draw your conclusion. Drawing a conclusion when your sample size is too small is called a **hasty generalization.** Audiences won't be persuaded by arguments based on small sample sizes. How many samples or examples are enough? That is hard to answer. You must analyze each speaking situation and make that decision as you prepare for different audiences and occasions. Some audiences will be convinced from only a few cases, while others will want a good deal of evidence before buying your conclusion. It just depends on the knowledge and attitudes of a given audience.

Second, you must ensure that the cases you present are typical. If you have cited evidence that seems out of the ordinary, your audience will unlikely be convinced by your argument. If you feel that your cases are atypical, further support your argument by offering some statistics. This will bolster your argument and will probably be more convincing for your audience.

Third, be careful how strong you make your conclusion. Remember, inductive reasoning is based on probability. You will never be able to examine every case in a given category. Therefore, refrain from presenting your conclusion to your audience as if it were a fact. You may want to qualify your argument. It may not be as powerful, but it is truthful and will be more persuasive to your audience.

Analogical Reasoning

Analogical reasoning is reasoning by comparison. You take two similar cases and argue that what is true about one is also true about the other. Analogical reasoning is well suited for presentations concerning issues of policy. When advocating solutions, it is easy to use analogical arguments. For example, a COM 114 group presentation argued that Purdue needed an updated public transportation system. They described the public transportation system used at the University of Kansas and showed how that system would be a solution to the transportation problems undergraduates face at Purdue. They proposed that what worked for the University of Kansas would also work for Purdue.

Tips for Using Arguments by Analogy   The key to using analogical reasoning well is to make sure the two things you are comparing are similar in important ways. Are the University of Kansas and Purdue similar in important ways? Are they roughly the same size? Are the transportation needs of the student populations similar? Are they both state-supported universities? Answers to these and other questions are important to examine. If your audience doesn't consider the two things you are comparing similar, then they won't be persuaded by your argument. Making an analogical argument about two issues that are not similar in important ways is called an invalid analogy.

Causal Reasoning

Causal reasoning attempts to establish a relationship between two events, such that one of the events caused or led to the other event. We engage in causal reasoning every day. We try to explain what caused the football team to lose their last game, or what caused the administration to turn off the fountain. Although we use causal reasoning every day, it isn't as simple as it seems. Proving that one event caused another is difficult to do. We generally consider two events causally related if the cause precedes the event in time, there is an empirical correlation between the

events, and the relationship between the two events is not found to be the result of some third event.[2]

Imagine that my knee hurts before it rains, and I proclaim that my knee pain causes rain. Criteria one is satisfied; knee pain before rain. Every time my knee hurts it rains. With criteria two, these things move or happen together. Criteria three asserts that the relationship between the two can't be caused by another variable. This example does not meet criteria three. My knee pain can be explained by the humidity that occurs prior to rain. The humidity associated with the incoming front causes the pain in my knee.

While this may seem like a ridiculous example, students often fall prey to this error in reasoning. Just because something occurs before something else doesn't mean the first event caused the second. While this is a necessary condition, it isn't sufficient. In fact, this mistake is so popular there is even a fallacy named for it: **post hoc ergo propter hoc** or "after this, therefore because of this."

Another key to remember when making causal arguments is that events sometimes have more than one cause. Oversimplifying the relationship between two events may lead your audience to question your reasoning. There is no escaping causal reasoning. We engage in it every day. However, it is important for you to realize that events are rarely so simple. Acknowledging this fact in your presentation will be appreciated by your audience.

Fallacies

Fallacies are errors in reasoning. You want to avoid fallacies in your presentation at all costs. As a critical audience member, you want to be aware of fallacies when they are presented to you. There are many types of fallacies. We have already examined some of them: hasty generalization; invalid analogy; and post hoc ergo propter hoc. Other popular fallacies with which you should be famil-

> **Another key to remember when making causal arguments is that events sometimes have more than one cause.**

iar include argument ad hominem, bandwagon, slippery slope, false dilemma, straw person, and red herring.

Argument Ad Hominem

Argument ad hominem is a Latin phrase meaning "against the person." An argument ad hominem occurs when irrelevant personal attacks are made about a person or group to which an individual belongs instead of the argument the person supports. Instead of attacking an argument an individual makes, a speaker will attack the person who made the claim.

> Of course Senator Smith's proposal includes raising taxes. What else can you expect from a bleeding heart liberal?

In this example, the speaker should address Senator Smith's proposal directly rather than call him a name. The focus has shifted from the issue to the character of the individual.

Bandwagon

This fallacy assumes that because something is popular it is right or the best. A speaker may say that because everybody else is doing it you should too—just jump on the bandwagon. Advertisers use this fallacy all of the time. Just because one brand is more popular than another doesn't mean it is better. You also see this argument used by politicians. They use polls in a similar way. Arguing that just because 72% of the population approves of the job the mayor is doing on developing the riverfront doesn't mean his or her strategy is correct or the best one. In order to evaluate the development plan, it must be examined and compared to other plans around the country. Just because something is popular doesn't make it right or wrong.

Slippery Slope

The slippery slope fallacy asserts that some action will inevitably lead to a chain of events that will end in a certain result. A speaker assumes that taking a step will ultimately lead to a second and third step, on down to an unwanted outcome. If a speaker claims that taking one step will inevitably lead to some disastrous outcome, then it is a slippery slope.

> If we allow the government to regulate handgun sales, it will lead to the regulation of the sale of rifles and shotguns. The next thing you know, the sale of all guns will be illegal and eventually the right to bear arms will be a thing of the past.

False Dilemma

A false dilemma, also known as a false dichotomy, gives the audience a choice between two options when really there are many more alternatives. It simplifies the situation when in reality the situation is rather complex.

> We either raise tuition or close all computer labs on campus.

We all know that the situation isn't that simple. There are a variety of ways to redistribute money on campus so that we can continue to fund the computer labs without raising tuition.

Straw Person

The straw person fallacy is committed when someone ignores a person's actual position and substitutes a weaker, distorted, or misrepresented version of that position, thereby making it easier to refute the opponent's position.

> Anti-gun organizations want to revoke the Second Amendment allowing citizens the right to bear arms.

In reality most anti-gun organizations don't want to revoke the Second Amendment. They usually want to increase background checks, waiting periods, and change regulations regarding gun registration.

Red Herring

A red herring is a fallacy in which an irrelevant topic is inserted into the discussion to divert attention away from the real issue. The fallacy gets its name from English fox hunts. The farmers, in an effort to keep fox hunters and their hounds from running through their crops, would drag a smoked herring with a strong odor along the edge of their fields. This threw the dogs off of the scent of the fox and kept them from destroying their crops.

> The university wants to increase the math requirement in the freshmen general education plan. How can we discuss general education requirements when parking is such an issue on this campus?

Politicians are often guilty of the red herring fallacy. In order to avoid controversial issues such as gun control, they will often change the subject so that they will not have to answer a question on a potentially controversial issue.

Using Pathos in your Presentation

Appeals to pathos, or appeals to emotion, are used in order to generate sadness, fear, elation, guilt, sympathy, or another emotion on the part of your audience. Emotional appeals add heart to your presentation. They can make a presentation more compelling. Emotional appeals are especially important in speeches of policy or value.[3] By arousing emotions in your audience members, they find it easier to identify with your presentation. Some common emotions aroused in presentations include fear,[4] anger, guilt, admiration, sympathy, and pride.

How can you effectively incorporate emotional appeals into your presentations? Emotional appeals can be communicated through language, supporting evidence, and delivery.

Emotional appeals add heart to your presentation.

Language

The use of emotion can be communicated through words that connotate emotion. By choosing select words packed with emotion, you can move your audience. Consider the following excerpt from a speech delivered by Kelly, a former COM 114 student:

> In March 1989, oil from the tanker Exxon Valdez **spilled** into the **pristine** Prince William Sound, **dumping** 11 million gallons of oil into one of Alaska's **most diverse** ecosystems. Because it happened in the spring, nature's **time of renewal,** the results were **tragic.** Twenty eight hundred sea otters, three hundred harbor seals, and nine hundred bald eagles, **the symbol of American freedom,** were killed.

By choosing certain words and phrases, the horror of this tragedy becomes more real for the audience. Had Kelly chosen to deliver the opening of her presentation in the following way, the impact would not have been the same.

> In March 1989, the tanker Exxon Valdez spilled 11 million gallons of oil into Prince William Sound, killing thousands of native species inhabiting the area.

The first opening has a much stronger impact on the audience because of the detail and the emotionally charged words that Kelly selected.

Be careful not to overdo it. A few emotionally charged words can go a long way for the audience. Overdoing it can draw the attention of the audience away from the message and onto the words themselves. Therefore, use words that pack emotion carefully.

Supporting Evidence

The use of narratives or extended examples to support your points can have a great emotional impact on an audience. Narratives and extended examples pull audiences into your presentations and naturally grow out of the content of your presentation. One key point to remember is you can't tell an audience how to feel; you have to show them. The example that follows shows how Dayna involved her audience emotionally in her presentation.

> Monica Jasmin was six months pregnant with her second son, Luke. She was being very careful about the food she was eating. She avoided caffeine and stayed away from unpasteurized cheeses. She thought she was eating nutritiously when she chose a turkey sandwich from a deli tray at her office. However, the turkey sandwich that Monica ate was infested with *Listeria monocytogenes,* a bacteria that can cause a disease called listeriosis. On December 13th, she developed a fever and severe muscle pain. Her husband Tim rushed her to the hospital, but it was too late. At 6:36 a.m. she lost their baby, Luke.

By using this narrative, Dayna is able to arouse an emotional response in her audience. This story puts a face on a little known but potentially devastating disease that can occur in pregnancy. By making us relate more to the topic, we are more involved and motivated to process her presenta-

> ## You should refrain from using emotional appeals when addressing questions of fact.

tion on food-borne illness. Without this vivid example, her speech would not have had the impact she was hoping for.

Delivery

Emotion can also be communicated through the delivery of your presentation. By incorporating pauses, facial expressions, and vocal variety into your presentation, you can also move your audience. Speak from your heart and your audience will feel your message. By demonstrating conviction and honesty, the language choices and narratives you have chosen will come alive for your audience. Remember, if you don't speak with conviction, your emotional appeals are likely to fall flat.

Using Pathos Ethically

Serious debate concerning the ethics of emotional appeals has ensued for many years. Some scholars advocate never using emotional appeals at all. They argue that emotional appeals have led to horrible human suffering. After all, Adolph Hitler used emotional appeals to promote hatred.

As long as emotional appeals are balanced with appeals to logic, it is perfectly acceptable to use them. Make sure that they are appropriate to the topic you are addressing. You should refrain from using emotional appeals when addressing questions of fact. They are inappropriate. Emotional criteria should not be applied to issues that are purely factual.[5]

However, you will be unlikely to move an audience to action without involving their hearts and minds. Just remember, all persuasive speeches should be built on evidence and sound reasoning. Emotional appeals should never be substituted for logic and good evidence.

Conclusion

Effective reasoning will have a strong impact on the success of your presentation. It is important that you learn how to use appeals to pathos, logos, and ethos well. Taking advantage of credibility by working on your competence and character will cause an audience to view your presentation more favorably. Credibility isn't enough. You must also appeal to the intellect of your audience by using logos or logic. Examine your evidence closely and use the type of reasoning (deductive, inductive, analogical, and casual) that is most effective for your type of supporting material. Remember to avoid fallacies as you construct your arguments. They can be devastating to your presentation. Finally, don't forget the impact of pathos, or emotional appeals. Emotional appeals can be quite compelling when combined with the other types of reasoning. However, your use of this appeal should be guided by good ethics.

Key Terms

Analogical Reasoning
Argument ad hominem
Bandwagon
Causal Reasoning
Credibility Ethos
Deductive Reasoning
Derived Credibility
Fallacy

False Dilemma
Hasty Generalization
Inductive Reasoning
Initial Credibility
Invalid Analogy
Logos
Major Premise
Minor Premise

Pathos
Post hoc ergo propter hoc
Red Herring
Slippery Slope
Straw Person
Syllogism
Terminal Credibility

Notes

1. O'Keefe, D. J. (2002). *Persuasion: Theory and research.* Thousand Oaks, CA: Sage.
2. Babble, E. (2001). *The practice of social research.* Belmont, CA: Wadsworth.
3. Lucas, S. (in press). *The art of public speaking.* New York: McGraw-Hill.
4. For more reading on fear appeals see Witte, K. (1992). Putting the fear back into fear appeals: The extended parallel process model (EPPM). *Communication Monographs* 61, 113–134.
5. Lucas. *The art of public speaking.*

Delivering the Presentation

Chapter Objectives

After reading this chapter, you should be able to:

- Explain the importance of good delivery to a successful presentation.

- Explain the characteristics of good delivery.

- Identify the four methods of delivery.

- Explain the guidelines of successful impromptu speaking.

- Explain the elements of vocal delivery that are vital to successful presentations.

- Discuss the aspects of physical delivery and their importance to presentational speaking.

Zoe, a former student, prepared thoroughly for her presentation. She found an interesting topic, conducted excellent research, did a thorough and accurate audience analysis, and used an organizational style tailored to the challenges her topic presented. In preparing for the presentation, Zoe could not have been more thorough. She volunteered to go first and couldn't wait to share her information with her peers. Her presentation went fine. She presented a well-researched and well-organized speech. However, after the presentation was over, I could see that she was extremely disappointed. I asked her what was wrong. She told me that although she felt good about the mechanics of her presentation, she didn't feel her audience paid attention or got excited about the possibilities of her proposal. I had to agree with Zoe. The class wasn't moved by the presentation as she had expected.

What went wrong? Although Zoe had excellent examples, flawless transitions, and moving testimony and arguments, she never connected with her audience. She stayed glued behind her notes and the lectern. She made little eye contact with her audience and was therefore unable to adapt to audience feedback.

What Zoe had failed to realize is that presentations contain two components: the verbal message and the nonverbal message. She had prepared thoroughly for the verbal portion of her presentation but had failed to focus on the nonverbal aspects. Simply put, Zoe had failed to reach her goal because of poor delivery.

The Importance of Good Delivery

As Zoe learned, it really doesn't matter how well crafted a presentation is; if the delivery is flat, the presentation will not achieve its potential. As you have been reading, a good presentation relies on solid content, effective organization, and convincing delivery. Good delivery provides three important elements to a presentation: it sets the tone for the presentation, makes the presentation more compelling, and helps illustrate the message for the audience.[1]

After participating as an audience member in a few presentations, it becomes easy to see why good delivery is important. But students often worry about how to incorporate effective delivery techniques into their actual presentations. By the end of this chapter, which examines the characteristics of effective delivery, guidelines for delivering a speech, and ways to optimize your vocal and physical delivery, this will be clear.

Characteristics of Effective Delivery

Effective Delivery Is Conversational

Although presentations are more formal than conversations, your presentation should maintain a conversational style. You want each audience member to feel that you are speaking directly to him or her, and not to a group of people. By establishing and maintaining eye contact and responding to audience feedback, you will be better able to connect with each member of the audience.

Another important feature of conversational style is expressiveness. Think about how you express your thoughts and emotions in conversations with your friends. What kinds of things do you do with your voice and face? Do you raise your eyebrows or smile? Whatever it is that you use to express yourself in everyday conversation, you should also use with an audience. Use vocal variety (see definition later in chapter), facial expressions, and an upright posture that indicates you are approachable and open. We will address each of these components later in the chapter and focus on skills that will help you develop a conversational style.

Effective Delivery Is Natural

One of the most important aspects of delivery is to be natural. Any vocal or nonverbal feature that distracts from the message should be avoided. Think about your natural conversational style. You want to be consistent with that style. If you use a lot of gestures when you speak, use them in your presentations as well. If you are a person who uses few, if any, gestures, don't add them to your presentation; it won't seem natural for you or to the audience and the presentation may seem forced. You want your delivery to be effective and engaging but almost go unnoticed. Natural delivery does not detract from the message or presentation, it enhances it.

Effective Delivery Is Varied

One of the most important aspects of effective delivery is that it is varied. It becomes very monotonous to listen to a speaker whose voice does not change in volume or pitch. Sometimes speakers develop a pattern of varied delivery that becomes predictable to the audience. For example, when they finish a final point, they will move to the other side of the room. Although they are making changes and varying their delivery, it is too predictable. We want the delivery to take the audience by surprise; anything less becomes monotonous.

Effective Delivery Enhances the Message

Good delivery enhances and adds impact to the message. As part of this process, delivery should help the audience interpret the message. Increased volume can emphasize an important point; a pause helps indicate that extra attention should be paid to an aspect in the presentation.

Unfortunately, in too many speeches, delivery detracts from the message. A speaker who speaks too softly distracts from the message, forcing audience members to strain to hear the words. Poor pronunciation and the use of slang words can also detract from the message. A presenter who paces from one end of the room to the other makes it very difficult for an audience to focus on the important elements of the lecture.

Methods of Delivery

To better understand elements of effective delivery, it is important to understand the different methods that are available: impromptu, manuscript, memorized, and extemporaneous. Each one of these methods has strengths and weaknesses. It is important that you analyze your situation and pick the method best suited for your situation.

Impromptu

The impromptu delivery method is probably the most common type of method used in presentational speaking. This method is characterized by little or no time for advanced preparation. We often call this type of speaking "off the cuff." Imagine that you are at a staff meeting and your boss asks you to report on developments in your division's current project. Obviously, you had no advanced warning that you were going to be asked to deliver this information, but now you are on the spot and must deliver a message that is both organized and effective—without having time for the usual preparation. It is important to know that there are certain skills you can learn that can make you more effective at an impromptu presentation. In addition to these skills, experience helps these unplanned presentations go more effectively.

Guidelines for Impromptu Speaking

Here are some guidelines that will help you organize and feel more confident with the impromptu method of delivery.

Step One: Prepare to Speak

You don't have to start speaking the minute you have been asked to. Take a deep breath, rise from your chair, and walk to the front of the room to the lectern. Use this time to gather and organize your thoughts.

Step Two: Determine your purpose

Try to develop one or two points as you walk to the lectern to begin speaking.

Think about what point or points you want to make. Because you will have a very limited amount of time in which to prepare and speak, focus on one issue that you know well and can adequately address. Avoid complex issues or ideas about which you have limited knowledge.

Step Three: Support your purpose

Support your purpose or points with examples, narratives, or other supporting evidence. Regardless of the type of evidence you choose, you want to provide specific details for your audience so that you justify your position or purpose.

Step Four: Prepare the introduction

Develop an introduction. A brief sentence will suffice in an impromptu presentation. You might refer to the event at which you are speaking or to another comment that has recently been made.

Step Five: Prepare the conclusion

Finally, conclude the presentation. One of the most common mistakes in this method of delivery is that the conclusion often rambles. Follow the guidelines in Chapter 4 for an effective ending (be brief, clear, and memorable). You want to come to a definite stop. Simply restate your point, or points, and end with a memorable thought or a call to action.

Keep these points in mind as you prepare for impromptu presentations:

■ **Don't rush**

Take your time before you start to speak. Make sure your thoughts are clearly laid out in your mind before you begin speaking. Also, speak slowly and don't rush through the presentation.

■ **Don't apologize**

Start your presentation with your introduction. Avoid statements such as, "You'll have to forgive me, I had little time to prepare today." Your audience will know this and they will not be expecting a masterpiece.

■ **Focus on the topic**

Keep the focus of your presentation on the topic at hand. Remember your purpose and don't stray from it. It is also important that you avoid any negative remarks. Keep your mind on your subject matter and keep negative thoughts at bay.

■ **Be Brief**

Remember, this is a brief presentation. Try to stay focused and avoid rambling. You don't have to say everything that you know about a particular topic. Choose your purpose, state your point or points, provide support, and then conclude.

■ **Foresee situations**

If at all possible, try to anticipate those situations in which you may be called on to speak. From experience, you may know that you will have to report on your division's progress at certain staff meetings. Plan in advance what you would like to say if the situation presents itself.

The strategies discussed above will help you keep impromptu speaking in perspective. With a little practice and a few strategies, anyone can be an effective impromptu speaker.

Manuscript

The manuscript method requires that you write out your speech word-for-word and deliver the presentation by reading directly from the actual manuscript.

Manuscript speaking is important when the exact wording of the presentation is paramount. For example, speeches of the President of the United States are written by professional speechwriters to address particular goals in particular situations. The president delivered one such speech to console the American people after the events of September 11, 2001. These speechwriters spend a great deal of time choosing the right phrases and words that will evoke specific feelings and emotions in a particular audience. Therefore, the exact wording is extremely important.

This type of delivery is the best method of choice when the stakes are high. A misspoken phrase can have significant ramifications for the president and could even affect national policy or security. Rarely, if ever, will you give a speech of this magnitude.

One drawback to manuscript speaking is that it is a difficult style to deliver well. As a presenter you want to connect with your audience. In order for this to happen, you must maintain good eye contact and vocal variety. These are hard to maintain when reading from a document. It takes many years of practice to deliver this style of speaking effectively. In addition, manuscript speaking does not allow the presenter the flexibility of adapting the presentation to the needs of his or her audience, which is very important to presentational speaking.

Memorized

Another style of delivery is to memorize the text of the speech and then simply recite it to your audience. As in the manuscript speech, the text of the presentation is written out word-for-word and the speech is delivered from memory.

> ### The extemporaneous presentation is a prepared and practiced method of delivery.

This type of style has many limitations. Numerous speakers who adopt this style lose their place in their speech and become flustered. Delivery in memorized presentations also seems very stiff, and an audience can usually tell when a speech is memorized. It lacks the vocal and physical variety normally found in other methods of delivery, such as the impromptu and extemporaneous methods. Much like the manuscript style, the memorized presentation limits your ability to adapt and therefore connect with your audience. This connection is something that is important to audiences, so you should consider this constraint when choosing your method of delivery.

Sometimes your instructor will recommend that you memorize certain elements of your presentation. For example, many instructors recommend memorizing the attention getter and the clincher. This ensures that you are able to make adequate eye contact at these critical points in the presentation. They may also recommend that you memorize some quotations or pieces of evidence.

Unless you are delivering a very short presentation, such as a toast at a wedding or an introduction for a speaker, the memorized style is probably not your best choice. The pitfalls that accompany this type of presentation outweigh most of the benefits.

Extemporaneous

The extemporaneous presentation is a prepared and practiced method of delivery. However, unlike manuscript and memorized methods, the speech is not written out word-for-word. You simply outline the main ideas of your presentation and use these as a memory aid as you deliver the presentation. Each time that the presentation is delivered, it is a bit different because you choose the exact wording of the presentation at the time you deliver the material. By providing the flexibility to choose the right words for the right situation, extemporaneous delivery allows the presenter to adapt to the audience. For example, imagine delivering a presentation to some colleagues within your organization. From their feedback you notice they are not following some of the supporting material you have provided. The extemporaneous style

allows you to go over this section of the presentation again, in a different way, in hopes of reaching those individuals in your audience.

In addition to providing the flexibility to adapt to your audience, the extemporaneous presentation also allows for more dynamic delivery. Because you are not tied to your notes or relying on your memory, you have the flexibility to maintain eye contact and use other delivery features that will make the presentation more interesting for your audience. Extemporaneous speaking is the preferred speaking style in today's organizations, and its popularity is the reason it is stressed in this course.

In the remaining sections of this chapter, we are going to examine aspects of vocal and physical delivery as well as give you some pointers on how to practice for your presentation.

Vocal Delivery

Sometimes speakers underestimate the power of the nonverbal aspects of vocal delivery. Like Zoe, they work very hard on researching, organizing, and practicing the speech, but they forget that their vocal delivery can enhance meaning and add impact to the presentation. Vocal characteristics such as volume, rate, pitch, pauses, enunciation, and pronunciation are all aspects of what we call paralanguage, or the nonverbal aspects of vocal delivery. These enhance the verbal message and therefore help illustrate the message for the audience. Practice using these skills to increase your effectiveness as a speaker.

Vocal Variety

The most important aspect of vocal delivery is vocal variety. As a speaker, you want to vary your volume, rate, pitch, and use of pauses to add impact to your presentation. In the section below, we discuss each of these issues, along with other elements of vocal delivery. The key to remember is to vary the use of all of these components.

Volume

One of the most important aspects in terms of intelligibility is speaking at a level at which you can be heard. In some speaking situations you will use an electronic device, such as a microphone, that will enhance your own voice and enable the audience to hear you no matter how softly you speak. However, many presentations you make will be done without the aid of electronics. Therefore, it is important for you to get a feel for how loudly to speak. I find that if you speak a little louder than you think is necessary, you are probably speaking at the right level. Once you begin your presentation, look around the room. Does the audience seem to be straining to hear you? Do the people sitting in the back of the room seem to be leaning forward in their chairs? If so, raise your volume. Most of the time speakers err on the side of speaking too softly rather than too loudly. However, some of us do have rather strong and booming voices. Check audience feedback to make sure they are comfortable with the level you are speaking. If they seem to be straining forward in their seats, you are probably speaking too softly. If they seem uncomfortable and are leaning back, you might lower your voice. When you practice, friends and family members can give you feedback on how effective your volume level is. Try to remember, however, that each speaking situation is unique. The size of the audience, along with the acoustics of the room, will make a difference in the volume you need to project. Attuning to audience feedback is probably the safest way to assure that you are speaking at a volume that is effective.

Rate

The typical American speaks about 180 words per minute. This range varies greatly throughout the United States. People in the South generally speak more slowly than people on the East Coast. Although we can process language much faster than this, this seems to be the rate most of us are used to and comfortable with in presentational situations. Therefore, you want to strive to fall somewhere around this figure. If you speak too fast, audience members may have a hard time following you. If you speak too slowly, audience members may find themselves wanting to finish your words and phrases for you rather than focusing on your message. Again, look for audience feedback; if members of the audience seem to be straining to hear you, you may be speaking too quickly.

Pitch

The pitch refers to the placement of your voice on the musical scale. Some of us have very low-pitched voices and some rather high-pitched voices. The important aspect of pitch is that it be varied. You want to mix the pitch of your voice to achieve a variety in tone. Otherwise, your speech will become very monotonous for your audience. You also want to be careful that you do not fall into a pattern of using pitch in the same way over and over again. For example, some women's voices rise in pitch at the end of a statement, turning every statement into a question. This can be very irritating for an audience.

One good way to examine the range of your natural pitch is to tape record yourself speaking. By listening to yourself, you can get a good idea of your vocal habits and the natural characteristics of your speaking voice. From this examination, you will gain a much better idea of how to vary the pitch of your speaking voice.

Pauses

Pauses are another tool you have to add dramatic impact to your delivery. After delivering an important point, pause for a second and let the audience think about what you have just said. The planned use of incorporating pauses into a presentation can have a big impact on its effectiveness. Remember, however, that there are two types of pauses—those that are planned and those that are unplanned.

Pauses that are unplanned are called **vocal fillers.** They are used when a speaker is trying to decide what to say next. These usually occur in the middle of a sentence or thought. We use them to fill in that "dead time" while we are mentally composing what we would like to say next. Some common vocal fillers are "um," "like," "you know," and "you know what I mean?" These vocal fillers are extremely distracting from the presentation. We usually insert them in a presentation when we are trying to fill small silences. As novice speakers, we are uncomfortable with silences and so we fill them with these vocal fillers. However, these should be avoided. Only those pauses that are planned and that add emphasis to your message should be used.

All of these nonverbal aspects of vocal delivery combine to add emphasis to important elements of your presentation. Say, for example, that you delivered the following statement to your audience: "According to **Ascribe,** a public interest newswire, 57 million pounds of ground beef, poultry, and deli meats were recalled in 2003 and 76 million people reported being victims of foodborne illness." You could emphasize these statistics in several ways. One strategy would be to pause briefly after delivering the statement. You could also raise the volume of your voice as you deliv-

> Mispronunciation of a word during your speech can ruin your credibility.

ered the statement. Regardless of the method you choose, this statement would have no impact if you did not vary your delivery.

Enunciation

Another important aspect of good vocal delivery is enunciation. You want to make sure that you deliver words clearly and distinctly so that the audience understands you. Many times, in casual conversation, we cut off the endings or beginnings of words. This is very common. We often say 'cause instead of because, or goin' instead of going. Although this is acceptable in casual conversation, the use of it in a formal presentation may cause an audience to question your competence and credibility.

Pronunciation

Mispronunciation of a word during your speech can ruin your credibility. Why should an audience consider you an expert in the field if you are mispronouncing key words related to your topic? It becomes imperative that you are certain of the pronunciation of unfamiliar or difficult words. If you are unsure, consult a dictionary.

It is easy to mispronounce even common words. Again, while acceptable in casual conversation, mispronunciation of everyday words is unacceptable in front of an audience. This type of mistake will not only call your competence into question, but can also confuse your audience. For example, many people say "affect" when they mean "effect." This difference in words can muddle an important point for an audience. The table on page 162 provides the proper pronunciation of many commonly misused words.

Physical Delivery

Another aspect of your presentation is the physical delivery, or how you present your body. How you gesture, move, make eye contact, and even dress are all essential features of the presentation. Let's examine each of these so that you can incorporate them effectively into your presentation.

Gestures

The use of gestures is one of those areas that cause novice speakers much concern. People never seem to know what to do with their hands. Often, speakers put their hands in their pockets and start playing with their change. Other times, speakers will tuck their hair behind their ears again and again. Sometimes speakers clinch their hands behind their backs. Not only are these gestures ineffective, they also distract from the message. Remember, one of the goals of delivery is to enhance the verbal message. If your gestures detract from rather than complement the message, they will be ineffective.

Commonly Mispronounced Words

Word	Correct Pronunciation	Incorrect Pronunciation
Across	a-CROSS	a-CROST
Athlete	ATH-leet	ATH-a-leet
Comfortable	COM-fort-a-ble	COMF-ta-ble
Espresso	Ess-PRESS-oh	ex-Press-oh
February	FEB-roo-air-y	Feb-yoo-air-y
Library	LIBE-rare-ee	LIB-air-ee
Nuclear	NUKE-lee-ar	NUKE-yoo-lar
Often	OFF-en	OFT-en
Probably	PRAH-bab-ly	PRAH-bal-ly
Supposedly	Sup-POSE-ed-ly	Sup-POSE-ab-ly
Toward	TOW-ward	TOR-ward

In order to illustrate or complement your verbal message, your gestures must appear natural. If you are a person who uses few gestures in natural conversation, then use few in your presentations. Gestures can add a great deal of impact to the presentation. However, as a novice speaker, you have more to worry about than incorporating gestures. Don't get caught up in incorporating gestures into your presentation. As you become an accomplished speaker, you will develop a style that works for you. One guideline to follow is this: if the gesture distracts from the message, do not use it.

Movement

Some common questions beginning students ask in this course are, Where do I stand? Should I walk around or stand still? Should I use the podium or not? Your instructor will provide guidelines for using the podium or lectern in your classroom. Outside of the classroom, it depends on the situation and the type of presentation.

Regardless of the speaking situation, there are a few guidelines that apply. Much like gestures, movement can add a good deal of impact to your presentation. However, it can also be very distracting. You must move with purpose to be effective. Many times novice speakers start to pace in front of their audience. You have probably seen professors use this same strategy. They walk from one side of the room to the other with no purpose. It is very distracting. We start concentrating on when they will cross the room rather than the verbal message itself.

> **Movement during your presentation can be very effective if you do it with purpose.**

Movement during your presentation can be very effective if you do it with purpose. Move to add impact to a particular or compelling point within the presentation. If you are standing behind a lectern, you might walk to the side of it to make an important point. You can also move during transitions to signal to the audience that you are moving from one point to another. No matter when you decide to move, it must be done with purpose.

Eye Contact

Eye contact is probably the most important component of physical delivery. It allows us to connect with our audience. Eye contact ensures that our presentation remains conversational and that members of the audience feel that we are addressing each of them individually.

Eye contact can be a bit uncomfortable for novice speakers. It may seem a bit strange to focus on members of the audience by looking directly at them. Therefore, many beginner speakers avoid eye contact. Instead they focus on their notecards and rarely look up at the audience.

Other speakers tend to favor one side of the room over the other. You may notice this phenomenon with some of your professors. They lecture to only one side of the room. If you are lucky enough to be sitting on their preferred side of the classroom or lecture hall, you feel that you have connected with them. If you are sitting on the side that received little or no eye contact, however, you will feel disconnected from the speaker. Favoring one side of the room or another is a very common mistake. If you think you are guilty of this common nonverbal delivery mistake, have friends watch your practice session and give you feedback, or videotape yourself to see.

In American culture, presenters who do not maintain eye contact with the audience are perceived as less trustworthy, competent, and concerned than those who maintain adequate eye contact. In the classroom situation, failure to make eye contact can be perceived as lack of preparation and even familiarity with your material. Therefore, when addressing your audience, it is important that you develop and implement this delivery strategy effectively.

You also want to make sure that your eye contact is effective. You need to look directly at audience members. A popular myth about presentational speaking is that a speaker should look over the heads of the audience to a spot on the wall. This will not be effective, and your audience will not perceive that you have made adequate eye contact. You must look directly into the faces of your audience members.

You cannot overestimate the importance of eye contact. Not only is it a tool for connecting with your audience, it also allows you to get feedback from your audience. Are they interested? Do they seem confused? With effective eye contact, you can gauge audience feedback and make necessary adaptations as the presentation progresses.

Appearance

A common question I receive from students is, What should I wear? There is no simple answer. Some research indicates that a professional appearance adds to your credibility.[2] However, simply putting on a suit regardless of the speaking situation is not a sure-fire way to increase your credibility. In fact, in some situations, this type of attire may actually hurt you. For example, suppose that you have been hired by the county outreach program to provide lectures to area farmers on new developments in pesticides. Showing up to one of these sessions dressed in a suit may hurt your credibility with this particular audience. Farmers will be dressed in work clothes and, in order to feel that you have credibility, they need to be able to relate to you and feel that you are similar to them. Appearance is an important part of this process.

You will want to dress professionally for the particular audience that you are addressing. What is professional attire for an accountant is not the same for a welder. Research indicates that being radically over- or underdressed for an occasion can lead to negative perceptions toward the speaker on behalf of the audience.[3] Thus, a good guideline is to dress slightly better than you anticipate your audience to be dressed.

Much like all the other aspects of nonverbal delivery, it is important that your appearance does not distract from your message. You want to present a comprehensive picture of competence. A professional appearance that takes into account the context can help you achieve this goal.

Practicing the Presentation

As in the example at the beginning of the chapter, you can plan, organize, and research an incredible presentation, but if your delivery is flat, all that planning will have been in vain. You simply have to practice your speech in order for it all to come together. In order for you to have enough time to rehearse thoroughly, you should complete your full-sentence outline, or preparation outline, three days before you plan to deliver your presentation.

Here are some guidelines to help you with your practice sessions.

Step 1: Practice aloud with your preparation or full-sentence outline. Check the outline for the following items: Is it too long or too short? Is it organized appropriately? Do you have adequate support for each idea? Once you have answered these questions and fixed any deficiencies, it is time to write the speaking outline. (Check the guidelines in Chapter 7.)

Step 2: Practice delivering your speech from your speaking outline. Rehearse the presentation several times until you are comfortable with the outline you have prepared. Go through the speech from beginning to end. Make sure you rehearse all aspects of the presentation. If you tell a narrative as the attention getter, make sure you practice the entire narrative. If you are using visual aids, they should be completed at this point and incorporated into the presentation. Remember, you should not be memorizing the speech, but becoming comfortable with the ideas of the presentation.

Step 3: Once the verbal message seems solid, start adding some of the aspects of delivery that will add impact to your presentation. Don't forget to mark delivery cues on your speaking outline so that you will be sure to incorporate them into your presentation. You might also try videotaping yourself, speaking into a tape recorder, or rehearsing in front of a mirror. All of these methods will help you get a good idea of what the speech will sound like to other people. However, the best way to determine how your presentation will be received is to present it to others. Ask your friends and family to act as audience members and to provide feedback. This will help you tweak those last-minute details.

Step 4: Put it all together. Try to replicate the actual speaking situation as closely as possible. If you are giving a classroom presentation, see if you can get access to your classroom and practice there. If you are giving a presentation to your organization, try to gain access to the conference room and have a quick run through. Practicing in the actual circumstances where you will be delivering the presentation is an excellent way to ensure that you are prepared.

The most important aspect of preparing for your presentation is to start early. If you don't leave yourself enough time to work through all of the little details of your presentation, your audience will know it. Lack of preparation time can also affect your confidence. So give yourself plenty of time to rehearse for your presentation.

Conclusion

The verbal content of your presentation is only one aspect of the message you are trying to convey to your audience. You simply cannot overestimate the impact that the nonverbal aspects of communication can have on your presentation. It is important that you pay close attention to both your vocal delivery (volume, rate, pitch, pauses, enunciation, and pronunciation) and physical delivery (gestures, movement, eye contact, and appearance). In order to put all of the aspects of your presentation together, you must leave yourself plenty of time to rehearse it. Guidelines for practicing your presentation include delivering your speech from the speaking outline, adding vocal and physical delivery cues, and practicing in circumstances similar to those of the actual presentation.

In general, you should strive to take the delivery of your message as seriously as you do the construction of the presentation.

Key Terms

Appearance	Manuscript delivery	Rate
Effective delivery	Memorized delivery	Vocal delivery
Enunciation	Movement	Vocal fillers
Extemporaneous delivery	Pauses	Vocal variety
Eye contact	Physical delivery	Volume
Gestures	Pitch	
Impromptu delivery	Pronunciation	

Notes

1. Ekman, P., & Friesen, W. (1969). The repertoire of nonverbal behavior: Categories, origins, usage, and coding. *Semiotica* 1, 49–98.
2. Morris, T. L., Gorham, J., Cohen, S. H., & Huffman, D. (1996). Fashion in the classroom: Effects of attire on student perceptions of instructors in college classes. *Communication Education* 45, 135–148.
3. Roach, K. D. (1997). Effects of graduate teaching assistant attire on student learning, misbehaviors, and ratings of instruction. *Communication Quarterly* 45 (3), 125–141.

CHAPTER 12

Presentation Aids

Chapter Objectives

After reading this chapter, you should be able to:

- Explain the major advantages of using visual aids in a speech.

- Apply the guidelines given in the chapter for preparing and presenting visual aids.

Because of the pervasiveness of computers, it is rare to see presentations in a professional context that do not make some use of presentation aids. In fact, most people think that they have to have some sort of presentation aid, such as a slick set of PowerPoint slides, or their presentation will be perceived as ineffective. Because computers make the creation of aids very easy, however, most people do not spend the time necessary to make good decisions about how to integrate them into their presentations.

We define a presentation aid as any item used to enhance the presentation itself. Examples of presentation aids include: physical objects, charts, graphs, maps, models, diagrams, audio-video material, photographs, etc. Aids can also be presented through a variety of mediums, such as overhead projectors, computers, and televisions. Regardless of the presentation aid's medium or type of content, the key to using them is that they must enhance understanding. Presentation aids cease to aid presentations when they detract from the presentation itself. It is very easy to use presentation aids inappropriately. This chapter will help you understand the different types of common presentation aids and how to integrate them successfully into presentations.

Functions of Presentation Aids

Presentation aids can function in a variety of ways. When used properly, presentation aids can have significant impact on the presentation and the speaker.

Increase Clarity and Retention

Presentation aids are used to enhance audience understanding. They can achieve this goal in three specific ways. First, they can clarify complex information. Large amounts of statistics and numerical information are difficult for an audience to process. By providing this information in a more concise manner, for example within a chart, the audience's ability to process the information and understand your material is greatly enhanced. Second, presentation aids help to illustrate abstract information. How could an audience be expected to understand the differences between Cubism and Impressionism if they didn't see examples of these types of art? Finally, presentation aids actually improve the memorability of the information in the presentation. Studies have shown that audiences will retain only 20% of what they hear. However, when an audience hears and sees the information a speaker presents, that number jumps to 50%[1].

Increase Presentation Effectiveness

Presentations that incorporate aids have also been shown to be more effective. Visual aids can actually increase the persuasiveness of a presentation. A study conducted by the University of Minnesota's School of Management and the 3M Corporation found that the use of visual aids can increase the persuasiveness of a presentation by up to 40%.[2]

Increase Speaker Effectiveness

Using presentation aids can actually affect the audience's perceptions of the speaker. Research has indicated that an average speaker will be perceived by the audience as better prepared, more credible, more professional and more dynamic than an average speaker who does not use presentation aids. Research has also indicated that communication apprehension is decreased for those speak-

> Charts graphically illustrate complex information so the meaning of the numbers is clearer to the audience.

ers who use presentation aids. The speaker can relax because the focus of the audience is directed toward the visual aid.

Types of Presentation Aids

Numerical Charts

Charts play a critical role in many presentations. Often, much of the information we need to illustrate is numerical in nature. Numerical data, especially tabular data, is very difficult to communicate verbally. "The primary purpose of any chart is to demonstrate relationships more quickly and more clearly than is possible using a tabular form."[3]

This makes charts perfect choices for oral presentations where audiences are limited in their ability to study complex sets of information. We are usually interested in displaying relative differences among numbers rather than the details of the specific numbers themselves. This is where charts can become very helpful.

Charts graphically illustrate complex information so the meaning of the numbers is clearer to the audience. In the context of an oral presentation, it is difficult for an audience member to carefully study a large table of rows and numbers. Not only is tabular information difficult to see, it is time consuming to process. To illustrate this, compare the following two ways of presenting the same information. The first figure represents the data in tabular form, while the second represents the same information in a chart. Though both are useful, the chart is easier to understand. In fact, you do not need to even know the exact numbers to see the general pattern of behavior. According to both the table and the chart, more users prefer to go directly to sites than to browse to them or search for them. Also, people are browsing to sites less over time. The exact numbers do not matter as much as the point they make.

How Do People Get to Web Sites

Year		
	2002	2003
Direct Navigation	50.12%	65.48%
Web Links	42.60%	21.04%
Search Engines	7.18%	13.46%

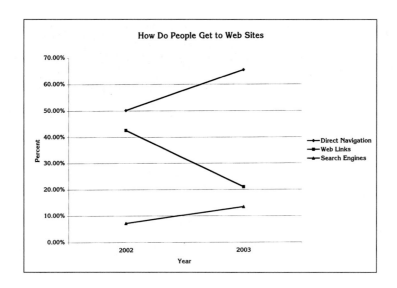

The key to using charts effectively is to know what type of chart to use based on the type of information you are trying to communicate. In this section we will cover three types of numerical charts: pie, bar, and line/column. All of these charts allow you to make different types of comparisons between and among numbers. Depending on the types of comparisons you need to make, you need to use different types of charts. Pie charts allow you to make comparisons between the relative sizes of different parts of a larger whole. Bar charts allow you to compare how different things rank in size. Line and column charts allow you to make comparisons of data over time, or to make comparisons about the frequency at which certain items are distributed. Though there are many additional types of charts, these are very popular and mastery of these will allow you to communicate many different types of numerical data clearly and succinctly. The following sections describe each type of numerical chart in more detail and provide tips on using them more effectively.

Pie Charts

Pie charts are one of the most popular types of charts. They are also very simple charts relative to some of the others. Often, we are interested in showing how different parts of something go together to make up a whole. Any time we are talking about parts of a whole, we are talking about percentages of the total. For instance, a pie chart might represent the percentage of students majoring in certain departments within a school or the percentage of sales accounted for by certain geographical regions, as seen in examples on page 173.

Bar Charts

Bar charts are extremely helpful when making comparisons among different types of items. These types of charts allow for easy visual ranking across items in a category. For instance, if I wanted to compare rabies vaccinations across geographical regions, I might use a bar chart like the following. In this example, it would be easy for your audience to recognize that the use of rabies vaccinations, for whatever reason, is more common in the South than in other regions.

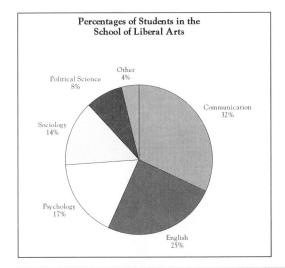

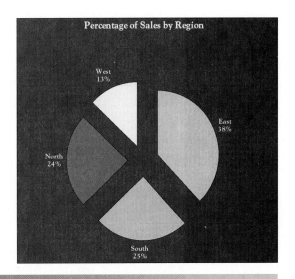

Pie Charts

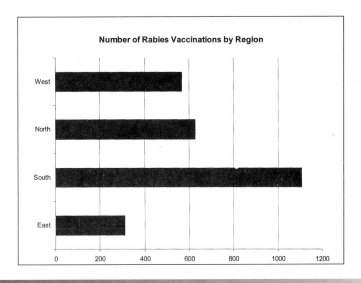

Bar Charts

Line/Column Charts

Line charts and column charts are most appropriate when one is comparing changes over time in a set of data. If the chart has few data points, under six or seven, a column chart is usually preferred. In a chart with many data points, line charts usually work best. The "How Do People Get to Web Sites" is a good example of a line chart, while the following is a good example of a column chart.

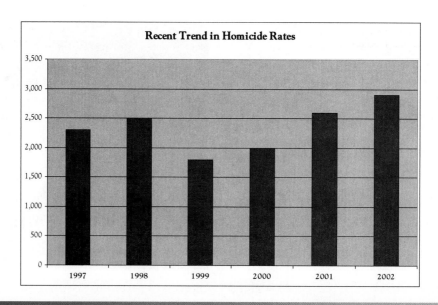

Line/Column Charts

Tips on Using Numerical Charts

1. Visually try to signify the most important numerical information by ranking (highest to lowest or lowest to highest) the information in the chart, or otherwise visually distinguishing important information.
2. Use high contrast colors.
3. Keep the number of segments in a pie chart at six or fewer. If you need more segments, you can often combine many smaller components into an "others" category.
4. Avoid creating a separate legend. Instead, put the labels in the appropriate positions in the chart.
5. Avoid using special effects, such as tilting to show perspective. This interferes with the ability to see proportions accurately.

Text Charts

Text charts list key ideas or phrases under a heading. Usually, this is the type of chart you see on text PowerPoint slides. They often use bullets and list items such as goals, function, guidelines, etc.

Maps

Maps organize information spatially. So, if you have arranged your main points in a spatial pattern, chances are you will need to use a map as a presentation aid. They are particularly helpful when you are trying to discuss geographically-oriented topics. They are also useful anytime you want to break information down by regions. Perhaps you are delivering a presentation on a recent flu outbreak and you want to demonstrate how it has spread across a particular state. Maps can also be used to provide directions within a speech.

The map in this example shows Kurdish territory in Iraq very clearly. Clarity is a key issue here. Maps often provide too much detail and make it hard for an audience to see the actual idea you are trying to communicate. Make sure your maps are easy to read like the one in this example.

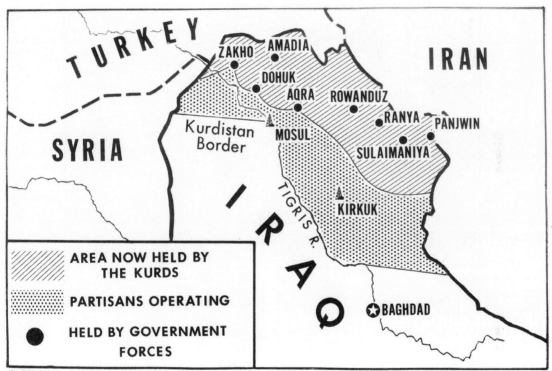

Diagrams

A diagram is a simple illustration that demonstrates the key ideas and how they relate to each other. Many times, we are trying to communicate the steps in a process. Diagrams are helpful in this endeavor. A student in COM 114 recently presented a speech on how banks process checks. He used a diagram to illustrate the steps in that process. Additional examples of diagrams can include flow charts and organizational charts.

The following diagram illustrates the bullet wound of President Reagan when he was shot by John Hinkley Jr. on January 20, 1981. This type of diagram drastically increases a person's ability to understand exactly what type of damage was caused by the bullet wound. As you will notice, the diagram is clearly labeled so that the audience can easily follow your explanation.

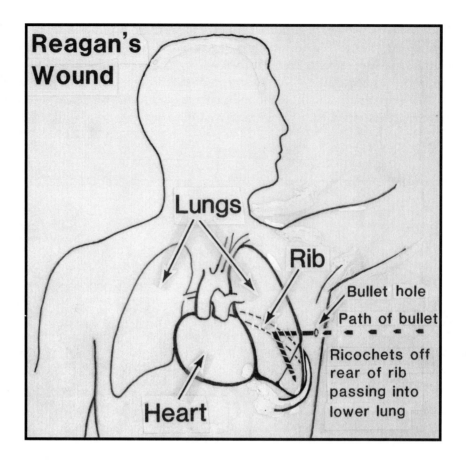

Photographs

Photographs can be very effective presentation aids. They illustrate events, people, or other objects more effectively than a speaker can do with words alone. Imagine trying to explain the architecture of Frank Lloyd Wright without showing some of his masterpieces. Oral descriptions cannot do his work justice. Unless an audience can see these beautiful works of art, they will not understand his genius.

Photos are easy to locate. They are all over the Internet. If you are going to use photographs, make sure they are very large and easy to see. The best way to do this is to scan them into a computer and print them out on transparencies, or include them in a PowerPoint presentation. If you don't have access to a scanner, a copy shop can copy a photo onto a transparency for you. Your audience would have to be very close to you to see an actual photograph of any size. To achieve maximum impact, take this extra step to ensure all audience members can see your aid.

Audio/Video

Audio and/or video can help bring presentations alive in ways that make your presentations very memorable. Some types of information benefit from audio/video information. We live in such a media saturated world that not including audio-video information often seems like an oversight for many audiences. Because audio-video information is so compelling, many people prefer getting news and entertainment from television than from reading newspapers or other sources of print information. Whether or not this is a good thing is something that is often debated, but the point is that you can often use this source of information to succinctly make points that are difficult to make with words. The primary difficulty with audio and video is that they entail using additional equipment, such as VCR's. If you have to use this type of equipment, you should be sure that your tapes are queued to the right spot prior to your presentation. You should also avoid trying to fast-forward or rewind to locate material during the presentation. The ideal solution is to capture this information digitally and play it using presentation software. This way you can completely control what your audience sees and hears.

Creating Multimedia Presentations

Most professional presentations today make use of what is called "presentation software" that makes use of computers and display devices, such as liquid crystal display (LCD) projectors. The most common software on the market today that creates these types of presentations is Microsoft PowerPoint, though other packages offer similar functionality. This type of software lets you create "slides" that can contain text, images, audio, video, and animations to help guide users through your presentation.

Presentation software is relatively easy to learn and all of you have probably seen many presentations that use this type of multimedia. Some of you may have even used this type of software before. In fact, if anything, presentation software is overused, or used ineffectively, because it is so pervasive and easy to use. The following sections will help you identify when and why you should use this type of tool, and when you should not.

Advantages to Using Presentation Software

There are several reasons to use presentation software. First, because presentation software provides you with visual information to support your presentation, you provide audiences with another exposure to your material that helps them retain important information. Secondly, presentation software breaks up the monotony of your presentation and adds visual interest to your information. Thirdly, by using this type of software, you can integrate different types of information into one standard format that you can easily manipulate during your presentation. For instance, if you need to use charts, sounds, and text to display different types of supporting information, you can do so entirely within a single set of slides, minimizing the need for multiple pieces of equipment. Lastly, presentation software often provides tools for creating speaking notes, outlines, and other types of materials, such as handouts or transparencies.

Using Presentation Software Effectively

Many people do not use PowerPoint and other tools to maximum advantage. One common mistake people make is to include way too much information on one slide. They often use PowerPoint

> One common mistake people make is to include way too much information on the slides.

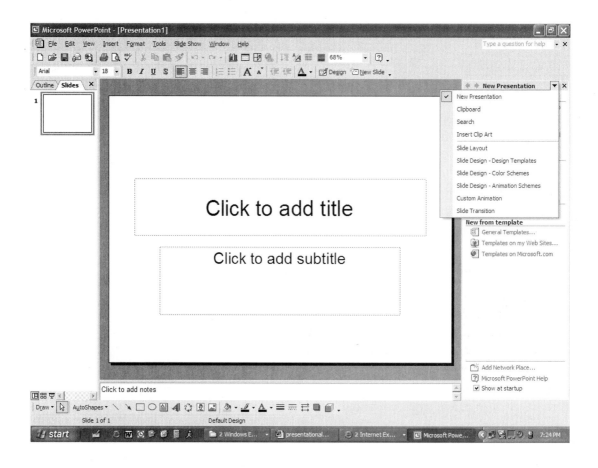

as a way to outline the whole presentation and then show that outline on their slides as they go. In this type of presentation, every point and subpoint in the presentation gets represented on slides and the speaker simply advances through all of these points as they move through the presentation. This creates a boring, text-heavy, and largely useless set of slides that do more to detract attention away from the speaker than anything else. When used this way, there are normally a very large number of slides, and this causes problems for the speaker because they always have to keep up with exactly where they are in the presentation and make sure the right slide, or part of slide, is showing. Many of you have probably seen presentations where the speaker had so many slides they end up playing catch-up with their slides because they forgot to advance them often enough as they were speaking. You don't want to be in this type of situation yourself. The following guidelines will help you create more effective PowerPoint presentations.

Keep Them Simple

Keep the number of slides to a minimum. Only put genuinely useful information that actually support your points on slides. In a 10-minute presentation, you should have no more than 4 or 5 slides. If you have more than that, you complicate what you have to keep up with during the presentation (working the slides instead of focusing on the audience) and are constantly shifting audience attention away from you. If an audience is continually wondering what the next slide will be, then they are not focusing on your message.

Use Only When Needed

Only show slides when you are specifically addressing them. This keeps the presentation focused on you rather than your presentation aid. PowerPoint lets you "blank" the screen with a simple keyboard command when you are not using the slide. People do not use this feature enough.

Use Effective Design Principles

When preparing your presentation slides, use high-contrasting colors, large font sizes, and consistent typefaces. Nothing is worse than a PowerPoint presentation with so much small text that the audience cannot read it easily. You should not have more than four to six words per line of text. Also, people find it easier to see large bright text (yellows and whites) on dark backgrounds (black and blues), than dark text on light backgrounds when it is projected onto a screen. The reverse is true for printed material. Finally, try to keep the number of fonts you use to a minimum. Choose one or two, and use them consistently across all slides.

Avoid Special Effects

Keep the special effects, such as slide transitions, sound effects and animations, to a minimum. Many amateur PowerPoint users load their presentations with so many pre-built special effects that their presentations become goofy and annoying. These features should always be used very sparingly. Other than the occasional subtle slide transition, these features do more harm than good, and should be avoided.

Avoid Standing in the Shadows

Remember, you are the presentation, not your PowerPoint slides. If the slides could speak for themselves, you could simply put your PowerPoint presentation up on the Web and allow your audience to read it for themselves. Because you are the focus of the presentation, avoid standing off to the side of the screen in the shadows. Because the lights are dimmed, the area to the side of the screen is usually very dark. It becomes easy for you, the presenter, to get lost. Don't let that happen. Make sure the room is well lit before you begin your presentation so that the audience can see you. This way they can identify you before you dim the lights. Make sure that you continue to connect with the audience even though the room is dark. Stay in the most well lit area in front. If the presentation contains a question and answer session, turn up the lights for that segment. Never forget, you are the presentation, not the presentation aids.

Tips for Designing Presentation Aids

Prepare Presentation Aids Carefully

Your presentation aids are a part of the overall effect of the presentation and deserve as much attention as all of the other parts of the planning process. Spend time carefully proofreading your presentation aids. Check spelling and grammar closely. Nothing can ruin your credibility more quickly than a typo. Create your presentation aids in advance so that you have ample time to catch mistakes. Get a friend to read over them for you. You can never check too closely.

Choose Fonts Carefully

When selecting fonts for projection, such as with a transparency or PowerPoint slide, choose sans-serif fonts. Examples include Helvetica or Arial. Serif fonts like Times, Times New Roman, or Palatino have soft edges that can make it difficult for audience members to read. [4]

Regardless of which font you decide to select, stick to just one. You can use features such as bold, color and size to add impact.

Font size should stay between 18 and 24. Anything larger than 24 points is overwhelming. However, audiences have trouble reading fonts smaller than 18.

Use Color

Color can be a very effective tool in a presentation. According to research, color can increase motivation and participation of an audience by up to 80 percent.[5] Color also enhances learning and improves retention by more than 75 percent.[6] Color advertisements outsell black and white advertisements by 88 percent.[7] This gives you some idea how important color can be.

While color can have a dramatic impact on a presentation, it is still important to use it with caution. Certain color combinations are not advisable due to deficiencies in color perception (color blindness)—red/green, brown/green, blue/black and blue/purple. These color combinations should always be avoided.[8]

As with any other element, color can be overdone. Be careful about overwhelming the audience with too much color. Color should be used to highlight certain key aspects that you want to draw attention to.

Keep Them Simple

Avoid putting too much information on a presentation aid. Each aid should contain only one idea or illustrate only one concept. If you need to use two different charts that have no relationship to each other, use separate presentation aids. Often times, students will put three different presentation aids on one transparency. Don't fall into this trap. This only confuses your audience. They will wonder why these three unrelated pictures are on the same transparency rather than focusing on your message.

When using text on a presentation aid, use only six lines of text per aid. Each line should be limited to six or seven words. This will keep your visual from overwhelming the audience.

Tips for Using Presentation Aids

Using presentation aids takes practice. They take time to prepare properly. However, if you invest time in creating them, and make good choices about what to use, then your presentation will benefit from their inclusion. The following tips will help make sure your use of presentation aids is as effective as possible.

Avoid Using the Chalkboard

By preparing your aids beforehand, the need for you to use items like a chalkboard to illustrate points is eliminated. Chalkboards or other tools for rapidly displaying information have their place, especially in regards to answering questions from the audience. However, they are not appropriate presentation aids. It is hard to write neatly when time is an issue. Turning one's back to the audience so that you can draw on the board will only interfere with your ability to connect to the audience. Even if you were able to prepare the drawing on the chalkboard ahead of time, it would lack the professionalism you are trying to achieve.

Practice, Practice, Practice

Use your presentation aids during practice sessions for your presentation. You should know exactly when to show them, and when you should remove them from view. This is easy if you keep your aids to a minimum. Having many presentation aids complicates your presentation and can be a source of confusion for you during the presentation.

Have a Backup Plan

Presentation aids that use technology are always prone to possible failure. You should have a backup plan in case of technical difficulties. You should construct your presentation so that if the technology doesn't work, you can still go on. Also, you can always bring an alternative version of your presentation aid. For instance, if you hope to use a computer to project PowerPoint slides, you might bring a backup set of transparencies to use as an alternative. If worse comes to worse, be prepared to deliver the presentation without them. As a speaker, you should always be prepared for this possibility.

Stay Focused on Your Audience

Many novice speakers get so caught up in making sure their presentation aid is working correctly that they end up speaking to their aid rather than to the audience. This is very common in PowerPoint presentations. By keeping your presentation aids simple, and practicing, you can use your aids successfully and still focus on your audience.

Avoid Passing Out Presentation Aids

Handouts are very tempting to create, and it is OK to use them. However, the mistake comes when you pass them out before or, worse, during your presentation. All this serves to do is distract your audience away from what you are saying. If at all possible, provide handouts at the end of your presentation if you want your audience to have something to refer to later. Also, avoid passing objects around. This causes even more confusion because people are seeing your objects at different times. Handouts and objects that are passed out usually cause more harm than good.

Display Presentation Aids Only When Explaining Them

Presentation aids are designed to attract the attention of our audience and that is exactly what they do. If you display an aid when you are not discussing it, some members of the audience will focus on the aid rather than the message you are delivering. So a good rule to follow is this— present the aid only when you are discussing it. After you have completed your explanation, remove the presentation aid. If it is a transparency, turn off the overhead projector; if it is a PowerPoint slide, black the screen.

Explain Your Presentation Aids

No matter how professional and clear your visual aids are, they cannot speak for themselves. You need to explain them to your audience. The audience doesn't know what to look for when examining your presentation aid. What is important about the presentation aid? Point that out to the audience. Even though it may be tempting, don't rush through the explanation of your presentation aid. You selected this material for a reason. Take the time to give your audience a thorough explanation.

Conclusion

Using presentation aids effectively can significantly aid an audience in understanding your message, if they are used effectively. Certain types of information, such as numerical information, can drastically benefit from the use of presentation aids. The key is to make sure that whatever you use actually adds meaning to your message. Gratuitous or ill-prepared visual aids will detract from your message, not enhance it.

Key Terms

Bar Charts
Charts
Diagrams

Line/Column Charts
Multimedia Presentations
Pie Charts

Presentational Aid

Notes

1. Pike, R. W. (1992). Creative training techniques handbook. Lakewood Books: Minneapolis, MN.
2. Vogel, R. D., Dickson, G. W., Lehman, J. A. (1986). Persuasion and the role of visual support: The 0M/3M Study (Minneapolis: University of Minnesota School of Management).
3. Zelanzny, G. (2001). Say it with charts (4th ed.). New York: McGraw-Hill.
4. Ayres, J. (1991). Using visual aids to reduce speech anxiety. Communication Research Reports, 72, 73–79.
5. Zelanzny, G. (2001).
6. InFocus Corporation, (2004). Using Fonts Effectively in Your Multimedia Presentation. Retrieved April 10, 2004, from *http://www.presentersuniversity.com/coursesarchivesfonts.php*
7. Green, R. E. (1984). The persuasive properties of color. Marketing Communications, October.
8. Loyola University School of Business, Chicago, IL. As reported in Hewlett-Packard's Advisor, June 1999.
9. 3M Corporation (1995). The Power of Color in Presentations. Retrieved April 10, 2004 from *http://www.3m.com/mettinnetwork/readingroom/meetingguide_power_color.html*

CHAPTER 13

Presenting as a Group

Chapter Objectives

After reading this chapter, you should be able to:

- Structure an effective group presentation

- Understand the importance of practicing as a group

- Conduct effective Q&A sessions

How to Present as a Group

In a recent episode of the NBC reality series "The Apprentice," one of the teams, Net Worth, lost a challenge due to a disorganized group presentation. Although their product line—a tech friendly clothing line designed for American Eagle—was as good as the competition's, their ability to present ideas as a team and persuade the executives of clothing manufacturer American Eagle to implement their product line was deficient. So ultimately, they were unable to sell their ideas to the client. In this situation, the executives from American Eagle said, "The poor presentation and the lack of research supporting their claims cost them the challenge."

Net Worth isn't alone. Too many times lack of group coordination before and during the presentation can have profound implications for the group. It may weaken your credibility, the credibility of the organization, or even cost you and your firm an account. Making sure that you know how to organize and present as a group is extremely important in today's business world. It is even an important skill in many of the courses you take during your college career. Think of all the courses in which a group presentation is required. Utilizing the steps and strategies outlined here will help ensure that you are successful in your future career and in your current academic career.

Preparing and Delivering the Group Presentation

Much of the presentation process is identical, whether you are preparing an individual presentation or a group presentation. Good group and individual presentations share many commonalities: there must be a clear goal, thorough audience analysis, adequate research to support your claims and clear organizational structure. The difference is that these activities must be coordinated throughout the group, which does present some unique challenges. There is also added difficulty in just how you make a uniform presentation when you have several speakers rather than just one. The following guidelines will help you overcome some of the challenges associated with coordinating and delivering effective group presentations. The guidelines are presented in two ways. First, each section presents the fundamentals that apply to a particular concept regardless of speaking context. Secondly, when appropriate, the concepts are applied to your actual group project in this course so that you can see how to incorporate them more effectively.

The Preparation Stage

Choose a Leader or Point Person

All group presentations and group projects will go more smoothly if one person acts as the liaison between the client and the other group members. This individual is responsible for knowing who is doing what and making sure the group has the resources it needs to accomplish the task at hand. The leader is also responsible for coordinating group meeting times, sharing contact information, and establishing group practice sessions. In short, the group leader is not an autocratic dictator demanding that his or her ideas and goals are carried out; rather, this individual makes sure the group stays on task and works to make sure that information is exchanged by all group members. The leader really serves as a group organizer or project manager.

In your group project for this class, the group leader will make sure all team members have exchanged phone numbers and e-mail addresses. The leader will also be the point person with your instructor. Although the entire group is responsible for ensuring the group's project is consistent with the instructor's assignment, the team leader is responsible for setting up those meetings and for follow-up e-mails between the group and the instructor. The leader will also be responsible for arranging meeting locations and practice sessions. He or she will also ensure that the group has the resources it needs, such as a computer, visual aids, etc. Although there are many other tasks that the group leader may undertake, these are the most common.

Establish the Goal

Once the group has decided on a leader, it can move toward establishing its goal. As with individual presentations, the goal for any group presentation must be very clear. Just what is it you want your audience to do, think or feel as a result of your presentation? Remember to establish this goal in light of time constraints and other environmental constraints. Will you really be able to accomplish your goals given the budget constraints, etc.? Once your group has decided on its goal, it becomes important that you think about who your audience is and how you can best achieve the goal.

In regards to the project in this course, you should think very carefully about your goal. Just what type of problem do you want to solve or what kind of problem can you realistically solve with about four weeks of preparation? This is a small amount of time to put together a presentation. You need to think about what you can realistically accomplish given your time and resource constraints. You will not be able to solve the university's parking problem, day-care issue, or transportation issue in this limited amount of time and with the budget constraints you have been given.

Your goal should be to tackle a problem that the university could actually implement. Several of the group presentations in this course have resulted in projects that Purdue has actually funded. One such project sought to strengthen international and domestic student relationships through university-sponsored social activities. The group received funding to form the Purdue Cultural Awareness Committee to coordinate and organize the activities. The goal of these social and educational activities was to increase cultural awareness and to promote student interaction through social gatherings.

Conduct Research

Once the group has a clearly established goal, it can begin to discuss research. As you saw in the opening narrative of this chapter, accounts are won and lost every day because of the research that supports a presentation. Net Worth's failure to work as a group also resulted in faulty research. Unlike Magna Corporation, which went out and surveyed individuals in the target market about what technological needs they had, Net Worth just guessed. In the end, the executives from American Eagle said that their lack of research and, therefore, knowledge of the market, hurt them considerably. In any type of presentation you make, you cannot underestimate the importance of solid research.

The nature of the group presentation in this course rests on good, solid research. Therefore, research is an issue for the entire group. Everybody should take an active role in the research process. Although you don't want to waste time replicating each other's work, you do want to make sure that you thoroughly research each aspect of the presentation. By having two or more individuals researching the same area, you lessen the chance of missing some vital piece of evidence.

Once the general research has been completed, you can ask certain individuals to go back and strengthen specific sections. For example, the Purdue Cultural Awareness Committee decided that once its research was collected, it needed to interview the associate dean responsible for diversity at Purdue; obviously, only one individual would need to go out and conduct this interview.

Assign Tasks

At this point the group needs to think about who has certain strengths on the team. In this course you have an advantage. You have seen each other present several times over the course of the semester, so you have a very good idea who on your team is strong in what area. Perhaps one of your team members is very strong in delivery skills; give them the most visible parts of the presentation to deliver. You will want to open and close the presentation with the strongest speaker in the group, so make sure that the group identifies that individual early. Maybe someone else is really good at organizational structure; have them coordinate and finalize the group outline. If someone is technically oriented, have them prepare the PowerPoint template and incorporate the visuals. Everybody in the group has strengths; use them to your advantage.

What you want to avoid, however, is a group presentation that looks like a series of individual presentations presented one after another rather than a group presentation. The presentation should draw on the group and its collective strengths. A team can deliver a much more powerful presentation than an individual. So take advantage of this aspect of working on a team.

In order to achieve a more cohesive presentation, you will want to be careful how you divide the workload. Don't divide the project in the following manner: one person conducts the research, one person constructs the PowerPoint, one person writes the introduction, one person the conclusion, and, finally, someone puts it all together. This will result in disaster. First of all, the introduction and conclusion should be written last, once the body is finalized.

Here is an example of how a group might proceed in assigning tasks. For the first group meeting each group member should be responsible for coming up with at least two ideas for the group project. The group should then meet face-to-face and discuss the pros and cons of each group member's proposals. Finally, at this meeting, the group should choose an idea for the project. At this point research becomes an important aspect. Everyone should be involved in conducting preliminary research. Have at least two group members cover each area of research to make sure that the group doesn't miss important details. Once the research has been conducted and you can answer important questions, then you can fine tune. You can determine what holes you have in your arguments and evidence and then decide how to fill those in. Filling in holes is usually a less daunting task. As mentioned before, it won't take the entire group to go out and interview key figures. At this point, that part of the research can be divided up among members.

Develop the Presentation Template

As this chapter has stressed, a group should look like a group when it presents. One element that will help you achieve this goal is a PowerPoint template. You can have one person design all the slides for the presentation or each individual can design their own. Regardless of how the presentation is put together, you will want it to appear as if one person designed the entire thing. So make sure that the group has designed a template that everyone can follow so that the presentation takes on a more uniform appearance. You will also want to make sure that font type and size are the same from slide to slide as well. If you prepare a template with enough detail, this step should already be done for you. Also, pay attention to the vocabulary used on each slide. Make sure each team member is using consistent language and abbreviations.

You can use one of the templates Microsoft supplies with its product or you can create your own. Creating your own template is relatively simple and makes the PowerPoint look custom and, therefore, professional. However, if you don't have the skills to customize the templates, don't try it. You will probably be better off with one of the Microsoft templates.

Design Presentation Format

Introductions

As with any other type of presentation, the group presentation will also have an introduction. Within the introduction, you must accomplish all of the tasks emphasized throughout this text: gain attention, establish credibility and relevance, introduce topic (thesis), preview main points, etc. However, you will have an additional component when presenting as a group: you will also have to introduce each group member and their role in the presentation and/or organization. The audience will want to know who each member is and what their role is. So simply saying, "This is Mary from marketing and she will discuss marketing," isn't good enough. Be specific about the point of Mary's segment. In order to achieve this goal, ask each speaker to write one sentence that encapsulates the most important idea in their section of the presentation. Use this material to help structure the introductions of each group member.

Speaker transitions

Transitions are an important element in any presentation. They become increasingly important in group presentations because they are the element that bridges one speaker to another. Good transitions can help unify the presentation while poor ones can make it seem like one individual presentation after another. According to Peter Giuliano, Chairman, Executive Communications Group, "Each presenter should wrap up his or her own segment, then establish a link to the next presenter."[1]

Here is an example: "You have seen from my examples and testimony that there is lack of cohesiveness between students in our department. I will now turn the podium over to Ken, who will discuss how we may be able to bridge some of these differences between students by employing some unique strategies."

In this example, the speaker has summed up the main point of his or her portion of the presentation and has previewed the main point of the following speaker. It is simply a directional transition with the addition of the name of the next speaker.

Question and Answer Session

The question and answer session is a vital part of the presentation. Make sure the group has a plan for how this section will be handled. There is nothing worse than ending with a Q&A session that was disorganized. The section on Q&A sessions in this chapter provides greater detail on this issue.

Practice the Presentation

No matter how much individuals practice their individual sections, you cannot overestimate the importance of the group practice session. At the bare minimum, a group should run through their presentation at least once—at full dress rehearsal level. This means a run-through from start to finish with no stops. This way you can tell how the group is doing on time, identify rough spots and determine if there are any oversights or replication in terms of material. All visual aids should be employed during the dress rehearsal and should be scrutinized one more time for typographical errors. It is also essential to ensure that all of your technology is working seamlessly. If possible, practice the presentation in the room where it will actually take place.

Don't leave your practice session to the last minute. The group needs to leave enough time to make adjustments if necessary. Remember, practice makes perfect. Although these group practice sessions may be difficult to coordinate, they will pay off!

The Actual Presentation

During the actual presentation, it is essential that all group members stay involved.[2] After all, if group members aren't interested in their presentation, why should the audience be interested? And believe it or not, the audience will be watching all members of the group, not just the person speaking, so it is essential that you show interest. Be very aware of your nonverbals; it is very easy to send negative messages to the audience with a sigh or a yawn.

In addition to appearing interested, you must also pay attention to the audience. Observing audience reaction can help in two ways. First, it can help you adapt to the needs of the audience during the presentation. For example, if during a team member's portion, you notice that he/she is losing the audience's attention, then modify your part of the presentation to compensate. Refer back to Chapter 11 for guidelines on how to adapt to the audience during the presentation. Second, it also helps to watch their reaction to various parts of the presentation. How are various messages being received by the audience?[3] For example, when your group presents information on cost, how does the audience react? Do they seem shocked or pleasantly surprised? This information can be very valuable to the group or organization later.

Unless it is absolutely necessary, resist leaning over and whispering to a team member. This shifts the attention and can call professionalism into question. And as Peter Giuliano, from Executive Communication Group, a consulting firm, warns, "The worst thing any team member can do, of course, is to show disagreement with what another presenter is saying."[4]

The Question and Answer Session

The question and answer session is as important as the presentation itself. It is the last thing the audience hears (recency effect) so it leaves a strong impression. Although most speakers consider the question and answer session an afterthought, it should be at the forefront of your preparation. Many decisions are made and perceptions formed during the Q&A. Accounts are won and lost over this often neglected component. A speaker or group who is unable to answer questions effectively can undermine the impact of a well prepared presentation. On the other hand, a speaker or group who answers questions well can strengthen the impact of the presentation and enhance credibility.

It is important to a successful presentation that you prepare thoroughly for the Q&A and that you put as much thought and energy into this component as any other. View the question and answer section as another avenue to reach your audience. You will be able to clarify positions or data, and explain details that you may have forgotten to include during the formal part of the presentation. Some guidelines for achieving a successful question and answer session are discussed in the following section.

Guidelines for an Effective Q&A

Prepare for the Q&A

Many times I am asked how can someone actually plan for a Q&A? After all, anything could happen, right? Actually, it may seem overwhelming at first, but you can actually do many things to prepare for the Q&A. They are much more predictable than you might first imagine. By anticipating questions and developing a plan, you will have more control over the Q&A than you first thought.

Anticipate Questions

Try to put yourself in the place of the audience. Really try to understand their position and perspective. From this vantage point, what questions do you think they could have about the material you presented? For example, sometimes a presentation is so limited by a time constraint that you may have to leave out important details. In this case, it would be easy to anticipate possible questions your audience might have. Obviously, they would ask follow-up questions requesting more detail. Another example is the hostile audience. With this type of audience, it will also be easy to predict where you and the audience differ in terms of attitudes, beliefs and behaviors. Once again, it would be easy to predict their objections and potential questions. Anticipate as many questions as you can and plan in advance how you will deal with these questions and concerns should they arise.

In the two scenarios discussed above, it is relatively easy to predict what an audience might ask; other times, it isn't as apparent. We are often so engrossed in our own material that it becomes difficult to imagine what an audience might find difficult or need further elaboration on. Get feedback from others to help you with this aspect of your presentation. If you can't think of questions a possible audience may have, ask friends and family to sit in on a practice session. Then solicit their questions. It is always a good idea to get as much practice on each aspect of the presentation as you can. Therefore, a trial run-through with an audience can achieve three goals: it can provide you with an additional practice session for the presentation itself, it can generate possible audience questions, and it can give you the experience of participating in a question and answer session before the real thing.

Have a Plan

If you are in a group situation, developing a plan for how you will handle the Q&A is essential. Will one person take all questions and divert them to the appropriate member of the team, or will all questions be directed at the team leader and answered by the team leader? Which ever way you decide to run the Q&A is fine. There is no prescribed plan that is best in all situations. However, it is essential that you have a plan. It looks completely unprofessional for several team members to jump in to answer the same question or to contradict one another. Make sure the session is as organized as possible and is as smooth as possible.

Answering Questions

Now that you know how to get prepared for the questions, you will need some strategies for delivering the answers to the questions. Follow the guidelines outlined below and your Q&A should run smoothly.

Keep Answers Concise and Direct

Answer each question as directly and as concisely as possible. Audiences appreciate a clear and direct response. If the answer is as simple as a yes or no, simply say so and move on to the next question. If you spend too much time on any one question, you may run short on time during the Q&A and some audience members may not have the opportunity to ask their questions.

Repeat Each Question

After each question is asked, repeat or rephrase the question for the entire audience. Oftentimes, it is difficult for other audience members to hear questions. There is nothing more frustrating than listening to a speaker answer a question that you didn't hear. Rephrasing or repeating a question also gives you some additional time to formulate your answer and allows you to make sure that you understood the question.

What if I Don't Know the Answer?

If you don't know the answer to a question, be honest. It is better to admit that you do not know than to talk around the issue, use fallacious reasoning or answer as if you are certain, when you are not. Imagine the credibility issues for you as a speaker if you answer a question incorrectly and someone in the audience knows the answer. This can be devastating.

Here are a few strategies that can help in these situations. First, you can always ask an audience member if they know the answer to the question. Let's imagine that you are delivering a presentation on "The Benefits of Alzheimer's Support Groups." The audience is made up of family members of Alzheimer's patients and local aging administrators and social workers who work with families who are experiencing this disease. Maybe someone asks you the question, "How many families in our county are currently using support groups?" Given that you are not from their particular county, you may not know the answer to this question. It would be perfectly acceptable to say, "I am not familiar with the numbers in this county. Does anyone in the audience have that information?" If not, say that is interesting and I will try to locate that information and get back to you. It is important to remember, however, that if you promise to get back to an audience member that you do. Your credibility can be called into question if you make empty promises.

What if No One Asks a Question?

This is a possibility. However, audience members suffer from communication apprehension just like speakers do. They often have questions; they just don't want to be the first to ask them. If after you open the floor for questions, there are none, simply say, "A question I am often asked is ..." and go ahead and answer the question. This will usually loosen an audience up and the questions will come streaming in.

With Whom Should I Make Eye Contact?

Make eye contact with the individual during the time they ask a question but speak to the entire audience when giving the reply. Also, avoid moving closer to the individual who asked the question as you give your response. These two strategies will keep the entire audience involved while you answer the question and, therefore, keep them interested.

Dealing with the Difficult Audience Member

Most audience members are polite, ask their question and are happy to go on their way. Sometimes, however, you will be confronted with the audience member who is intent on monopolizing the entire session, engaging you in a debate or some other inappropriate behavior. The most important thing to remember here is to never lose your cool. Handle these situations as delicately as possible. However, it is important to remember that you are in control. Don't be afraid to assert yourself and redirect negative behavior and energy.

It is a mistake to engage this audience member in a one-on-one dialogue. Allow audience members one question and one follow-up question. It is up to you to maintain control of the session. If, after answering their second question, it becomes clear that they are going to ask another one, simply look out to the entire audience and ask if someone else has a question. "Does anyone else have a question?"

Another option is to simply tell the audience member that you find this discussion interesting and perhaps you could talk after the presentation is over. Explain that you want to ensure that everyone in the audience has had a chance to have their questions answered and simply move to the next question.

Often, an audience member will respond with a loaded question. These are questions that are worded so that any response will appear negative. For example, "What are you doing with all the money you are making from our salary cuts?" Stephen D. Boyd, Ph.D., a noted communication consultant, says, "Don't answer a loaded question; defuse it before you answer."[5] He uses the following example as an illustration. Suppose an audience member asks the following question, "What are you doing with all the money you are making from increased prices?" Simply reply, "I understand your frustration with the recent rate increase. I believe what you are asking is, 'Why such a sudden increase in rates?'" Then go on to answer that question. By answering a loaded question, you will just set yourself up for conflict.

Stay Confident

Many times individuals find the Q&A threatening. Whereas you have control over the formal aspect of the presentation, you have less control over questions the audience may ask. It is true that oftentimes audience members may ask difficult questions and try to challenge you or your ideas; however, if you have thought about the Q&A and planned in advance, you can handle these issues effectively and with confidence.

In my own experience as an audience member, a communication instructor and communication consultant, I have seen the speaker shrink two inches when he or she opens the floor for questions. Remember, this is a great opportunity for you to sell yourself, your ideas, your product or even your company. Stand up straight. Look audience members directly in the eye and exude the confidence that you have demonstrated throughout your presentation.

Provide Closure

Just as your presentation comes to a clear ending, so also should your Q&A session. You want to maintain control as much as possible. If you run out of time for additional questions, tell the audience that you are out of time and close the session. If it seems that all questions have been answered, simply respond by saying, "If there are no more questions, I would like to thank you for your time and participation." Regardless of whether you run short or long, always thank the audience for their participation and thoughtful questions. Then provide a very short one or two sentence wrap-up statement that sums up your thoughts or the conclusion of your presentation. You want to have the final word. Take the opportunity to leave the audience on a positive note.

Conclusion

This chapter is a guide to keep you from encountering the problems experienced by Net Worth that were described in the opening paragraphs. As Net Worth experienced, group presentations can present some unique challenges. As long as the group prepares thoroughly by choosing a leader, establishing a clear goal, conducting good research, and utilizing each member's strengths, the group presentation can be effective. In order to achieve success, it is important that the group function as a team rather than a collection of individuals. Using design templates, effective introductions, adequate transitions, and group practice sessions are the means through which groups can achieve the necessary uniformity to be successful.

Question and answer sessions are extremely important to the presentation. Often overlooked, they are a great opportunity for you to clarify your position and strengthen your connection to your audience. In order to be successful, you need to plan ahead for the Q&A and then maintain control of the session. By managing questions effectively and having the last word, a question and answer session can enhance the credibility of the speaker.

Notes

1. Giuliano, P. (2005, Winter). Ask the expert: Team or group presentations. The Total Communicator, 3(1). Retrieved May 10, 2005, from http://totalcommunicator.com/vol3_1/expert2.html.
2. Newborne, E. (2002). Tag-Team Pitches: Group presentations are a different ball game Here's how to play. Sales and Marketing Management, (3), 154.
3. Giuliano, P. (2005, Winter). Ask the expert: Team or group presentations. The Total Communicator, 3(1). Retrieved May 10, 2005, from http://totalcommunicator.com/vol3_1/expert2.html.
4. When it's time to present as a team. The Total Communicator, 2(1). Retrieved May 10, 2005, from http://totalcommunicator.com/vol2_1/team_article.html.
5. Boyd, S. D. (2004). The presentation after the presentation. Techniques, 79(3), 42–3.

Photo Credits

Chapter 8

    p. 104 © Ronnie Kaufman/CORBIS
    p. 108 © R.W. Jones/CORBIS

Chapter 9

    p. 118 © Larry Downing/Reuters NewMedia Inc./CORBIS
    p. 120 Natalie Behring-Chisholm/Getty Images
    p. 127 © Douglas Graham/CORBIS SYGMA

Chapter 10

    p. 138 Mark Wilson/Getty Images
    p. 142 © Farrell Grehan/CORBIS

Chapter 11

    p. 152 Robert Mecea/Getty Images
    p. 158 © Dan Levine/AFP/CORBIS
    p. 162 © Tim Graham/CORBIS

Chapter 12

    p. 168 © Daniel Lippitt/CORBIS SYGMA
    p. 172 © Bettmann/CORBIS
    p. 173 © Bettmann/CORBIS

Chapter 13

    p. 184 © Tom & Dee Ann McCarthy/CORBIS
    p. 188 © Royalty-Free/CORBIS
    p. 190 © Rob Lewine/CORBIS

Assignments and Forms

Career Informative Presentation
Point Value: 100 points
Length: 3 minutes
My presentation date: _____

In this assignment, you are to uncover the types of presentations you might be asked to make in your future career choice. This may be done through library research, newspaper articles, textbooks, or through interviews with those in the career. You should identify the specific types of presentations (informative, explanatory, or persuasive) you might be asked to give, in what possible scenarios these might occur, and to what possible target audiences such presentations might be geared.

It is important that you present the material in an appropriate organizational pattern for an oral presentation. You must have an introduction, body, and conclusion. This will help your audience understand and retain the information you provide. You also will be asked to pay specific attention to your delivery. Simple presentations are an excellent opportunity to become comfortable speaking in front of an audience. They also provide opportunities to practice such delivery techniques as eye contact, hand gestures, tone and volume without having to worry about sharing a large volume of knowledge.

Specific Requirements:
- Inform audience of the types of presentations you might make in a future career
- Time limit: 3 minutes. If your speech goes over the time criteria, you will be penalized 10 points, so practice your speech.
- Cite any sources of your research
- Develop a thesis statement
- Pick an appropriate organizational pattern
- Develop an appropriate introduction and conclusion
- Use an extemporaneous speaking style. This means that you are not to read your speech or to memorize your speech, but are to talk to the audience from notes. You must be concerned with both physical and vocal delivery.
- A typed full-sentence outline of your presentation is due on _____. Your instructor must approve your outline before you can deliver your presentation. If you do not turn in an outline before your speaking date, you will not be able to deliver your presentation.
- You must also meet any additional requirements as outlined in class by your instructor.

Evaluation:
Your presentation should meet the requirements of a properly presented informative presentation.
- Preparation of the full-sentence outline
- Topic guidelines met
- Proper speech structure (introduction, body, conclusion)
- Appropriate organizational pattern
- Refined delivery

OUTLINE CHECKLIST: Career Presentation

SPEAKER: _____   **TIME LIMIT:** _____
TOPIC: _____   **SITUATION/AUDIENCE:** _____

___ yes no ___		***SPECIFIC PURPOSE:***
___ yes no ___		1. Is it stated as an infinitive phrase?
___ yes no ___		2. Does it contain only one idea?
___ yes no ___		3. Does it use clear and concise language?
		4. Is the focus clearly defined?
Score: _____		

___ yes   no ___
___ yes   no ___
___ yes   no ___
___ yes   no ___

Score: _____

SPECIFIC PURPOSE:
1. Is it stated as an infinitive phrase?
2. Does it contain only one idea?
3. Does it use clear and concise language?
4. Is the focus clearly defined?

___ yes   no ___
___ yes   no ___
___ yes   no ___

Score: _____

THESIS STATEMENT:
1. Is the focus clearly defined?
2. Are main points previewed?
3. Is it written as a complete sentence?

___ yes   no ___

INTRODUCTION:
Contains all necessary components: attention getter, credibility statement, relevance, thesis?

___ yes   no ___
___ yes   no ___
___ yes   no ___
___ yes   no ___

Attention getter
- Is it appropriate for topic?
- Is it appropriate for selected audience?
- Does it have impact?
- Is it appropriate in length?

___ yes   no ___
___ yes   no ___

Credibility statement
- Does it sound professional/believable?
- Does it point out personal experience/interest?

___ yes   no ___
___ yes   no ___

Relevance statement
- Does the statement create an immediate need to listen?
- Is it appropriate for the selected audience?

___ yes   no ___

Thesis (see above)
- Make sure thesis is same in introduction as written above.

Score: _____

___ yes   no ___

TRANSITION:
1. Is there a directional transition between introduction and body?

Score: _____

___ yes no ___	**ORGANIZATION:**	
___ yes no ___	1. Is the appropriate organizational pattern used?	
___ yes no ___	2. Are the main points significant?	
___ yes no ___	3. Are the main points balanced?	
___ yes no ___	4. Do the main points contain one distinct idea?	
___ yes no ___	5. Are they written as complete sentences?	
___ yes no ___	6. Are there directional transitions between main points?	
___ yes no ___	7. Are the subpoints organized correctly?	
___ yes no ___	8. Do the points coordinate?	
___ yes no ___	9. Is there correct subordination?	

Score: _____

___ yes no ___	**EVIDENCE:**
___ yes no ___	1. Does each main point have sufficient evidence?
___ yes no ___	2. Is evidence appropriate for selected audience?
___ yes no ___	3. Is evidence timely?
___ yes no ___	4. Are a variety of types of supporting materials used?
___ yes no ___	5. Is evidence from credible sources?
___ yes no ___	6. Is evidence cited appropriately?
___ yes no ___	7. Does evidence actually support main points/conclusion/arguments?

Score: _____

___ yes no __	**ARGUMENTS:**
___ yes no ___	1. Do arguments follow sound reasoning?
___ yes no ___	2. Is fallacious reasoning avoided?
	3. Do arguments make appropriate appeals (logs, ethos, pathos)?

Score: _____

___ yes no ___	**VISUAL AIDS:**
___ yes no ___	1. Are visual aids included in outline?
___ yes no ___	2. Is explanation included on how visual aid enhances/explains information?
	3. Are visual aids appropriate?

Score: _____

___ yes no ___	**TRANSITION:**
	1. Was there a directional transition from the body to the conclusion?

Score: _____

___ yes no ___	**CONCLUSION:**
___ yes no ___	1. Is thesis restated?
	2. Does conclusion contain a clincher?
	• Is it memorable?
___ yes no ___	• Is it appropriate for selected audience?
	3. Did conclusion (erroneously) introduce new information?

Score: _____

___ yes no ___	**LENGTH/STYLE:**
___ yes no ___	1. Can material be covered in time frame allotted?
	2. Was outline typed?

Score: _____

___ yes no ___	**BIBLIOGRAPHY/REFERENCE PAGE:**
___ yes no ___	1. Citations meet the minimum requirement in number?
	2. Citations use the appropriate style/format (APA/MLA)?

Score: _____

OUTLINE CHECKLIST: Career Presentation

SPEAKER: _____ **TIME LIMIT:** _____
TOPIC: _____ **SITUATION/AUDIENCE:** _____

___ yes no ___ ___ yes no ___ ___ yes no ___ ___ yes no ___ **Score:** _____		***SPECIFIC PURPOSE:*** 1. Is it stated as an infinitive phrase? 2. Does it contain only one idea? 3. Does it use clear and concise language? 4. Is the focus clearly defined?
___ yes no ___ ___ yes no ___ ___ yes no ___ **Score:** _____		***THESIS STATEMENT:*** 1. Is the focus clearly defined? 2. Are main points previewed? 3. Is it written as a complete sentence?
___ yes no ___ ___ yes no ___ ___ yes no ___ ___ yes no ___ ___ yes no ___ ___ yes no ___ ___ yes no ___ ___ yes no ___ ___ yes no ___ ___ yes no ___ **Score:** _____		***INTRODUCTION:*** Contains all necessary components: attention getter, credibility statement, relevance, thesis? ***Attention getter*** • Is it appropriate for topic? • Is it appropriate for selected audience? • Does it have impact? • Is it appropriate in length? ***Credibility statement*** • Does it sound professional/believable? • Does it point out personal experience/interest? ***Relevance statement*** • Does the statement create an immediate need to listen? • Is it appropriate for the selected audience? ***Thesis (see above)*** • Make sure thesis is same in introduction as written above.
___ yes no ___ **Score:** _____		***TRANSITION:*** 1. Is there a directional transition between introduction and body?

___ yes no ___	***ORGANIZATION:***	
___ yes no ___	1. Is the appropriate organizational pattern used?	
___ yes no ___	2. Are the main points significant?	
___ yes no ___	3. Are the main points balanced?	
___ yes no ___	4. Do the main points contain one distinct idea?	
___ yes no ___	5. Are they written as complete sentences?	
___ yes no ___	6. Are there directional transitions between main points?	
___ yes no ___	7. Are the subpoints organized correctly?	
___ yes no ___	8. Do the points coordinate?	
___ yes no ___	9. Is there correct subordination?	
Score: ___		

___ yes no ___	***EVIDENCE:***
___ yes no ___	1. Does each main point have sufficient evidence?
___ yes no ___	2. Is evidence appropriate for selected audience?
___ yes no ___	3. Is evidence timely?
___ yes no ___	4. Are a variety of types of supporting materials used?
___ yes no ___	5. Is evidence from credible sources?
___ yes no ___	6. Is evidence cited appropriately?
___ yes no ___	7. Does evidence actually support main points/conclusion/arguments?
Score: ___	

___ yes no ___	***ARGUMENTS:***
___ yes no ___	1. Do arguments follow sound reasoning?
___ yes no ___	2. Is fallacious reasoning avoided?
___ yes no ___	3. Do arguments make appropriate appeals (logs, ethos, pathos)?
Score: ___	

___ yes no ___	***VISUAL AIDS:***
___ yes no ___	1. Are visual aids included in outline?
___ yes no ___	2. Is explanation included on how visual aid enhances/explains information?
___ yes no ___	3. Are visual aids appropriate?
Score: ___	

___ yes no ___	***TRANSITION:***
	1. Was there a directional transition from the body to the conclusion?
Score: ___	

___ yes no ___	***CONCLUSION:***
___ yes no ___	1. Is thesis restated?
	2. Does conclusion contain a clincher?
	• Is it memorable?
	• Is it appropriate for selected audience?
___ yes no ___	3. Did conclusion (erroneously) introduce new information?
Score: ___	

___ yes no ___	***LENGTH/STYLE:***
___ yes no ___	1. Can material be covered in time frame allotted?
	2. Was outline typed?
Score: ___	

	BIBLIOGRAPHY/REFERENCE PAGE:
___ yes no ___	1. Citations meet the minimum requirement in number?
___ yes no ___	2. Citations use the appropriate style/format (APA/MLA)?
Score: ___	

SPEECH EVALUATION FORM: Career Presentation

Speaker: _____   Time Limit: _____
Topic: _____   Length of Speech: _____

Section total ____/____	**Introduction:** (Captured attention, stated thesis, relevance, credibility, transition) **Strengths:** **Weaknesses:**
Section total ____/____	**Body:** (Organization, transitions, sources, visual aids, language) **Strengths:** **Weaknesses:**
Section total ____/____	**Conclusion:** (Transition, restated thesis, clincher) **Strengths:** **Weaknesses:**
Section total ____/____	**Delivery:** (eye contact, vocal variety, physical delivery, extemporaneous, rehearsed) **Strengths:** **Weaknesses:**
Section total ____/____	**Other:** (Audience analysis, timely, creative) **Strengths:** **Weaknesses:**

Comments

Major Strengths:

Areas Needing Improvement:

Total Points/Grade:

Event Presentation
Point Value: 100 points
Length: 3 minutes
My Presentation Date: _____

You are to deliver a **3 minute,** polished, well-rehearsed speech that follows the basic guidelines of speech organization. You are to choose an event in your life that has affected you in some important way. Maybe you took a mission trip to Honduras or had dinner with Mohammad Ali and something important about who you are or about your life has never been the same. Tell your audience about the event and how it changed your goals, beliefs, behaviors, routines, etc. More specifically, you will want to select two ways this event has changed your life and make those your main points. Then go back and develop those two main points by adding examples, short narratives etc. This is not a speech on a sensitive issue rather it will aid your classmates' attempts at audience analysis for later presentations. Do not select a topic that was emotionally difficult or may be uncomfortable for you to address in front of an audience. There are many events that change our lives or impact how we act, think or behave in important ways that are not too intimate to discuss in front of a group (e.g., getting a puppy, the birth of a sibling, brush with greatness, reading a certain book, etc.).

Specific Requirements:
- Inform audience who you are (unique aspects of your character) as opposed to what you are (information such as your name, age, major, etc.).
- Time limit: 3 minutes. If your speech goes over the time criteria, you will be penalized 10 points, so practice your presentation.
- Cite any sources of your research.
- Develop a thesis statement.
- Pick an appropriate organizational pattern.
- Develop an appropriate introduction and conclusion.
- Use an extemporaneous speaking style. This means that you are not to read your speech or to memorize your speech, but are to talk to the audience from notes. You must be concerned with both physical and vocal delivery.
- A typed full-sentence outline of your presentation is due on _____. Your instructor must approve your outline before you can deliver your presentation. If you do not turn in an outline before your speaking date, you will not be able to deliver your presentation.
- You must also meet any additional requirements as outlined in class by your instructor.

Evaluation:
Your presentation should meet the requirements of a properly presented informative presentation.
- Preparation of the full-sentence outline
- Topic guideline met
- Proper presentation structure (introduction, body, conclusion)
- Appropriate organizational pattern
- Refined delivery

OUTLINE CHECKLIST: Event Presentation

SPEAKER: _____   **TIME LIMIT:** _____

TOPIC: _____   **SITUATION/AUDIENCE:** _____

____ yes no ____		***SPECIFIC PURPOSE:***
____ yes no ____		1. Is it stated as an infinitive phrase?
____ yes no ____		2. Does it contain only one idea?
____ yes no ____		3. Does it use clear and concise language?
		4. Is the focus clearly defined?
Score: _____		

____ yes no ____		***THESIS STATEMENT:***
____ yes no ____		1. Is the focus clearly defined?
____ yes no ____		2. Are main points previewed?
		3. Is it written as a complete sentence?
Score: _____		

INTRODUCTION:

____ yes   no ____   Contains all necessary components: attention getter, credibility statement, relevance, thesis?

Attention getter

- ____ yes   no ____   • Is it appropriate for topic?
- ____ yes   no ____   • Is it appropriate for selected audience?
- ____ yes   no ____   • Does it have impact?
- ____ yes   no ____   • Is it appropriate in length?

Credibility statement

- ____ yes   no ____   • Does it sound professional/believable?
- ____ yes   no ____   • Does it point out personal experience/interest?

Relevance statement

- ____ yes   no ____   • Does the statement create an immediate need to listen?
- ____ yes   no ____   • Is it appropriate for the selected audience?

Thesis (see above)

- ____ yes   no ____   • Make sure thesis is same in introduction as written above.

Score: _____

TRANSITION:

____ yes   no ____   1. Is there a directional transition between introduction and body?

Score: _____

___ yes no ___	**ORGANIZATION:**	
___ yes no ___	1. Is the appropriate organizational pattern used?	
___ yes no ___	2. Are the main points significant?	
___ yes no ___	3. Are the main points balanced?	
___ yes no ___	4. Do the main points contain one distinct idea?	
___ yes no ___	5. Are they written as complete sentences?	
___ yes no ___	6. Are there directional transitions between main points?	
___ yes no ___	7. Are the subpoints organized correctly?	
___ yes no ___	8. Do the points coordinate?	
___ yes no ___	9. Is there correct subordination?	

Score: _____

___ yes no ___	**EVIDENCE:**
___ yes no ___	1. Does each main point have sufficient evidence?
___ yes no ___	2. Is evidence appropriate for selected audience?
___ yes no ___	3. Is evidence timely?
___ yes no ___	4. Are a variety of types of supporting materials used?
___ yes no ___	5. Is evidence from credible sources?
___ yes no ___	6. Is evidence cited appropriately?
___ yes no ___	7. Does evidence actually support main points/conclusion/arguments?

Score: _____

___ yes no ___	**ARGUMENTS:**
___ yes no ___	1. Do arguments follow sound reasoning?
___ yes no ___	2. Is fallacious reasoning avoided?
___ yes no ___	3. Do arguments make appropriate appeals (logs, ethos, pathos)?

Score: _____

___ yes no ___	**VISUAL AIDS:**
___ yes no ___	1. Are visual aids included in outline?
___ yes no ___	2. Is explanation included on how visual aid enhances/explains information?
___ yes no ___	3. Are visual aids appropriate?

Score: _____

___ yes no ___	**TRANSITION:**
	1. Was there a directional transition from the body to the conclusion?

Score: _____

___ yes no ___	**CONCLUSION:**
___ yes no ___	1. Is thesis restated?
	2. Does conclusion contain a clincher?
	• Is it memorable?
	• Is it appropriate for selected audience?
___ yes no ___	3. Did conclusion (erroneously) introduce new information?

Score: _____

___ yes no ___	**LENGTH/STYLE:**
___ yes no ___	1. Can material be covered in time frame allotted?
	2. Was outline typed?

Score: _____

___ yes no ___	**BIBLIOGRAPHY/REFERENCE PAGE:**
___ yes no ___	1. Citations meet the minimum requirement in number?
	2. Citations use the appropriate style/format (APA/MLA)?

Score: _____

OUTLINE CHECKLIST: Event Presentation

SPEAKER: _____   **TIME LIMIT:** _____

TOPIC: _____   **SITUATION/AUDIENCE:** _____

___ yes no ___	***SPECIFIC PURPOSE:***
___ yes no ___	1. Is it stated as an infinitive phrase?
___ yes no ___	2. Does it contain only one idea?
___ yes no ___	3. Does it use clear and concise language?
	4. Is the focus clearly defined?
Score: _____	

___ yes no ___	***THESIS STATEMENT:***
___ yes no ___	1. Is the focus clearly defined?
___ yes no ___	2. Are main points previewed?
	3. Is it written as a complete sentence?
Score: _____	

___ yes no ___	***INTRODUCTION:*** Contains all necessary components: attention getter, credibility statement, relevance, thesis?
	Attention getter
___ yes no ___	• Is it appropriate for topic?
___ yes no ___	• Is it appropriate for selected audience?
___ yes no ___	• Does it have impact?
___ yes no ___	• Is it appropriate in length?
	Credibility statement
___ yes no ___	• Does it sound professional/believable?
___ yes no ___	• Does it point out personal experience/interest?
	Relevance statement
___ yes no ___	• Does the statement create an immediate need to listen?
___ yes no ___	• Is it appropriate for the selected audience?
	Thesis (see above)
___ yes no ___	• Make sure thesis is same in introduction as written above.
Score: _____	

___ yes no __	***TRANSITION:*** 1. Is there a directional transition between introduction and body?
Score: _____	

___ yes no ___		**ORGANIZATION:**
___ yes no ___		1. Is the appropriate organizational pattern used?
___ yes no ___		2. Are the main points significant?
___ yes no ___		3. Are the main points balanced?
___ yes no ___		4. Do the main points contain one distinct idea?
___ yes no ___		5. Are they written as complete sentences?
___ yes no ___		6. Are there directional transitions between main points?
___ yes no ___		7. Are the subpoints organized correctly?
___ yes no ___		8. Do the points coordinate?
___ yes no ___		9. Is there correct subordination?
Score: ___		

	EVIDENCE:
___ yes no ___	1. Does each main point have sufficient evidence?
___ yes no ___	2. Is evidence appropriate for selected audience?
___ yes no ___	3. Is evidence timely?
___ yes no ___	4. Are a variety of types of supporting materials used?
___ yes no ___	5. Is evidence from credible sources?
___ yes no ___	6. Is evidence cited appropriately?
___ yes no ___	7. Does evidence actually support main points/conclusion/arguments?
Score: ___	

	ARGUMENTS:
___ yes no __	1. Do arguments follow sound reasoning?
___ yes no __	2. Is fallacious reasoning avoided?
___ yes no ___	3. Do arguments make appropriate appeals (logs, ethos, pathos)?
Score: ___	

	VISUAL AIDS:
___ yes no ___	1. Are visual aids included in outline?
___ yes no ___	2. Is explanation included on how visual aid enhances/explains information?
___ yes no ___	3. Are visual aids appropriate?
Score: ___	

	TRANSITION:
___ yes no ___	1. Was there a directional transition from the body to the conclusion?
Score: ___	

	CONCLUSION:
___ yes no ___	1. Is thesis restated?
___ yes no ___	2. Does conclusion contain a clincher?
	• Is it memorable?
	• Is it appropriate for selected audience?
___ yes no ___	3. Did conclusion (erroneously) introduce new information?
Score: ___	

	LENGTH/STYLE:
___ yes no ___	1. Can material be covered in time frame allotted?
___ yes no ___	2. Was outline typed?
Score: ___	

	BIBLIOGRAPHY/REFERENCE PAGE:
___ yes no ___	1. Citations meet the minimum requirement in number?
___ yes no ___	2. Citations use the appropriate style/format (APA/MLA)?
Score: ___	

SPEECH EVALUATION FORM: Event Presentation

Speaker: _____   Time Limit: _____

Topic: _____   Length of Speech: _____

Section total ____ / ____	**Introduction:** (Captured attention, stated thesis, relevance, credibility, transition) **Strengths:** **Weaknesses:**
Section total ____ / ____	**Body:** (Organization, transitions, sources, visual aids, language) **Strengths:** **Weaknesses:**
Section total ____ / ____	**Conclusion:** (Transition, restated thesis, clincher) **Strengths:** **Weaknesses:**
Section total ____ / ____	**Delivery:** (eye contact, vocal variety, physical delivery, extemporaneous, rehearsed) **Strengths:** **Weaknesses:**
Section total ____ / ____	**Other:** (Audience analysis, timely, creative) **Strengths:** **Weaknesses:**

Comments

Major Strengths:

Areas Needing Improvement:

Total Points/Grade:

SPEECH EVALUATION FORM: Event Presentation

Speaker: _____   Time Limit: _____

Topic: _____   Length of Speech: _____

Section total _____ / _____	**Introduction:** (Captured attention, stated thesis, relevance, credibility, transition) **Strengths:** **Weaknesses:**
Section total _____ / _____	**Body:** (Organization, transitions, sources, visual aids, language) **Strengths:** **Weaknesses:**
Section total _____ / _____	**Conclusion:** (Transition, restated thesis, clincher) **Strengths:** **Weaknesses:**
Section total _____ / _____	**Delivery:** (eye contact, vocal variety, physical delivery, extemporaneous, rehearsed) **Strengths:** **Weaknesses:**
Section total _____ / _____	**Other:** (Audience analysis, timely, creative) **Strengths:** **Weaknesses:**

Comments

Major Strengths:

Areas Needing Improvement:

Total Points/Grade:

OUTLINE CHECKLIST: News Presentation

SPEAKER: _____   TIME LIMIT: _____

TOPIC: _____   SITUATION/AUDIENCE: _____

___ yes no ___		***SPECIFIC PURPOSE:***
___ yes no ___		1. Is it stated as an infinitive phrase?
___ yes no ___		2. Does it contain only one idea?
___ yes no ___		3. Does it use clear and concise language?
		4. Is the focus clearly defined?

Score: _____

THESIS STATEMENT:

___ yes   no ___   1. Is the focus clearly defined?

___ yes   no ___   2. Are main points previewed?

___ yes   no ___   3. Is it written as a complete sentence?

Score: _____

INTRODUCTION:

___ yes   no ___   Contains all necessary components: attention getter, credibility statement, relevance, thesis?

Attention getter

___ yes   no ___   • Is it appropriate for topic?

___ yes   no ___   • Is it appropriate for selected audience?

___ yes   no ___   • Does it have impact?

___ yes   no ___   • Is it appropriate in length?

Credibility statement

___ yes   no ___   • Does it sound professional/believable?

___ yes   no ___   • Does it point out personal experience/interest?

Relevance statement

___ yes   no ___   • Does the statement create an immediate need to listen?

___ yes   no ___   • Is it appropriate for the selected audience?

Thesis (see above)

___ yes   no ___   • Make sure thesis is same in introduction as written above.

Score: _____

TRANSITION:

___ yes   no __   1. Is there a directional transition between introduction and body?

Score: _____

___ yes no ___ ___ yes no ___ ___ yes no ___ ___ yes no ___ ___ yes no ___ ___ yes no ___ ___ yes no ___ ___ yes no ___ ___ yes no ___ **Score:** ___	***ORGANIZATION:*** 1. Is the appropriate organizational pattern used? 2. Are the main points significant? 3. Are the main points balanced? 4. Do the main points contain one distinct idea? 5. Are they written as complete sentences? 6. Are there directional transitions between main points? 7. Are the subpoints organized correctly? 8. Do the points coordinate? 9. Is there correct subordination?
___ yes no ___ ___ yes no ___ ___ yes no ___ ___ yes no ___ ___ yes no ___ ___ yes no ___ ___ yes no ___ **Score:** ___	***EVIDENCE:*** 1. Does each main point have sufficient evidence? 2. Is evidence appropriate for selected audience? 3. Is evidence timely? 4. Are a variety of types of supporting materials used? 5. Is evidence from credible sources? 6. Is evidence cited appropriately? 7. Does evidence actually support main points/conclusion/arguments?
___ yes no ___ ___ yes no ___ ___ yes no ___ **Score:** ___	***ARGUMENTS:*** 1. Do arguments follow sound reasoning? 2. Is fallacious reasoning avoided? 3. Do arguments make appropriate appeals (logs, ethos, pathos)?
___ yes no ___ ___ yes no ___ ___ yes no ___ **Score:** ___	***VISUAL AIDS:*** 1. Are visual aids included in outline? 2. Is explanation included on how visual aid enhances/explains information? 3. Are visual aids appropriate?
___ yes no ___ **Score:** ___	***TRANSITION:*** 1. Was there a directional transition from the body to the conclusion?

___ yes   no ___
___ yes   no ___
 	
___ yes   no ___
 	
Score: ___
	CONCLUSION:
	1. Is thesis restated?
	2. Does conclusion contain a clincher?
	    • Is it memorable?
	    • Is it appropriate for selected audience?
	3. Did conclusion (erroneously) introduce new information?

___ yes no ___ ___ yes no ___ **Score:** ___	***LENGTH/STYLE:*** 1. Can material be covered in time frame allotted? 2. Was outline typed?
___ yes no ___ ___ yes no ___ **Score:** _____	***BIBLIOGRAPHY/REFERENCE PAGE:*** 1. Citations meet the minimum requirement in number? 2. Citations use the appropriate style/format (APA/MLA)?

OUTLINE CHECKLIST: Event Presentation

SPEAKER: _____   TIME LIMIT: _____
TOPIC: _____   SITUATION/AUDIENCE: _____

____ yes no ____	***SPECIFIC PURPOSE:***	
____ yes no ____	1. Is it stated as an infinitive phrase?	
____ yes no ____	2. Does it contain only one idea?	
____ yes no ____	3. Does it use clear and concise language?	
	4. Is the focus clearly defined?	

Score: _____

____ yes no ____	***THESIS STATEMENT:***
____ yes no ____	1. Is the focus clearly defined?
____ yes no ____	2. Are main points previewed?
	3. Is it written as a complete sentence?

Score: _____

____ yes no ____	***INTRODUCTION:***
	Contains all necessary components: attention getter, credibility statement, relevance, thesis?

Attention getter
____ yes no ____	• Is it appropriate for topic?
____ yes no ____	• Is it appropriate for selected audience?
____ yes no ____	• Does it have impact?
____ yes no ____	• Is it appropriate in length?

Credibility statement
____ yes no ____	• Does it sound professional/believable?
____ yes no ____	• Does it point out personal experience/interest?

Relevance statement
____ yes no ____	• Does the statement create an immediate need to listen?
____ yes no ____	• Is it appropriate for the selected audience?

Thesis (see above)
____ yes no ____	• Make sure thesis is same in introduction as written above.

Score: _____

____ yes no ____	***TRANSITION:***
	1. Is there a directional transition between introduction and body?

Score: _____

	ORGANIZATION:
___ yes no ___	1. Is the appropriate organizational pattern used?
___ yes no ___	2. Are the main points significant?
___ yes no ___	3. Are the main points balanced?
___ yes no ___	4. Do the main points contain one distinct idea?
___ yes no ___	5. Are they written as complete sentences?
___ yes no ___	6. Are there directional transitions between main points?
___ yes no ___	7. Are the subpoints organized correctly?
___ yes no ___	8. Do the points coordinate?
___ yes no ___	9. Is there correct subordination?
Score: ___	
	EVIDENCE:
___ yes no ___	1. Does each main point have sufficient evidence?
___ yes no ___	2. Is evidence appropriate for selected audience?
___ yes no ___	3. Is evidence timely?
___ yes no ___	4. Are a variety of types of supporting materials used?
___ yes no ___	5. Is evidence from credible sources?
___ yes no ___	6. Is evidence cited appropriately?
___ yes no ___	7. Does evidence actually support main points/conclusion/arguments?
Score: ___	
	ARGUMENTS:
___ yes no ___	1. Do arguments follow sound reasoning?
___ yes no ___	2. Is fallacious reasoning avoided?
___ yes no ___	3. Do arguments make appropriate appeals (logs, ethos, pathos)?
Score: ___	
	VISUAL AIDS:
___ yes no ___	1. Are visual aids included in outline?
___ yes no ___	2. Is explanation included on how visual aid enhances/explains information?
___ yes no ___	3. Are visual aids appropriate?
Score: ___	
	TRANSITION:
___ yes no ___	1. Was there a directional transition from the body to the conclusion?
Score: ___	
	CONCLUSION:
___ yes no ___	1. Is thesis restated?
___ yes no ___	2. Does conclusion contain a clincher?
	• Is it memorable?
	• Is it appropriate for selected audience?
___ yes no ___	3. Did conclusion (erroneously) introduce new information?
Score: ___	
	LENGTH/STYLE:
___ yes no ___	1. Can material be covered in time frame allotted?
___ yes no ___	2. Was outline typed?
Score: ___	
	BIBLIOGRAPHY/REFERENCE PAGE:
___ yes no ___	1. Citations meet the minimum requirement in number?
___ yes no ___	2. Citations use the appropriate style/format (APA/MLA)?
Score: ___	

Explaining Information Presentation
Point Value: 150
Length: 5 to 6 minutes
My Presentation Date: _____

In today's information age we are often faced with presenting difficult or challenging information to an audience who may have little experience with the ideas we are presenting. It becomes particularly important that we can take these ideas and express them in an understandable way to audiences with varying levels of information. In this assignment you will be asked to choose a difficult topic and explain it in detail to your audience. You will want your audience to be able to grasp and remember the material in your presentation after hearing it only once. In order to do this effectively it is important that you draw analogies between your audiences' experiences and the material you are presenting in your presentation. This assignment requires excellent audience analysis in order to provide information at a level the audience can process and understand. It is your job to analyze your audience effectively so that your presentation is effective.

Specific Requirements

- Presentation must use one of the strategies discussed in class: elucidating explanations, quasi-scientific explanations, or transformative explanations.
- Time Limit: 5-6 minutes. *If your speech does not meet the time criteria, you will be penalized ten points.*
- Base the speech on at least six sources of research published within the last year. At least five of these sources must be cited correctly within your speech. **Web cites do not count as published material.** *All material citied on your bibliography must be turned in to your instructor the day of your presentation. Failure to do so will result in a ten point penalty.*
- Adequately explain the ideas of the presentation by fully developing main points with concrete supporting material.
- Relate unfamiliar ideas to what the audience knows and values.
- Develop a thesis that meets the criteria discussed in class and in the textbook (full sentence, one distinct idea etc…).
- Develop two or three main points. Main points should meet class criteria (balance, mutually exclusive, etc.) and fit one of the organizational patterns discussed in class.
- Present well-reasoned and well-documented evidence for your main points.
- Appropriate development of an introduction and conclusion.
- Demonstrate skillful use of transitions.
- Refined delivery: Your speaking style should be extemporaneous. This means that you are not to read your speech, or to memorize your speech, but are to talk to the audience and adapt to the audience as you speak. Work for both effective physical and vocal delivery.

- A *typed* sentence outline of the speech along with a bibliography of your six sources. These must be submitted through your Web CT account to your instructor. Due Date: _____. **Your outline must be approved by your instructor before you can deliver your presentation. If you fail to have your outline approved by your instructor before your assigned speaking day you will lose your opportunity to speak and will receive a ZERO on this assignment.**
- You must also meet any additional requirements as outlined in class by your instructor.

Evaluation:

Your speech should meet the requirements of a properly presented informative speech.

G. Preparation of the sentence outline and bibliography.
H. Analysis of the topic and audience.
I. Organization of speech.
J. Research
K. Use of evidence and appeals
L. Refined Delivery

Remember, practice, practice, practice!!!!! Good Luck.

OUTLINE CHECKLIST:
Explaining Information Presentation

SPEAKER: _____ _____   **TIME LIMIT:** _____

TOPIC: _____ _____   **SITUATION/AUDIENCE:** _____

___ yes no ___	**SPECIFIC PURPOSE:**	
___ yes no ___	1. Is stated as an infinitive phrase?	
___ yes no ___	2. Does it contain only one idea?	
___ yes no ___	3. Does it use clear and concise language?	
	4. Is the focus clearly defined?	
Score: _____		

	THESIS STATEMENT:
___ yes no ___	1. Is the focus clearly defined?
___ yes no ___	2. Are main points previewed?
___ yes no ___	3. Is it written as a complete sentence?
Score: _____	

___ yes no ___	**INTRODUCTION:** Contains all necessary components: attention getter, credibility statement, relevance, thesis?
	Attention getter
___ yes no ___	• Is it appropriate for topic?
___ yes no ___	• Is it appropriate for selected audience?
___ yes no ___	• Does it have impact?
___ yes no ___	• Is it appropriate in length?
	Credibility statement
___ yes no ___	• Does it sound professional/believable?
___ yes no ___	• Does it point out personal experience/interest?
	Relevance statement
___ yes no ___	• Does the statement create an immediate need to listen?
___ yes no ___	• Is it appropriate for the selected audience?
	Thesis (see above)
___ yes no ___	• Make sure thesis is same in introduction as written above.
Score: _____	

	TRANSITION:
___ yes no ___	1. Is there a directional transition between introduction and body?
Score: _____	

	EXPLANATION:
___ yes no ___	1. The appropriate explanatory pattern was employed?
___ yes no ___	2. Explanation was presented with clarity?
Score: _____	

235

___ yes no ___	**ORGANIZATION:** 1. Is the appropriate organizational pattern used?	
___ yes no ___	2. Are the main points significant?	
___ yes no ___	3. Are the main points balanced?	
___ yes no ___	4. Do the main points contain one distinct idea?	
___ yes no ___	5. Are they written as complete sentences?	
___ yes no ___	6. Are there directional transitions between main points?	
___ yes no ___	7. Are the subpoints organized correctly?	
___ yes no ___	8. Do the points coordinate?	
___ yes no ___	9. Is there correct subordination?	
Score: ___		

___ yes no ___	**EVIDENCE:** 1. Does each main point have sufficient evidence?
___ yes no ___	2. Is evidence appropriate for selected audience?
___ yes no ___	3. Is evidence timely?
___ yes no ___	4. Are a variety of types of supporting materials used?
___ yes no ___	5. Is evidence from credible sources?
___ yes no ___	6. Is evidence cited appropriately?
___ yes no ___	7. Does evidence actually support main points/conclusion/arguments?
Score: ___	

___ yes no ___	**ARGUMENTS:** 1. Do arguments follow sound reasoning?
___ yes no ___	2. Is fallacious reasoning avoided?
___ yes no ___	3. Do arguments make appropriate appeals (logs, ethos, pathos)?
Score: ___	

___ yes no ___	**VISUAL AIDS:** 1. Are visual aids included in outline?
___ yes no ___	2. Is explanation included on how visual aid enhances/explains information?
___ yes no ___	3. Are visual aids appropriate?
Score: ___	

___ yes no ___	**TRANSITION:** 1. Was there a directional transition from the body to the conclusion?
Score: ___	

___ yes no ___	**CONCLUSION:** 1. Is thesis restated?
___ yes no ___	2. Does conclusion contain a clincher? • Is it memorable? • Is it appropriate for selected audience?
___ yes no ___	3. Did conclusion (erroneously) introduce new information?
Score: ___	

___ yes no ___	**LENGTH/STYLE:** 1. Can material be covered in time frame allotted?
___ yes no ___	2. Was outline typed?
Score: ___	

___ yes no ___	**BIBLIOGRAPHY/REFERENCE PAGE:** 1. Citations meet the minimum requirement in number?
___ yes no ___	2. Citations use the appropriate style/format (APA/MLA)?
Score: ___	

OUTLINE CHECKLIST:
Explaining Information Presentation

SPEAKER: _____ **TIME LIMIT:** _____

TOPIC: _____ **SITUATION/AUDIENCE:** _____

___ yes no ___	___ yes no ___	

SPECIFIC PURPOSE:

___ yes no ___   1. Is it stated as an infinitive phrase?
___ yes no ___   2. Does it contain only one idea?
___ yes no ___   3. Does it use clear and concise language?
___ yes no ___   4. Is the focus clearly defined?

Score: _____

THESIS STATEMENT:

___ yes no ___   1. Is the focus clearly defined?
___ yes no ___   2. Are main points previewed?
___ yes no ___   3. Is it written as a complete sentence?

Score: _____

INTRODUCTION:

___ yes no ___   Contains all necessary components: attention getter, credibility statement, relevance, thesis?

Attention getter

___ yes no ___   • Is it appropriate for topic?
___ yes no ___   • Is it appropriate for selected audience?
___ yes no ___   • Does it have impact?
___ yes no ___   • Is it appropriate in length?

Credibility statement

___ yes no ___   • Does it sound professional/believable?
___ yes no ___   • Does it point out personal experience/interest?

Relevance statement

___ yes no ___   • Does the statement create an immediate need to listen?
___ yes no ___   • Is it appropriate for the selected audience?

Thesis (see above)

___ yes no ___   • Make sure thesis is same in introduction as written above.

Score: _____

TRANSITION:

___ yes no ___   1. Is there a directional transition between introduction and body?

Score: _____

EXPLANATION:

___ yes no ___   1. The appropriate explanatory pattern was employed?
___ yes no ___   2. Explanation was presented with clarity?

Score: _____

___ yes no ___		**ORGANIZATION:**
___ yes no ___		1. Is the appropriate organizational pattern used?
___ yes no ___		2. Are the main points significant?
___ yes no ___		3. Are the main points balanced?
___ yes no ___		4. Do the main points contain one distinct idea?
___ yes no ___		5. Are they written as complete sentences?
___ yes no ___		6. Are there directional transitions between main points?
___ yes no ___		7. Are the subpoints organized correctly?
___ yes no ___		8. Do the points coordinate?
___ yes no ___		9. Is there correct subordination?

Score: ___

EVIDENCE:

___ yes no ___   1. Does each main point have sufficient evidence?
___ yes no ___   2. Is evidence appropriate for selected audience?
___ yes no ___   3. Is evidence timely?
___ yes no ___   4. Are a variety of types of supporting materials used?
___ yes no ___   5. Is evidence from credible sources?
___ yes no ___   6. Is evidence cited appropriately?
___ yes no ___   7. Does evidence actually support main points/conclusion/arguments?

Score: ___

ARGUMENTS:

___ yes no ___   1. Do arguments follow sound reasoning?
___ yes no ___   2. Is fallacious reasoning avoided?
___ yes no ___   3. Do arguments make appropriate appeals (logs, ethos, pathos)?

Score: ___

VISUAL AIDS:

___ yes no ___   1. Are visual aids included in outline?
___ yes no ___   2. Is explanation included on how visual aid enhances/explains information?
___ yes no ___   3. Are visual aids appropriate?

Score: ___

TRANSITION:

___ yes no ___   1. Was there a directional transition from the body to the conclusion?

Score: ___

CONCLUSION:

___ yes no ___   1. Is thesis restated?
___ yes no ___   2. Does conclusion contain a clincher?
         • Is it memorable?
         • Is it appropriate for selected audience?
___ yes no ___   3. Did conclusion (erroneously) introduce new information?

Score: ___

LENGTH/STYLE:

___ yes no ___   1. Can material be covered in time frame allotted?
___ yes no ___   2. Was outline typed?

Score: ___

BIBLIOGRAPHY/REFERENCE PAGE:

___ yes no ___   1. Citations meet the minimum requirement in number?
___ yes no ___   2. Citations use the appropriate style/format (APA/MLA)?

Score: ___

SPEECH EVALUATION FORM: Explaining Information

Speaker: _____　　　Time Limit: _____
Topic: _____　　　Length of Speech: _____

Section total _____ / _____	**Introduction:** (Captured attention, stated thesis, relevance, credibility, transition) **Strengths:** **Weaknesses:**
Section total _____ / _____	**Body:** (Organization, transitions, sources, visual aids, language, complex material explanation, appropriate explanatory method) **Strengths:** **Weaknesses:**
Section total _____ / _____	**Conclusion:** (Transition, restated thesis, clincher) **Strengths:** **Weaknesses:**
Section total _____ / _____	**Delivery:** (eye contact, vocal variety, physical delivery, extemporaneous, rehearsed) **Strengths:** **Weaknesses:**
Section total _____ / _____	**Other:** (Audience analysis, timely, creative) **Strengths:** **Weaknesses:**

Comments

Major Strengths:

Areas Needing Improvement:

Total Points/Grade:

SPEECH EVALUATION FORM: Explaining Information

Speaker: _____   Time Limit: _____
Topic: _____   Length of Speech: _____

Section total	Introduction: (Captured attention, stated thesis, relevance, credibility, transition) **Strengths:** **Weaknesses:**
Section total ___ / ___	**Introduction:** (Captured attention, stated thesis, relevance, credibility, transition) **Strengths:** **Weaknesses:**
Section total ___ / ___	**Body:** (Organization, transitions, sources, visual aids, language, complex material explanation, appropriate explanatory method) **Strengths:** **Weaknesses:**
Section total ___ / ___	**Conclusion:** (Transition, restated thesis, clincher) **Strengths:** **Weaknesses:**
Section total ___ / ___	**Delivery:** (eye contact, vocal variety, physical delivery, extemporaneous, rehearsed) **Strengths:** **Weaknesses:**
Section total ___ / ___	**Other:** (Audience analysis, timely, creative) **Strengths:** **Weaknesses:**

Comments

Major Strengths:

Areas Needing Improvement:

Total Points/Grade:

Persuasive Presentation
Length: 5 to 6 minutes
Point Vale: 200
My Presentation Date: _____

Assignment overview

On this round, you will be asked to deliver a presentation on a question of fact, value or policy. It is important that you use the correct organizational pattern for your speech type. Check the class readings so that you can ensure that you use the appropriate one. The focus of this presentation is on making and evaluating arguments. Specifically, you'll be expected to use examples, statistics, and expert testimony for supporting material as well as weave these elements together in a way that provides complete and logical documentation and reasoning for the key ideas in your speech. You will need to demonstrate effective reasoning skills by using good solid arguments that are free from fallacies. You will also need a visual aid.

Specific Requirements

- Time Limit: 5-6 minutes. *If your speech does not meet the time criteria, you will be penalized ten points.*
- Base the speech on at least six sources of research. At least five of these sources must be cited correctly within your speech. **Web cites do not count as published material.** *All sources included on bibliography must be turned in to your instructor the day of your presentation. Failure to do so results in loss of ten points.*
- Summarize the major arguments of your view.
- Present well-reasoned and well-documented evidence for the major arguments.
- Avoid bias in presenting arguments or characterizing conflicting views
- Effective use of a visual aid. Ask the following questions: is it necessary and does it enhance audience understanding? Is it professional and free from errors?
- Refined delivery: Your speaking style should be extemporaneous. This means that you are not to read your speech, or to memorize your speech, but are to talk to the audience and adapt to the audience as you speak. Work for both effective physical and vocal delivery.
- A _typed_ sentence outline of the speech along with a bibliography of your sources. These must be submitted through your WEBCT account to your instructor. Due date: **November 4th** **Your outline must be approved by your instructor before you can delivery your presentation. If you fail to have your outline approved by your instructor before you assigned speaking day you will lose your opportunity to speak and will receive a ZERO on this assignment.**
- You must also meet any additional requirements as outlined in class by your instructor.

Areas for Evaluation:
Your speech should meet the requirements of a properly presented persuasive speech.
M. Preparation of the sentence outline and bibliography.
N. Analysis of the topic and audience.
O. Organization of speech.
P. Research
Q. Use of evidence and appeals
R. Refined Delivery

Remember, practice, practice, practice!!!!! Good Luck.

OUTLINE CHECKLIST:
Persuasive Presentation

SPEAKER: _____ **TIME LIMIT:** _____

TOPIC: _____ **SITUATION/AUDIENCE:** _____

___ yes no ___	***SPECIFIC PURPOSE:***	
___ yes no ___	1. Is it stated as an infinitive phrase?	
___ yes no ___	2. Does it contain only one idea?	
___ yes no ___	3. Does it use clear and concise language?	
	4. Is the focus clearly defined?	

Score: _____

___ yes no ___	***THESIS STATEMENT:***
___ yes no ___	1. Is the focus clearly defined?
___ yes no ___	2. Are main points previewed?
	3. Is it written as a complete sentence?

Score: _____

___ yes no ___	***INTRODUCTION:*** Contains all necessary components: attention getter, credibility statement, relevance, thesis?
	Attention getter
___ yes no ___	• Is it appropriate for topic?
___ yes no ___	• Is it appropriate for selected audience?
___ yes no ___	• Does it have impact?
___ yes no ___	• Is it appropriate in length?
	Credibility statement
___ yes no ___	• Does it sound professional/believable?
___ yes no ___	• Does it point out personal experience/interest?
	Relevance statement
___ yes no ___	• Does the statement create an immediate need to listen?
___ yes no ___	• Is it appropriate for the selected audience?
	Thesis (see above)
___ yes no ___	• Make sure thesis is same in introduction as written above.

Score: _____

___ yes no __	***TRANSITION:*** 1. Is there a directional transition between introduction and body?

Score: _____

		ORGANIZATION:
___ yes	no ___	1. Is the appropriate organizational pattern used?
___ yes	no ___	2. Are the main points significant?
___ yes	no ___	3. Are the main points balanced?
___ yes	no ___	4. Do the main points contain one distinct idea?
___ yes	no ___	5. Are they written as complete sentences?
___ yes	no ___	6. Are there directional transitions between main points?
___ yes	no ___	7. Are the subpoints organized correctly?
___ yes	no ___	8. Do the points coordinate?
___ yes	no ___	9. Is there correct subordination?
Score: ___		
		EVIDENCE:
___ yes	no ___	1. Does each main point have sufficient evidence?
___ yes	no ___	2. Is evidence appropriate for selected audience?
___ yes	no ___	3. Is evidence timely?
___ yes	no ___	4. Are a variety of types of supporting materials used?
___ yes	no ___	5. Is evidence from credible sources?
___ yes	no ___	6. Is evidence cited appropriately?
___ yes	no ___	7. Does evidence actually support main points/conclusion/arguments?
Score: ___		
		ARGUMENTS:
___ yes	no __	1. Do arguments follow sound reasoning?
___ yes	no __	2. Is fallacious reasoning avoided?
___ yes	no __	3. Do arguments make appropriate appeals (logs, ethos, pathos)?
Score: ___		
		VISUAL AIDS:
___ yes	no ___	1. Are visual aids included in outline?
___ yes	no ___	2. Is explanation included on how visual aid enhances/explains information?
___ yes	no ___	3. Are visual aids appropriate?
Score: ___		
		TRANSITION:
___ yes	no ___	1. Was there a directional transition from the body to the conclusion?
Score: ___		
		CONCLUSION:
___ yes	no ___	1. Is thesis restated?
___ yes	no ___	2. Does conclusion contain a clincher?
		• Is it memorable?
		• Is it appropriate for selected audience?
___ yes	no ___	3. Did conclusion (erroneously) introduce new information?
Score: ___		
		LENGTH/STYLE:
___ yes	no ___	1. Can material be covered in time frame allotted?
___ yes	no ___	2. Was outline typed?
Score: ___		
		BIBLIOGRAPHY/REFERENCE PAGE:
___ yes	no ___	1. Citations meet the minimum requirement in number?
___ yes	no ___	2. Citations use the appropriate style/format (APA/MLA)?
Score: ___		

OUTLINE CHECKLIST:
Persuasive Presentation

SPEAKER: _____   **TIME LIMIT:** _____

TOPIC: _____   **SITUATION/AUDIENCE:** _____

___ yes no ___	***SPECIFIC PURPOSE:***	
___ yes no ___	1. Is it stated as an infinitive phrase?	
___ yes no ___	2. Does it contain only one idea?	
___ yes no ___	3. Does it use clear and concise language?	
___ yes no ___	4. Is the focus clearly defined?	
Score: _____		

___ yes no ___	***THESIS STATEMENT:***
___ yes no ___	1. Is the focus clearly defined?
___ yes no ___	2. Are main points previewed?
___ yes no ___	3. Is it written as a complete sentence?
Score: _____	

___ yes no ___	***INTRODUCTION:*** Contains all necessary components: attention getter, credibility statement, relevance, thesis?
	Attention getter
___ yes no ___	• Is it appropriate for topic?
___ yes no ___	• Is it appropriate for selected audience?
___ yes no ___	• Does it have impact?
___ yes no ___	• Is it appropriate in length?
	Credibility statement
___ yes no ___	• Does it sound professional/believable?
___ yes no ___	• Does it point out personal experience/interest?
	Relevance statement
___ yes no ___	• Does the statement create an immediate need to listen?
___ yes no ___	• Is it appropriate for the selected audience?
	Thesis (see above)
___ yes no ___	• Make sure thesis is same in introduction as written above.
Score: _____	

___ yes no ___	***TRANSITION:*** 1. Is there a directional transition between introduction and body?
Score: _____	

		ORGANIZATION:
___ yes	no ___	1. Is the appropriate organizational pattern used?
___ yes	no ___	2. Are the main points significant?
___ yes	no ___	3. Are the main points balanced?
___ yes	no ___	4. Do the main points contain one distinct idea?
___ yes	no ___	5. Are they written as complete sentences?
___ yes	no ___	6. Are there directional transitions between main points?
___ yes	no ___	7. Are the subpoints organized correctly?
___ yes	no ___	8. Do the points coordinate?
___ yes	no ___	9. Is there correct subordination?
Score: ___		
		EVIDENCE:
___ yes	no ___	1. Does each main point have sufficient evidence?
___ yes	no ___	2. Is evidence appropriate for selected audience?
___ yes	no ___	3. Is evidence timely?
___ yes	no ___	4. Are a variety of types of supporting materials used?
___ yes	no ___	5. Is evidence from credible sources?
___ yes	no ___	6. Is evidence cited appropriately?
___ yes	no ___	7. Does evidence actually support main points/conclusion/arguments?
Score: ___		
		ARGUMENTS:
___ yes	no ___	1. Do arguments follow sound reasoning?
___ yes	no ___	2. Is fallacious reasoning avoided?
___ yes	no ___	3. Do arguments make appropriate appeals (logs, ethos, pathos)?
Score: ___		
		VISUAL AIDS:
___ yes	no ___	1. Are visual aids included in outline?
___ yes	no ___	2. Is explanation included on how visual aid enhances/explains information?
___ yes	no ___	3. Are visual aids appropriate?
Score: ___		
		TRANSITION:
___ yes	no ___	1. Was there a directional transition from the body to the conclusion?
Score: ___		
		CONCLUSION:
___ yes	no ___	1. Is thesis restated?
___ yes	no ___	2. Does conclusion contain a clincher?
		• Is it memorable?
		• Is it appropriate for selected audience?
___ yes	no ___	3. Did conclusion (erroneously) introduce new information?
Score: ___		
		LENGTH/STYLE:
___ yes	no ___	1. Can material be covered in time frame allotted?
___ yes	no ___	2. Was outline typed?
Score: ___		
		BIBLIOGRAPHY/REFERENCE PAGE:
___ yes	no ___	1. Citations meet the minimum requirement in number?
___ yes	no ___	2. Citations use the appropriate style/format (APA/MLA)?
Score: ___		

SPEECH EVALUATION FORM: Persuasive Presentation

Speaker: _____   Time Limit: _____

Topic: _____   Length of Speech: _____

Section total _____ / _____	**Introduction:** (Captured attention, stated thesis, relevance, credibility, transition) **Strengths:** **Weaknesses:**
Section total _____ / _____	**Body:** (Organization, transitions, sources, visual aids, language, well-reasoned arguments, avoided fallacies) **Strengths:** **Weaknesses:**
Section total _____ / _____	**Conclusion:** (Transition, restated thesis, clincher) **Strengths:** **Weaknesses:**
Section total _____ / _____	**Delivery:** (eye contact, vocal variety, physical delivery, extemporaneous, rehearsed) **Strengths:** **Weaknesses:**
Section total _____ / _____	**Other:** (Audience analysis, timely, creative) **Strengths:** **Weaknesses:**

Comments

Major Strengths:

Areas Needing Improvement:

Total Points/Grade:

SPEECH EVALUATION FORM: Persuasive Presentation

Speaker: _____ Time Limit: _____

Topic: _____ Length of Speech: _____

Section total _____ / _____	**Introduction:** (Captured attention, stated thesis, relevance, credibility, transition) **Strengths:** **Weaknesses:**
Section total _____ / _____	**Body:** (Organization, transitions, sources, visual aids, language, well-reasoned arguments, avoided fallacies) **Strengths:** **Weaknesses:**
Section total _____ / _____	**Conclusion:** (Transition, restated thesis, clincher) **Strengths:** **Weaknesses:**
Section total _____ / _____	**Delivery:** (eye contact, vocal variety, physical delivery, extemporaneous, rehearsed) **Strengths:** **Weaknesses:**
Section total _____ / _____	**Other:** (Audience analysis, timely, creative) **Strengths:** **Weaknesses:**

Comments

Major Strengths:

Areas Needing Improvement:

Total Points/Grade

Small Group Presentation
Length: 50 Minutes
Point Value: 200 Points
My Group's Presentation Day: _____

For this assignment you will need to take everything you have learned this semester and apply it to this presentation. You will draw on your delivery skills, organizational abilities, reasoning and argumentation skills, critiquing skills, as well as your ability to interact and communicate effectively in small groups. This presentation will require some role-playing.

The situation:

Purdue President Martin Jischke controls the distribution of funds from an incentive grant pool. You are part of a group who has a particular campus concern but has lacked the funds necessary to address the problem. Your group sees this as an opportunity to bring some of its ideas to the public forefront and actually make a difference. President Jischke will be entertaining several proposals from other groups. Previously, President Jischke funded a proposal to create the Purdue Cultural Awareness Committee to help unite various campus ethnic groups and promote diversity, and a proposal to fund the creation of video public service announcements and posters to promote exposure to Purdue's Sexual Harassment Network.

Your task:

Your group is competing for these incentive grant resources. The maximum amount to be applied for is $2,000. So you will develop and present a proposal. Remember, you will be competing for the resources so your proposal must be compelling and persuasive. You will present your proposal to President Jischke's appointed committee and your instructor. The committee will be comprised of other classmates. While your instructor will be responsible for grading the assignment, the committee will have an input in the final appraisal of the proposal.

SPECIFIC REQUIREMENTS

You and four or five other classmates will form some type of group (activist group, neighborhood group, college organization etc.) or use an existing organization. You are to select a need or problem this organization wants to address and propose a solution to that need/problem. Each group should get their topic/need/problem approved by their instructor before beginning to work on the project.

- Every person in the group should take a **speaking** part in the presentation and have knowledge of the proposal.
- Each presentation will follow the problem-solution format discussed in class. Pay particular attention to the need, plan, and practicality issues related to questions of policy.
- The last part of the presentation will consist of a question and answer session with the selection committee (members of the class). The committee should try their best to find problems with the proposal. So, the presenting group must cover every possible angle of the problem and solution. Be sure you are prepared to defend health, social, economic, environmental, etc. concerns.
- The group has the entire class period for the presentation and question and answer session.
- Every class member will also serve on a selection committee. As a member of this committee, you will be required to ask very thoughtful and knowledgeable questions about other group's proposals and provide a critique of the proposal.

If there is a shirker in your group, you (NOT your instructor) will need to deal with him/her. That is, it will be the responsibility of the group to set up rules pertaining to attending planning meeting(s), who will do what, sanctions for not doing what was expected, etc. The group will sign a group contract and every member will be held to the behavioral guidelines as outlined by that contract. My suggestion is to get these issues settled as soon after group formation as possible so that come presentation day when Billie Bob doesn't show up or shows up unprepared, the group will have a known procedure for dealing with Billie Bob!!!!

RECEIVING CREDIT

You may receive a total of 200 points for participating in this assignment. Point breakdown is as follows: **Criteria for Group Presentation** (160 points): All group members will receive the same score for this portion of the assignment.

1. **Presentation and Group Effectiveness** (125 points)
   - Creativity and vividness of presentation.
   - How well you engaged the audience. The best way to fulfill this criteria is to use a variety of methods to present your ideas-rather than rely solely on a lecture approach, use videos, have handouts, ANYTHING to break the monotony of a string of individual presentations.
   - Perceived productivity of the group – Did you accomplish your task? How informative and persuasive is the information? Was the presentation well-organized?
   - Perceived cohesiveness of the group – How well did the group members seem to work together? Did everyone take an active part?
   - Elements of Effective Speaking (all those things we have talked about all semester long).
     - Organization
     - Effective use of evidence
     - Refined delivery
     - Audience Analysis
     - Appropriate use of Visual Aids
2. **Executive Summary of the proposal:** This is just the outline of the presentation. (25 points)
3. **Feedback from the committee members** (10 points)

Criteria for Individual Evaluation (40 points) Individual scores will be assigned for this portion
1. **Individual presentation skills:** Basically, I will be evaluating your delivery on the presentation, how well you answered questions from the committee, and your overall demeanor during your group's presentation. (15 points)
2. **Group Evaluation Questionnaire:** Each member is to complete the attached questionnaire regarding contributions of each group member in an honest and thorough manner. My evaluation of this questionnaire will be based on the thoroughness of your responses. (5 points)
3. **Individual contributions to the group:** Based on your own group member's responses to the group evaluation questionnaire. Did your group say you participated and were a good group member? (10 points)
4. **Committee Member Responsibilities:** Were you prepared with <u>thoughtful and thorough</u> questions during one other group's presentation? Your thorough and honest critique of the other group's proposal and presentation (10 points)

Small Group Presentation
Group Evaluation Form

Speaker: _____   Time Limit: _____
Topic: _____   Length of Speech: _____

Introduction:
1. _____Captured attention
2. _____Stated thesis
3. _____Related topic to audience
4. _____Established credibility
5. _____Previewed main points
6. _____Provided transition to body
7. Other comments:

Body:
1. _____Organized main points clearly and logically
2. _____Included transitions between main points
3. _____Used accurate, relevant and timely supporting materials in sufficient quantity
4. _____Citied sources accurately in speech
5. _____Used relevant, professional visual aids that enhanced audience understanding
6. _____Used visual aids appropriately
7. _____Used an oral language style appropriate to topic and audience
8. Other comments:

Conclusion:
1. _____Provided transition to conclusion
2. _____Restated thesis
3. _____Summarized main points
4. _____Ended with a memorable final thought (clincher)
5. Other comments:

Question and Answer Section:
1. _____Rephrased questions
2. _____Answered questions clearly and completely
3. _____Answered questions succinctly
4. _____Q&A was well organized and professional
5. Other comments:

Overall Group Assessment:
1. _____Project demonstrated creativity
2. _____Accomplishment of group persuasive and informative goals
3. _____Presentation demonstrated group cohesiveness
4. _____Transitioning from one speaker to another was smooth
5. Other comments:

Evaluation of Proposal
1. _____Proposal clearly identified and defined community issue/problem
2. _____Proposal presented a clear plan for dealing with issue
3. _____Proposal presented a practical solution
4. Other comments:

Comments

Major Strengths:

Areas Needing Improvement:

Overall Evaluation:

Total Points/Grade:
Presentation Score   _____
Executive Summary   _____
Committee Evaluation _____
Total Group Score   _____

Index